International Political Economy Series

Series Editor
Timothy M. Shaw
University of Massachusetts
Boston, MA, USA

Emeritus Professor
University of London
London, UK

The global political economy is in flux as a series of cumulative crises impacts its organization and governance. The IPE series has tracked its development in both analysis and structure over the last three decades. It has always had a concentration on the global South. Now the South increasingly challenges the North as the centre of development, also reflected in a growing number of submissions and publications on indebted Eurozone economies in Southern Europe. An indispensable resource for scholars and researchers, the series examines a variety of capitalisms and connections by focusing on emerging economies, companies and sectors, debates and policies. It informs diverse policy communities as the established trans-Atlantic North declines and 'the rest', especially the BRICS, rise.

NOW INDEXED ON SCOPUS!

More information about this series at
https://link.springer.com/bookseries/13996

Chang Kyung-Sup

Transformative Citizenship in South Korea

Politics of Transformative Contributory Rights

Chang Kyung-Sup
Sociology
Seoul National University
Seoul, Republic of Korea

ISSN 2662-2483   ISSN 2662-2491 (electronic)
International Political Economy Series
ISBN 978-3-030-87689-0   ISBN 978-3-030-87690-6 (eBook)
https://doi.org/10.1007/978-3-030-87690-6

© The Editor(s) (if applicable) and The Author(s), under exclusive license to Springer Nature Switzerland AG 2022
This work is subject to copyright. All rights are solely and exclusively licensed by the Publisher, whether the whole or part of the material is concerned, specifically the rights of translation, reprinting, reuse of illustrations, recitation, broadcasting, reproduction on microfilms or in any other physical way, and transmission or information storage and retrieval, electronic adaptation, computer software, or by similar or dissimilar methodology now known or hereafter developed.
The use of general descriptive names, registered names, trademarks, service marks, etc. in this publication does not imply, even in the absence of a specific statement, that such names are exempt from the relevant protective laws and regulations and therefore free for general use.
The publisher, the authors and the editors are safe to assume that the advice and information in this book are believed to be true and accurate at the date of publication. Neither the publisher nor the authors or the editors give a warranty, expressed or implied, with respect to the material contained herein or for any errors or omissions that may have been made. The publisher remains neutral with regard to jurisdictional claims in published maps and institutional affiliations.

Cover credit: Rob Friedman/Stockphoto.com

This Palgrave Macmillan imprint is published by the registered company Springer Nature Switzerland AG
The registered company address is: Gewerbestrasse 11, 6330 Cham, Switzerland

*The resarch and writing in the current work have been supported by
the National Research Foundation of Korea Grant
(NRF-2014S1A5B1018229)*

CONTENTS

Part I Historico-Political Contours of Citizenship

1   Introduction: Transformative Citizenship
    in Perspective   3
2   State-Society Relations and Citizenship Regimes
    in East Asia   27
3   Political Citizenship Without Democratic Social
    Representation   55

Part II Citizenship as Transformative Contributory
         Rights

4   Developmental Citizenship and Its Discontents   89
5   Social Citizenship Between Developmental Liberalism
    and Neoliberalism   111
6   Education as Citizenship, or Citizenship by Education   139
7   Reproductive Contributory Rights: From Patriarchal
    to Patriotic Fertility?   163
8   Ad Hoc Cultural Citizenship: Neotraditional
    to Multicultural (Non)transition   175
9   Risk Citizenship in Complex Risk Society   193

Part III Whither Post-Transformative Citizenship

10 Transformative Citizenship, Transformative
    Victimhood   213

Notes   223
References   257
Index   281

Foreword:
Transformative Contributory Rights and Successful Societies

When dealing with citizenship, political science tends to look at rights to passports, arrangements for free and fair voting systems, legitimate opposition, and the independence of the media. These conditions in effect define a functional democracy as much as citizenship. Legal theory has focused more on human rights than citizenship. Law recognizes that every right implies a duty. If I have a right to freedom of speech, I have a duty to protect the independence of the media and in modern times to be vigilant against the spread of fake news and conspiracy theories. However, there is no widely recognized charter of human duties to match human rights. These ideas about rights are often identified with the Protestant Reformation and the origins of liberal theory in Britain in the seventeenth century.

Against this background, sociology came rather late to the debate. We can claim that the critical development in the sociology of citizenship came with a lecture given by T. H. Marshall to University of Cambridge in 1949. This lecture got published as *Citizenship and Social Class and Other Essays* in 1950. He identified juridical, political, and socioeconomic rights as they had evolved in Britain between the seventeenth and nineteenth centuries. This historical development can be said to have resulted in the welfare state within the framework of a democratic system. As such, this system came on the back of Keynesian economics, the Beveridge Report that became the basis of the National Health System, and the Education Act which created the foundations of a universal educational system. Although this British development created the basis of citizenship rights within the context of a welfare state, these developments were not peculiar to Britain and we can find similar developments taking place in Germany and the Scandinavian societies of northern Europe.

The developments pointed to an important transformation of capitalism in providing workers and their families with some level of protection against the harsh realities of unemployment resulting from sickness, old age, the business cycle, and predatory employers. This system was based on the idea of contributory rights which play a large part in Professor Chang's account of citizenship in modern South Korea. This idea expresses the principle that, in return for activities that contribute to the survival and development of society, workers and their dependents will benefit from the activities of the state in sustaining welfare, medical, and educational institutions that in turn underpin a civilized existence. More specifically, the duties of the citizen are to pay taxes on the basis of income, to make contributions to society through, for example, jury or military service, and to support the growth of society through family formation and reproduction. The idea of civility was an important aspect of this early development of citizenship. I have argued that these three supports of citizenship have been eroded by neoliberal economics, the decline of collective welfare as an ideal, the military conscription in favor of privatized military forces, and cultural changes around divorce, reproduction, and gender identity (Turner, 2001).

We cannot satisfactorily study citizenship as a concept in isolation from a range of related ideas such as civilization, city and civility, and courtesy. In any case, citizenship is a measure of inclusion, solidarity, and civility. In Western social and political theory, these are highly interconnected concepts. Edward Shils (1958) also emphasized civility as a key component of democracy, especially regarding the conduct of business within a parliamentary system. The notion of "contributory tights" underlines this relationship. One can elaborate this argument to point out that in a society where civility is respected and prized, there is also a certain level of trust toward politicians, lawyers, teachers, and other public servant, and correspondingly, the citizen is both respected and shown respect. Disrespect may be, at the interpersonal level, one reliable indication that all is not well in public life.

The idea of contributory rights has been developed primarily by sociologists and offers a distinctive tradition quite separate from both political theory and law. To emphasize this distinctive tradition, I shall refer to taxation and its demographic component. Barrington Moore in *Social Origins of Dictatorship and Democracy* (1966) identified three routes to democracy through agrarian class struggle. His basic theory was summarized as "no bourgeoisie, no democracy" in the transition to modernity with special reference to the relationships between feudal landowners and peasants. Moore's thesis can also be presented as "no taxation, no democracy" indicating that withholding tax can be an important political strategy to influence governments. There are different versions of this argument, but there is evidence that democracies flourish where there is an effective taxation system that can deliver state-supported benefits to citizens. By contrast in poor societies with failing economies on the basis of rentier state, there is a weak middle class. What is known as "rentierism" also supports a predatory elite and governments run by clientelism (Herb, 2005). These factors combine to inhibit both the development of democracy and widespread enjoyment of citizenship rights. However, in developed economies with a functioning democracy, the wealthy will adopt various strategies of "wealth defence" (Winters, 2017) to defend their assets from the state. The use of off-shore tax havens is an obvious example.

Moore's thesis was particularly relevant to the English and French transitions to democracy and capitalism, but his argument has also been applied to Korea by Gi-Wook Shin (1998) who argues that "agrarian conflict theory" is important in explaining the origins of modern Korean society. The growth of agrarian class conflict before the 1960s explains why Korean landlords diverted their investment out of agrarian production into the growing urban industrial sector.

Another important dimension to the sociology of citizenship comes from demography. Population growth and health are obvious measures of a successful society. In *Successful Societies*, Peter Hall and Michele Lamont (2009: 2) take population health "as a proxy for social well-being". Their approach finds support in the research of Anne Case and Angus Deaton (2017) who examined declining life expectancy and increasing morbidity rates in the United States. These indicators point to declining health conditions with special reference to white Non-Hispanic males due to low educational achievement, drug abuse, suicide, and homicide.

Demography has not, however, played a sufficiently large role in most theories of citizenship. One exception is to be found in the work of Gunnar Myrdal. In the 1930s, Myrdal and his wife Alva Myrdal published several articles on population issues. In "Population Problems and Policies" (1938), they noted that, given the decline in fertility in Sweden, by the 1970s there would be a rapidly aging population and a declining workforce. The result would be a general decline in economic growth and increasing political unrest. In their proposition, the ideal was that the size of the family should be related to the need for "a constant population stock". However, while family size was a matter of personal choice rather than reflecting the demands of the state, they argued that the family is one of the best guarantees of individual happiness. Myrdal returned to a similar theme in his *Asian Drama* (1968) where in Volume II on "Population Prospects" he concluded that, with falling mortality and fertility remaining largely unchanged, there would be a population explosion in Asia that would have negative effects on economic development.

In the contemporary situation and in all developed societies, there has been what demographers describe as the third demographic transition combining a low fertility rate with widespread availability of contraception, an erosion of the family system with divorce on demand, public acceptance of gay marriage, the growth of female labor in the workforce, and a rapidly ageing population. A society needs a Total Fertility Rate (TFR) of 2.1 to achieve population replacement. The TFR refers to the anticipated births of a woman in her "child-bearing years" between 15 and 49. Many Asian societies are well below replacement. For example, South Korea now has one of the lowest TFRs in the world at 0.84 in 2020, while Niger at 7.0 is one of the highest. The long-term implications for South Korea are a shrinking and aging population which has serious implications for its continued economic growth and for its military capability. Japan also suffers from similar problems with a TFR at 1.4 in 2020. The figure for Singapore was 1.1 in 2020.

I have emphasized this demographic dimension to contributory rights, because it has been a traditional assumption that there is an implied duty that adults through marriage should reproduce in order to sustain the economy and the well-being of the community. As the Myrdals observed, reproduction increases the individual happiness of adult citizens, but the consequence is the reproduction of the society. I would go further to suggest that population replacement can be adopted as a measure of successful societies.

Demographers have argued that once a society has arrived at a TFR level well below the baseline figure of 2.1, it is almost impossible to reverse the trend. If we combine this demographic development with the growth of privatized medicine and education, the decline of compulsory military service accompanied by its growing privatization, and changes in the taxation system of post-Keynesian economies, the traditional bases of contributory rights of a welfare system are disappearing leaving behind an increasingly privatized and individualized system of rights. Perhaps one extreme development in this trend is the ability to buy citizenship if an individual can make a substantial economic contribution to a society. This development is also referred to as "investment citizenship", whereby through an investment plan people can receive an additional passport by a fast track. This practice is widespread. Vanuatu, for example, offers a citizenship oath online via a zoom conference.

One might argue controversially that there are ultimately only two important questions for social science: Can we define "successful societies" and can we explain social and political success? While there are many attempts to answer such questions, satisfactory and convincing answers are few and far between (Stone and Turner, 2020). Perhaps the first point to establish is that the analysis of happiness can be discovered at the very foundations of political theory in Aristotle's discussion of *Eudaimonia* or happiness in the *Nicomachean Ethics* where he says in Book 1 Chapter 4 that happiness is what "the political art aims at" (Aristotle, 2011:1095a16). While he notes that there is general agreement that happiness is the goal of human life, there is no agreement about what it is. The notion of *Eudaimonia* is in fact mistakenly translated as "happiness" and is better understood as "well-being" or "flourishing". We might legitimately infer that for Aristotle a flourishing society is one in which citizens flourish in the context of a safe and secure *polis*. The point of this legacy is that well-being is more than merely personal satisfaction. It is always connected to larger social structures and I would argue, following Chang Kyung-Sup's account of contributory rights, that individual well-being is grounded in a flourishing form of citizenship.

There are any number of indices that are used, both explicitly and implicitly, to measure individual happiness and social and political success, such as economic growth, crime rates, house prices, demographic measures of fertility and longevity, and environmental measures to regulate pollution. In terms of legal and political theory, human rights, rule of law, transparency, the absence of corruption, the role of opposition parties, and the acceptance of opposition as a necessary aspect of a functioning democracy are regarded as basic conditions of liberal democracies.

Despite these tangible achievements in attempts to study successful societies and human happiness, sociologists have remained skeptical about the validity of the enterprise. One standard objection is that these measures are culturally specific coming as they do from Western social science. It is perhaps ironic that the small kingdom of Bhutan, under the guidance of King Jigme Singye Wangchuck in 1972, was the first society to replace Gross Domestic Product with Gross Domestic Happiness as a more relevant, richer, and holistic measure of individual and social well-being. Its diverse indicators include health, living standards, cultural diversity, and good governance that go beyond a simple psychological measure of satisfaction. South Korea does not achieve satisfactory results on happiness (Doh and Chung, 2020). The low level of reported happiness in modern-day South Korea offers further evidence to support Professor Chang's account of the strains of rapid industrialization on the well-being of its citizens.

We can pursue this argument to propose that a successful society is one in which the well-being of individuals is deeply connected to their involvement in the civil sphere as citizenships of a common political community. A society is successful when its citizens believe that their many diverse contributions to society—through taxation, public service, formation of families, and the raising of children—are respected and rewarded by communal approbation, and by governmental policies that contribute to the education of their children, care for their elderly parents, the security of the community, the upkeep of the environment, and so forth. In other words, there is some tangible equivalence between the performance of certain critical duties (voting, payment of taxes, military service, jury service, and communal involvement) and the enjoyment of rights.

This commentary brings me to three obvious questions: Is South Korea a successful society and more specifically what does the history of citizenship in South Korea tell about the well-being of its citizens? Are there further lessons to be drawn from other authoritarian societies that have been successful? At many levels, South Korea is an extraordinary society that has been shaken by many profound internal and external forces including the division of the peninsula and the devastation of the Korean War.

By any standards, it has had a long history of military conflict, colonialism, and militarism. Korea was annexed by Japan in 1910 and then divided in 1948. The Korean War lasted between 1950 and 1953. Under American military influence, it is troubled by problematic and dangerous neighbors. Under these circumstances, its economic growth and social development have been extraordinary. However, as Professor Chang demonstrates, the social and political costs of this transformation have been considerable. The strains of transformative citizenship have included assassination, hardship, and political instability. The demographic transition of South Korea is in many respects a litmus test of these social and political strains. Seoul has a population of just under ten million and is praised for its architecture, transport system, and security, but at the same time the countryside has been denuded of population as young people migrate to the city for employment. As I have indicated, South Korea, alongside Singapore, Hong Kong, and Japan, has a demographic crisis. As South Korean women become highly educated, employed, and single, the import of foreign wives from neighboring societies such as Vietnam has radically changed traditional patterns of agriculture, family life, and population stability. This demographic pattern is also slowly converting South Korea into a multicultural society. Can this demographic transition—with a shrinking and aging population—be sustained without future social and political conflict?

Professor Chang has taken the idea of contributory rights to develop a dynamic picture of Korean politics and society over the last 60 years. This compelling study of South Korea from the Korean War to the present day of uncertainty and danger on the Korean Peninsula is an account of the trials and tribulations of citizenship in this dynamic society. The idea of citizenship and contributory rights provides a powerful explanatory framework of the success and failures of democracy from war to post-war development amid the rise of *chaebol* and family capitalism, the modern-day instability of trade wars between the United States and China, and the emergence of North Korea as an unpredictable nuclear power. *Chaebol* have been the distinctive feature of South Korean capitalist development with family ownership and management plus close ties to the government. The result has been a South Korean power elite and a massive concentration of wealth.

Despite the complexity of the society and its turbulent history, Professor Chang has developed a remarkably coherent view of South Korea through the lens of an ever-changing pattern of citizenship through its developmental and transformative stages. He also provides useful comparisons with developments elsewhere in Asia, especially with Japan. In fact, bureaucratic authoritarian politics has been common under economic development strategies in both Latin America and

Asia. Economic liberalism did not include political liberalism. Another comparison would include Singapore which can be described as a form of soft authoritarianism. Under the firm guidance of Lee Kuan Yew, the People's Action Party exercised continuous rulership. Singapore has enjoyed economic growth and social stability, but at the cost of traditional democratic values and institutions. The paradox of Singapore has been the use of the law to subdue criticisms of the state and its ruling family. Thus far, its bourgeoisie has been willing to forego the luxury of liberal freedoms in favor of stability and economic growth with the benefit of foreign workers who have limited rights to pensions, job security, or welfare benefits. The Singapore elite may not worry too much about its declining fertility rate while it has ample supplies of labor from neighboring Malaysia, Indonesia, and Thailand.

Chang Kyung-Sup has, by refashioning much of the legacy of citizenship studies from T. H. Marshall onward, produced a book of the utmost importance, not just for the study of South Korea, but for an analysis of Asian development in the last century and into this century. South Korea is perhaps the best example of rapid twentieth-century economic growth, but at the cost of democratic entitlements and under conditions of exploitative labor. Can South Korea continue its successful development with its demographic decline, dependence on foreign brides, the difficulties with its neighbors, its lopsided urban development, and its entanglement with American foreign policy? The survival of its system of contributory rights will no doubt play an important role in its ability to respond effectively to these various challenges.

Bryan S. Turner
Australian Catholic University
Banyo, Australia

REFERENCES

Aristotle. 2011. *Aristotle's Nicomachean Ethics*. Chicago and London: The University of Chicago Press (translated by Robert C. Bartlett and Susan D. Collins).

Case, Anne, and Angus Deaton. 2017. "Mortality and Morbidity in the 21 Century." *Brookings Papers on Economic Activity*, 2017(Spring): 397–443.

Doh, Young Yim, and Ji-Bum Chung. 2020. "What Types of Happiness Do Korean Adults Pursue?'" *International Journal of Environment Research and Public Health* 17(5): 1502–1518.

Hall, Peter, and Michele Lamont. 2009. "Introduction." Peter Hall and Michele Lamont, eds., *Successful Societies: How Institutions and Culture Affect Health*, pp. 1–22. Cambridge: Cambridge University Press.

Herb, Michael. 2005. "No Representation without Taxation? Rents, Development, and Democracy." *Comparative Politics* 37(3): 297–316.

Marshall, T. H. 1950. *Citizenship and Social Class and Other Essays*. Cambridge: Cambridge University Press.

Moore, Barrington. 1966. *Social Origins of Dictatorship and Democracy: Lord and Peasant in the Making of the Modern World*. Boston, MA: Beacon Press.

Myrdal, Gunnar. 1968. *Asian Drama: An Inquiry into the Poverty of Nations*. New York: Pantheon Books.

Myrdal, Gunnar, and Alva Myrdal. 1938. "Population Problems and Policies." *Annals of the American Academy of Political and Social Science* 197 (May 1938): 200–215.

Shils, Edward. 1958. "Ideology and Civility: On the Politics of the Intellectual." *Sewanee Revue* 66(3): 450–480.

Shin, Gi-Wook. 1998. "Agrarian Conflict and the Origins of Korean Capitalism." *American Journal of Sociology* 103(5): 1309–1351.

Stones, Rob and Bryan S. Turner. 2020. "Successful Societies: Decision-Making and the Quality of Attentiveness." *British Journal of Sociology* 71(1): 183–200.

Turner, Bryan S. 2001. "The Erosion of Citizenship." *British Journal of Sociology* 52(2): 189–209.

Winters, Jeffrey A. 2017. "Wealth Defense and the Complicity of Liberal Democracy." *Nomos* 58: 158–225.

Preface

My initial interest in the subject of citizenship was engendered by the chronic discrepancies between the legal-ideological declaration of liberal individual(ist) rights in South Korea's national constitution and other formal politico-legal documents and the practical hiatus by politicians, technocrats, public intellectuals, and journalists even in alluding to the notion of citizenship itself. Apparently, South Korea's public elites have perceived or understood—but not denied—citizenship in fundamentally (and interestingly) different ways from their Western counterparts. Many years of analytical efforts to decipher such potential differences in the politico-epistemological dimension have led me to devise various complementary concepts or "ideal types" in pertinently grasping at South Korean social and political realties as are, rather than being obsessed or saddened with the supposed anomalies vis-à-vis the customarily referenced Western experiences and institutions. Ultimately, I began to find myself endeavoring to advance the whole (sub)discipline of citizenship studies into a more cosmopolitan direction by emphasizing a scientific necessity to thoroughly and sensitively reflect the long historical processes and complicated local and international conditions of Asian nations' sociopolitical transformations. Given that citizenship, as a converging point of research on democratization, neoliberalization, and globalization/cosmopolitanization, has suddenly become perhaps the most rapidly growing field of sociological enquiry in East Asia, I am strongly motivated to develop an innovatively integrative citizenship perspective on this world region's distinct sociocultural and political economic conditions.

In so doing, I have been enormously encouraged and supported by Prof. Bryan S. Turner, who has served simultaneously as a crucial source of so many inspiring ideas (some of which are valuably used in this book) and as an earnest collaborator in advancing citizenship issues in East Asia in terms of academic conferences, publications, lectures, and so forth. Above all, we successfully produced together *Contested Citizenship in East Asia: Developmental Politics, National Unity, and Globalization* (Chang Kyung-Sup and Bryan S. Turner, eds., 2012, Routledge) after a related international conference in Seoul. Chapters 2 and 4 in the current book have respectively been modified and updated from my articles in this coedited book, "Different Beds, One Dream? State-Society Relationships and Citizenship Regimes in East Asia" and "Developmental Citizenship in Perspective: The South Korean Case and Beyond". Besides, as the founding editor of the subdiscipline's core journal, *Citizenship Studies*, Turner gave me the honor of serving on the journal's editorial board and subsequently on the journal's advisory board. I guest-edited a special issue of *Citizenship Studies* in 2012, on "South Korea: Politics and Culture of Citizenship", and another special issue in 2020, on "Developmental Citizenship in China: Economic Reform, Social Governance, and Chinese Post-Socialism". For the current work, Turner's scholarship on citizenship serves as a sort of "bridge over troubled water" in dealing with various complicated analytical and epistemological matters embedded in the actually existing conditions of sociopolitical relations and practices.

On the other hand, I would like to acknowledge my intellectual debt to the late Ulrich Beck, whose innovative scholarship has been crucially useful in my exploration of comparative modernities and other related issues. Chapter 9 in this book, "Risk Citizenship in Complex Risk Society", although I cannot show it to him now, reflects many years of close interaction and collaboration between us, particularly through a European Research Council (ERC) project. The current Coronavirus pandemic has made humanity so anxiously witness and experience what Beck explained as "world risk society" and infallibly points to an urgent scholarly (and political) necessity to explore cosmopolitan citizenship in all possible directions. This book on South Korea's characteristic national transformative citizenship, unfortunately, leaves such latest scholarly necessity somewhat untouched. Nonetheless, I do hope this work can help fortify the theoretical and empirical platform for lifting citizenship studies above the hitherto dominant focus on Euro-American experiences and perspectives—that is, what Beck so earnestly emphasized and promoted as "methodological cosmopolitanism" in his final years.

I also would like to thank Dr. Chang Gwi-Yon for collaborating with me earnestly in an earlier study on South Korean democracy and labor politics. While this study was separately published (in Korean) many years ago, many of its rich outcomes have been essentially reflected in Chapter 3 in this book, "Political Citizenship without Democratic Social Representation". As implied in the current book, the deeply gloomy conclusion and prospect about South Korea's working-class politics in the previous work seem to be even more valid now.

When ready to write some of the core chapters of this book, I was invited by University of Cambridge as a Visiting Fellow (and later a life member) of Clare Hall (College) in spring and summer 2019. The university's wonderfully comfortable and intellectually stimulating environment enabled me to make serious progress toward a rough early draft of this book, as the formal outcome of my visiting fellowship research at Clare Hall. Presenting some of the materials in this study at the invited seminars with the university's sociology department and Clare Hall (College) was enormously useful in organizing and refurbishing various critical parts in the book. Sarah Franklin, Manali Desai, John B. Thompson, and Ha-Joon Chang personally shared their time to advice and support me during my term with Cambridge.

Also, colleagues at St Antony's College, University of Oxford—Takehiko Kariya, Hugh Whittaker, and Roger Goodman in particular—warmly invited me during this period and offered their valuable opinions on my work. They later on decided to hold a special international seminar in 2020, in which this work could have been presented. While the Coronavirus pandemic forced its postponement, I eagerly look forward to discussing the current work with them and many other colleagues at Oxford before too long.

In September 2019, I had a privilege of giving a special invitation speech at the Academy of the Kingdom of Morocco (in Rabat, Morocco), which offered me an extremely valuable opportunity to comparatively discuss many issues in this book, particularly with so many distinguished Moroccan and Arabic scholars. I am much thankful to Dr. El Mostafa Rezrazi, among many other colleagues, at the Academy for his deep interest in my work and kind hospitality. I also had somewhat earlier opportunities to present parts of this book's substance in the invited lectures at University of Edinburgh and University of Oxford, thanks to the kind arrangements by Lynn Jamieson, the then British Sociological Association (BSA) president. In addition, I am likewise grateful to Stevi Jackson at University of York, Peter Abrahamson at University of Copenhagen, Laurence Roulleau-Berger at University of Lyon, Rajni Palriwala and Do-Young Kim at University of Delhi, Yong-Chool Ha at University of Washington, Emiko Ochiai at Kyoto University, Hiroshi Kojima at Waseda University, Piao Guang-Xing at Minzu University of China, Raymond Chan at City University of Hong Kong, and Hyaeweol Choi at Australian National University (formerly), for similar lecture invitations at their respective universities on various topics analyzed in this book.

As carefully indicated in various parts of this book, my thesis of transformative citizenship is presented not as an exclusive or unique characteristic of South Korean development and modernization, but as a highly generic sociopolitical and political economic property of most postcolonial nations with a *collective will to catching-up*. In fact, the number and varieties of such nations have constantly increased, in particular, including now the so-called (post-socialist) "transition" societies. I have had a special interest in global varieties of what is analyzed as *developmental citizenship* in Chapter 4 in this book. I was so fortunately joined by a very productive group of mostly East Asian scholars—Alvin So, Lee Dong-Jin, Yoon Jong-Seok, Park Woo, Jeong Jong-Ho, James K. Wong, Moon Woojong, Erik Mobrand, Shen Hsiu-Hua, Jeong Jong-Ho, and Robert Easthope—in exploring the structural features and diverse domains of developmental citizenship in post-socialist China through an international conference at the Institute for China Studies, Seoul National University, in 2018, and the annual special issue of *Citizenship Studies* in 2020 (to be also published as an edited book, *Developmental Citizenship in China: Economic Reform, Social Governance, and Chinese Post-Socialism*, by Routledge in early 2022). I am deeply grateful to these colleagues for contributing their invaluable observations and insights to the new citizenship approach to contemporary China (and a host of other post-socialist nations across the world).

My pursuit of citizenship issues in East Asia has required myself to learn from many more leading scholars in this area as they have effectively contributed to innovating sociology and other social sciences for much better fit with the rapidly and fundamentally changing social realities in the new century. Needless to say, such learning has been valuably utilized in preparing this book. In this regard, I am much grateful to Yoon In-Jin, Seol Dong-Hoon, Kim Hyun-Mee, Arif Dirlik, Ching Kwan lee, Gu Shengzu, Choe Hyun, Ito Peng, Michael Seth, Seungsook Moon, Kong Suk-Ki, Lee Chulwoo, Lee Hyunok, Song Yoo-Jean, Sung Minkyu, Park Myoung-Kyu, Jung Keun-Sik, Kim Seok-ho, and many other colleagues.

Since the substantive topics in the individual chapters of this book cover a full spectrum of social issues, it is simply impossible to acknowledge all my scholarly debts to so many teachers, colleagues, and collaborators who have kindly supported me in understanding and researching the concerned issues. Nonetheless, I would like to express my sincere thanks to: Cho Heung-Sik, Shin Kwang-Yeong, Eun Ki-Soo, Song In-Ha, Lee Joonkoo, Shim Doobo, Han Joon, Lee Cheol-Sung, Lee Keun, Lee Hyeon Jung, Chin Meejung, Lee Jung Hee, Dietrich Rueschemeyer, Paget Henry, Chang Gwi-Yon, Zhang Yi, Ito Peng, Kim Taekyoon, Park Tae-Gyun, Chang Dae-oup, Kim Se-Kyun, Lim Hyun-Chin, Kim Myoung Soo, Cho Youngdal, Kwon Hyeong-ki, Chua Beng Huat, Youna Kim, Kim Kyong-Dong, Yoon Sang-Chul, Elizabeth Thurbon, Sophia Seung-Yoon Lee, Shin Wook-Hee, Kim Eui-Young, Ahn Mi-Young, Pietro Masina, GöranTherborn, C. P. Chandrasekhar, Kim Hong-Jung, Han Sang-Jin, Hong Doo-Seung, Shin Yong-Ha, Park Keong-Suk, Bae Eun-Kyung, Chang Dukjin, Kim Chul-Kyu, Kim Heung-Ju, Han Wan-Sang, Kwon Tae-Hwan, Kwon Hyunji, Choo Jihyun, Song Ho-Keun, Ham In-Hee, Chin Seung-Kwon, John Lie, Hagen Koo, Nancy Abelmann, Pieter Boele Van Hensbroek, Linda Weiss, Ben Fine, Tat Yan Kong, Sven Hort, and many others.

Finally, I greatly thank Timothy M. Shaw and Anca Pusca, respectively, Palgrave Macmillan's academic and executive editor in charge of the publisher's prestigious International Political Economy (IPE) series. The marvelously satisfactory experiences in publishing in the same IPE series my earlier authored book, *Developmental Liberalism in South Korea: Formation, Degeneration, and Transnationalization* (2019) and my coedited volume, *Developmental Politics in Transition: The Neoliberal Era and Beyond* (with Ben Fine and Linda Weiss, 2012), have continued with the current book thanks to their enthusiastic support. Also, I am so grateful to Uma Vinesh at the publisher for offering me wonderful logistical and editorial service, and appreciate the superb effort of the publisher's production team.

Chang Kyung-Sup

About This Book

South Korea's postcolonial history has been replete with dramatic societal transformations through which it has seemingly emerged with a fully blown modernity, or compressed modernity. While both the state and civil society were severely unstable with their own survival remaining in question, the volatile internal conditions and international environments required them to hurriedly embark on rapid civilizational and developmental transitions. Paradoxically, such transformations were often pursued as a strategic means to overcome the sociopolitical dilemmas stemming from the inchoate, dependent, and even illegitimate nature of the state machinery and dominant social order. There have arisen the transformation-oriented state, society, and citizenry for which each transformation becomes an ultimate purpose in itself, the processes and means of the transformations constitute the main sociopolitical order, and the transformation-embedded interests form the core social identity. In this milieu, a distinct mode of citizenship has been engendered in terms of *transformative contributory rights*. Citizenship as transformative contributory rights can be defined as effective and/or legitimate claims to national and social resources, opportunities, and/or respects that accrue to each citizen's contributions to the nation's and/or society's collective transformative goals. In South Korea's aggressive and precipitous societal transformations, its citizens have been exhorted or have exhorted themselves to intensely engage in each of such transformations, so that their citizenship has been very much framed and substantiated by the conditions, processes, and outcomes of such collective transformative engagements. This book concretely and systematically analyzes how such transformative dynamic has respectively shaped South Koreans' developmental, social, educational, reproductive, and cultural citizenship.

Acronyms

BSA	British Sociological Association
CEO	Chief Executive Officer
CFEPH	China Financial and Economic Publishing House
CIA	Central Information Agency
Covid 19	Coronavirus Disease 2019
CSR	Corporate Social Responsibility
DLP	Democratic Labor Party
DMZ	Demilitarized Zone
EPB	Economic Planning Board
ERC	European Research Council
G7	Group of Seven
GDP	Gross Domestic Product
GONGO	Government-Organized Non-Governmental Organization
ICT	Information and Communication Technology
IMF	International Monetary Fund
IRAA	Imperial Rule Assistance Association
IUCN	International Union of Conservation for Nature
KCIA	Korea Central Information Agency
KCTU	Korean Confederation of Trade Unions
KDI	Korea Development Institute
KHEI	Korea Higher Education Research Institute
KICE	Korea Institute for Curriculum and Evaluation
KIDI	Korea Insurance Development Institute
KMT	Kuomintang or Guomindang
KOSIS	Korean Statistical Information Service
K-pop	Korean Popular Music

KREI	Korea Rural Economic Institute
KRIVET	Korea Research Institute for Vocational Education and Training
KSO	Korea Statistical Office
KWDI	Korea Women's Development Institute
LDP	Liberal Democratic Party
MOE	Ministry of Education
MOGEF	Ministry of Gender Equality and Family
MOPAS	Ministry of Public Administration and Safety
NEC	National Election Commission
NGO	Non-Governmental Organization
NPO	Non-Profit Organization
NSO	National Statistical Office
OECD	Organisation for Economic Cooperation and Development
PCASPP	Presidential Committee on Ageing Society and Population Policy
PRC	People's Republic of China
PSPD	People's Solidarity for Participatory Democracy
ROK	Republic of Korea
SAT	Scholastic Ability Test
SKY	Seoul National University, Korea University, Yonsei University
SMEs	Small and Medium-sized Enterprises
SRI	Statistics Research Institute
TFR	Total Fertility Rate
UK	United Kingdom
UN	United Nations
UNDP	United Nations Development Programme
USA	United States of America
USSR	Union of Soviet Socialists Republics
WTO	World Trade Organization
WWII	World War II

LIST OF FIGURES

Chapter 4

Photo 1   Presidential candidate Lee Myung-Bak addressing the Republic of Korea 747 Supporters Association, 7 August 2000   98

Chapter 5

Fig. 1   Proportions benefitting from social insurances and fringe benefits by employment status after the national financial crisis   129

Chapter 8

Fig. 1   Growth and composition in international marriages in South Korea   186
Photo 1   "Korea-Vietnam/Philippines Family Video Reunion" organized by Ministry of Public Administration and Safety (MOPAS)   187
Photo 2   Children shouting, "Let us do away with the word, "multicultural"!"   189
Photo 3   Vietnam students in South Korea protesting against international marriage brokers' racist and sex-selling practices and South Korean society's neglect   190

Chapter 9

Photo 1 The collapse of Sampoong Department Store, 29 June 1995   195

LIST OF TABLES

Chapter 3

| Table 1 | Rate of overlap between DLP and KCTU union members (as of June 2002) | 73 |
| Table 2 | The first election results of the British Labour Party and the Democratic Labor Party in South Korea | 75 |

Chapter 4

| Table 1 | Main election pledges of presidential candidates in the authoritarian political era | 93 |
| Table 2 | Offense assessment factors for business crimes committed by ruling shareholder families and professional managers of business conglomerates (*chaebol*) | 102 |

Chapter 5

| Table 1 | Social expenditure trend in South Korea vs OECD average (% GDP) | 117 |

Chapter 6

| Table 1 | OECD countries with higher proportions of population aged 25–34 with tertiary education (latest: 2018 or before) | 141 |

Table 2 SKY university students by familial income strata in the first
semester of 2018 (SKY: Seoul National University, Korea
University, Yonsei University) 158

Chapter 7

Table 1 Countries with the world's highest and lowest levels
of total fertility rate in 2018 166

Chapter 8

Table 1 Family life cycle distribution of rural households on the eve
of the sudden increase in international marriages 184

PART I

Historico-Political Contours of Citizenship

CHAPTER 1

Introduction: Transformative Citizenship in Perspective

1 INTRODUCTION

"The return of the nation-state" is apparent all around the globe that has been literally blanketed by a new type of Coronavirus. Amid most countries' shutdown of national borders and pressure for various aliens' repatriation, humanity is hurriedly reshuffled (again) by the politico-administrative identification regime of national citizenship. Ironically, the legal imposition of each person's restrictive physical belonging according to national citizenship has revealed vastly diverse conditions of basic citizenship rights in the modern nation-states. In a sense, the new Coronavirus has functioned as a powerful analytical tool (or a litmus test if you would prefer) in concretely and systematically divulging the variegated national conditions of citizenship rights across the world—perhaps, more persuasive and realistic than any of the previous theoretical and empirical studies by human social scientists on this essential issue.

Such seems to be particularly the case regarding South Korea, a country whose successful actions to curb the Coronavirus epidemic have been earnestly praised by numerous foreign media and political leaders. It has even served as a model reference with which many foreign governments have been scolded in comparison by many influential journalists and experts. This development may well help to substantially make up for the country's hitherto embarrassment at the frequent international as well as domestic criticisms concerning its defective social security system and concomitant human sufferings (as manifested in terms of its globally scandalous levels of household indebtedness, old-age poverty, suicide, low fertility, and so forth). At least, the strong practicality of South Korea's universal health insurance program has been demonstrated before the whole world as it has enabled the government to take timely and aggressive actions in tracking down Coronavirus diffusion in human interactions and hospitalizing every each infection-diagnosed individual with no immediate public or private financial worries. However, far more complex aspects of its citizenship rights have been revealed in the country's initial reaction to the epidemic's outbreak and subsequent preparation for the hoped post-Coronavirus era.

South Korea's modern history has been replete with national or nation-shocking disasters caused politically, socially, industrially, and ecologically, often with complex international entanglement. Each of these disasters has produced a game-changer effect in the state-citizen relations, whether temporarily or permanently. That is, South Korean citizens, who are ordinarily contentious and defiant as shown vividly in determined mass protests against the state almost every day, suddenly get ready to be mobilized and regimented by the government in order to expeditiously overcome the imminent or ongoing crises.

In the current "COVID-19" situation, the government instantly summoned civilian experts in the biomedical industry to virtually order them to develop Coronavirus test instruments almost overnight and relentlessly organized technicians in the ICT industry to instantly build the digital information system for tracking down actual and potential routes of Coronavirus diffusion through human movements and interactions (Kim and Kim, 2020). The government did not even bother to strongly persuade ordinary citizens to understand and accept the emergency necessity for their (digital) subjection to the unprecedented public intrusion into privacy, not to mention the medical necessity for their virtual house-arrest for two weeks if found having been in a certain vicinity of any infected person (Löw and Knoblauch, 2020). When the Sincheonji (New World) cult incident broke out in Daegu City in early 2020, involving thousands of its members who were simultaneously diagnosed of Coronavirus infection and thereby drove the city's medical system into a near collapse, it took only a phone call by the prime minister to Samsung before many other private firms lined up to offer the government's use of their social facilities for accommodating the so-called light symptom patients of infection. (These rather lucky patients accounted for a large majority of the Coronavirus patients in Daegu, given the cult's exceptional success in winning over youth under the chronic employment crisis.) At the same time, when several hundreds of doctors, nurses, and other medical personnel immediately "volunteered" to serve in Daegu, they were readily dispatched to specially (re)organized medical units for Coronavirus-infected patients, many of which are privately controlled, though nominally non-profit, hospitals. In a society where the government rarely receives open praise from society, civilian experts and organizations as well as ordinary citizens all of a sudden turned into earnest and devoted collaborators in the current national exigency of "overcoming the Coronavirus crisis".

Does this attest to what American sociologist, Peter Evans, characterizes as the state's "embedded autonomy" in South Korean development—or perhaps the state's embedded capacity in that the state's autonomy sounds somewhat out of context in a practically state-created political economy? The South Korean government is already busy *reinventing the Coronavirus crisis into another national transformation*, namely a neodevelopmental industrial drive under the borrowed but somewhat Koreanized slogan of "the fourth industrial revolution". The apparently impressive contributions of the biomedical and ICT industries to the country's globally celebrated success (so far) in a uniquely inventive system of quarantine—accompanied by frequent phone calls from foreign state leaders to beg for prioritized export of South Korean firms' Coronavirus test kits and other related equipment—seem to have so excited economic technocrats and their otherwise shy president, Moon Jae-In, that he triumphantly declared an ambitious industrial policy plan to urgently help develop these industries as new centers of export promotion with huge financial and regulatory support. "Turn a crisis into an opportunity" has been perhaps the most favored catchword to so many political and industrial leaders in South Korea, now practically including Moon. On his return from the G7+4 Summit in the UK, Moon emphatically remarked during his cabinet meeting (22 June 2021) as below:

> Despite the painful history and geopolitical difficulties, our people never got frustrated or despaired, but achieved both dazzling economic growth and democracy so as to become a globally recognized country… The

Republic of Korea continues to advance forward. It challenges ceaselessly by turning crisis into opportunity and keeps opening the future… The dynamics and creativity of our people and enterprises have served as the driving force for innovations and led development by leaps and bouns in such diverse areas as high-tech industry, science and technology, and culture and art It is dreaming of the leap from a catching-up nation to a leading nation. (https://www.korea.kr/news/stateCouncilList.do)

The still developmentalist state's aggressively expressed willingness to crown the concerned industries as possible new champions of national economic developmentalism could not but be an unexpected boon to them. (This was all the more so if one considers that Moon shyly excused himself during the noisy quarrel between his developmentalist economic technocrats and the ruling political party over the universal or income-selective boundary of even a very modest sum of one-time disaster relief allowance in the summer of 2020.)

The Coronavirus crisis will eventually end sooner or later in South Korea (and in any other societies), but by then it will have transformed into a new society with another compressed layer of modernity added on to the existing multiple compressed layers of modernity, or *compressed modernity* as explained in my earlier work (Chang, K., 1999, 2010a, 2010b). Continual societal crises in South Korea have served as the sociopolitical platform for (mostly yet controversially successful) national transformations, as evinced by its robust democracy, advanced industrial economy, and rich and diverse culture, coupled with various chronic symptoms of social despair (as vividly described in the Oscar-awarded movie, *Parasite*). Most broadly, the nation's postcolonial and post-war existence—as an entity economically exploited under decades of Japanese colonialism, physically burnt down nationwide by the Korean War, and militarily threatened by North Korea (along with its next door communist patrons, China and the Soviet Union)—constituted a crisis in itself. South Koreans' citizenship as rights, duties, and identities in relation to the state and society needs to be seriously probed against the country's almost normalized situation of recurrent societal crises and the transformative nature of state-citizen relations attuned to the progressive overcoming of such crises. This book, framed through the concept/theory of *transformative contributory rights*, has been written precisely in that direction.

2 Transformative Contributory Rights: South Korean Modernity, Transformative Collectivism, and Citizenship

Koreans, and other East Asians, are known to be collectivist or, interchangeably but arguably speaking, communitarian. If seen in a modern historical context, South Koreans' being collectivist is far from a unique phenomenon. Even without summoning the arguable ancestral heritages, they have been *existentially collectivist* due to their subjection, as an irreducible ethnic nation, to Japan's racist capitalist colonialism, Americans' neocolonialist military occupation, an (ethno)nationalist inter-Korea war, nationalist development and modernization, and so forth (Lie, J., 1998). Under all these drastic, often internationally driven, collective experiences, their survival has necessitated the ethos of "If united, we survive; if divided, we die".[1] The scales and traits of the main historical factors for their turbulent existence have required them to pursue both immediate survival and long-term prosperity in collectivist manners. Such practical collectivism—or collectivism as social practice—has been most critically defined, indoctrinated, and reproduced by the state, both when led by the conservative and the arguably progressive forces. The South Korean state, however, has confronted with quite contentious civil society, which ironically has its own strong collectivist aspiration for becoming the state itself whether in nationalist-socialist or social democratic terms. Despite its many distinct elements and aspects, South Koreans' existential collectivism is a generically shared trait of most postcolonial peoples.

Citizenship, the supposedly quintessential sociopolitical component of liberal modernity, has existed in South Korea along with such collectivist conditions of survival and prosperity. It is in this context that citizenship, paradoxically, has rarely been politically articulated, socially debated, or even academically researched in this now proudly democratic nation. Even the word "citizen" (*simin* if literally translated) is not comfortably accepted in public discourses and academic writings.[2] *Simin* is usually understood as a physical-administrative subject of city resident, whereas an ordinary city is devoid of any such historico-civilizational status as in Europe (i.e., the historically founded social arena of free industrial and merchant class).[3] In circumstances where citizen would be referred to in a liberal Western society, *gukmin*—meaning "nation person" literally or "national"—has been uttered.[4] This notion of citizenship is aptly related to what Bryan S. Turner observes as follows:

> The first form [of citizenship] occurs where there is a strong connection between state formation and the emergence of citizenship as national membership. National citizenship has typically assumed the character of ethno-nationalism and was important in nation-building activities from the nineteenth century onwards. In Asia, this type of citizenship was closely related to the so-called developmental state, and in Latin America national citizenship was also connected to nation-building activities of dominant elites… In both South Korea and Japan, military elites were influential in driving the agenda of ethno-nationalism and social modernization during the period of state formation. (Turner and Chang, 2012: 243)

When a South Korean is referred to as a *gukmin*, he/she implicitly becomes a "state person" as well, and thereby subject to all kinds of taken-for-granted rules, orders, duties, and even morals implicitly or explicitly devised and promoted by the state and its quasi-technocratic intellectual and media functionaries.[5] The nation (*gukga* or, interchangeably, *nara*) is perceived as an amalgamated institution encompassing in effect all of the historical ethnicity of *hangyeore*, modern civil society, and the legal-bureaucratic state.

In a fundamental paradox, the state itself has been legally defined by strict stipulations on modern liberal democracy. The Republic of Korea—launched in 1948 after the political model of the United States—was, institutionally speaking, one of the most advanced democratic polities at that time. Postcolonial South Korean society simply could not look back to its precolonial polity and was advised, and forced, to instantly study and adopt the American systems of politics as well as economy, education, and so forth (Cumings, 1981; Mobrand, 2019; Park, T., 2008). Thereby arose an on-paper liberal polity in which the state is existentially justified in respect of its contractually reciprocal relationship with *all individual citizens*. At least in law, each citizen was duly positioned to reciprocate with the state in terms of fully democratic citizenship rights and duties.[6]

The practical utility of the advanced liberal—by definition, individualist—polity legally declared as such, however, was fundamentally collectivist from the very beginning. "Free democracy" adopted and protected therein implied every citizen's collective duty of rejecting communism and all its associated ideas, policies, institutions, groups, and persons (sometimes including friends, families, and relatives). Such collectivist duty, scarily codified in the National Security Law, has chronically overridden all citizens' individual(ist) rights or claims on such rights. During many years under the military's dictatorship, in practice, communism was often identified as any acts or thoughts that oppose the military-led anti-communist state (Kim, D., 2006). That is, citizens could claim their citizenship rights, including very basic civil freedom, only if they obeyed the dictatorial, and proudly nationalist, military state (Moon, S., 2005). At the same time, the same state successfully orchestrated a sort of nationalist industrialization in which capitalism was defined as a collective national venture and each citizen was exhorted to participate virtually as a national political duty. Under all these circumstances, calling a citizen *gukmin*, instead of *simin*, and being called as such were epistemologically accustomed to. On the other hand, citizen (*simin*), as a sort of *reflexive* concept derived from complex European experiences, has been too much an intellectual and/or academic property alien to ordinary people.[7] Civil society activists, on the basis of their hard won experiences against the authoritarian state, have used *simin* more often than social scientists, who feel somewhat burdened in qualifying the term in the South Korean context.[8]

Nothing seemed to be fundamentally changing even after the military retreated from politics (Choi, J., 2002). South Koreans have kept being called *gukmin* and have rarely asserted themselves as individual(st) claimers of sovereign socioeconomic rights, if any. Ironically, when the national financial crisis broke out in 1997–1998, they were collectivistically summoned again by the then proudly democratic state leadership (under Kim Dae-Jung) to sacrifice their jobs and even help to "collect gold" (to be changed into foreign currencies) for "saving the national economy first" (Chang, K., 2019, Ch. 3). In fact, it was the clumsy mimicry by Kim Young-Sam's "civilian government" (*munminjeongbu*) of the Park Chung-Hee-style nationalist developmental drive that had caused the unprecedented national economic fiasco. Subsequently, the two politically less conservative, albeit socioeconomically neoliberal, administrations, under Kim Dae-Jung and Roh Moo-Hyun, respectively, did attempt to acknowledge and promote some of individual citizens' irreducible citizenship rights, but fell short of developmentally rehabilitating the national economy with a broad popular basis (conceptualized below in this book as *developmental citizenship*).

Consequently, in the next two presidential elections, South Koreans (re)turned to the collective developmentalist pledges of two Park Chung-Hee marketers, Lee Myung-Bak (a famous industrialist in the Park Chung-Hee era) and Park Geun-Hye (a daughter of Park Chung-Hee), respectively. However, upon their policy failure in delivering such pledges, besides many alleged and revealed personal corruption scandals, millions of South Koreans took to the streets in the globally televised spectacles of "candlelight protests", chanting "Daehanminguk is a democratic republic, and sovereignty rests with *gukmin*".[9] (In Park Geun-Hye's case, a secret crony's political/administrative interference and personal corruption even led to her impeachment.) Lee and Park, and even all other post-military presidents, seem to have made South Koreans gradually become disenchanted with nationalist or state-centered collectivist agendas. But this does not (and cannot) mean that citizens are finally determined or enabled to instead deal with the state on an individualistic contractual basis. Instead, a widespread tendency is to withdraw from the public sphere and even from the publicly normalized or encouraged type of private life (for instance, working, marrying, and procreating).

Does South Korea's above sociopolitical trajectory imply that its people's citizenship has always been an empty shell? In spite of such sociopolitical intransigence, the country has undergone quite stunning levels and spans of modern civilizational and developmental transformations which I have theorized and analyzed as *compressed modernity* in many earlier writings. Compressed modernity is defined as *a civilizational condition in which economic, political, social and/or cultural changes occur in an extremely condensed manner in respect to both time and space, and in which the dynamic coexistence of mutually disparate historical and social elements leads to the construction and reconstruction of a highly complex and fluid social system* (Chang, K., 2017a). South Korean life since the nation's liberation in 1945 from the Japanese colonial rule has been replete with dramatic institutional, developmental, sociopolitical, and ethnonational transitions in which each and every South Korean's citizenship status has dramatically formed and changed in conjunction with the state's—and sometimes civil society's—collectivist purposes. That is, *a distinct regime of citizenship embedded in transformative collectivism has evolved out of South Korea's compressed modernity*.

Under compressed modernity, incessant and abrupt societal transformations have dictated South Koreans to confront not only the difficulties inherent in such changes but, more critically, the troubles ensuing from the crude institutional conditions for managing them.[10] While both the state and civil society were immature and unstable with their own survival remaining in question, the internal conditions and international environments required them to embark on, among other changes, rapid institutional and techno-scientific modernization and aggressive economic development. In fact, such transformations were often pursued in order to strategically trounce the sociopolitical dilemmas stemming from the inchoate, dependent, and even illegitimate nature of the state machinery and dominant social order. There have arisen *the transformation-oriented state, society, and citizenry to which each transformation becomes an ultimate purpose in itself, the processes and means of the transformations constitute the main sociopolitical order, and the transformation-embedded interests form the core social identity*. While these transformations have usually been circumstantially necessitated or even dictated, the dominance of the collectivist transformative order is apparently analogous to what Max Weber (1946) expounded as the means-end reversal under modernity.

In this milieu, a distinct mode of citizenship has been engendered in terms of *transformative contributory rights*. "Contributory rights" is Bryan S. Turner's definition of citizenship—in particular, social rights as compared to individual or human rights—in modern democracies (Turner, 2001; Isin and Turner, 2007). It is contributory because "effective claims against a society are made possible by the contributions that citizens have made to society typically through work, war, or parenting" (Isin and Turner, 2007: 12). He further observes:

> Despite its inherited character, citizenship is often based on some notion of the reciprocity between duties and rights on the one hand, and on achievement, striving, and effort on the other. We can therefore regard citizenship as a system of contributory rights in which there is, albeit approximately, some relationship between our contributions to a community and what we receive back in return. (Turner and Chang, 2012: 245)

Similarly, citizenship as transformative contributory rights can be defined as *effective and/or legitimate claims to national and social resources, opportunities, and/or respects that accrue to each citizen's contributions to the nation's or society's collective transformative purposes*.

The purpose of this book is to show that, as South Korea has been aggressively and precipitously engaged in institutional and technoscientific modernization, economic development, political democratization, economic and sociocultural globalization, and, mostly recently, ethnonational reformation, its citizens have been exhorted or have exhorted themselves to intensely engage in each of these transformations, and their citizenship, constituted by identities, duties, and rights, has been very much framed and substantiated by the conditions, processes, and outcomes of such *collective transformative engagements*. Transformative contributory rights, or transformative citizenship, constitute a citizenship regime of compressed development and modernization in South Korea, and basically in most of postcolonial developing nations. It reflects an instrumentalist sociopolitical order of South Korea, and many other postcolonial nations, under compressed modernity, and requires a systematic amendment of the Marshallian theory of democratic citizenship evolution (Marshall, 1964).

3 SOUTH KOREA/EAST ASIA IN CITIZENSHIP PERSPECTIVE

In recent years, East Asia has served as a fertile ground for imagining or advocating paradigmatic alternatives to the so-called Western modernity. The conceptual and/or theoretical alternatives in this regard include among others "the developmental state" (Wade, 1990; Amsden, 1989, 1994; Weiss, 1998), politics with "Asian values" (Kim, D., 1994; Zakaria and Lee, 1994), paternalistic management and team production (Dore, 1973; Ohno, 1988; Whittaker, 1990), family-controlled business and society (Carney and Gadajlovic, 2003; Kang, M., 1996; Chang, K., 2010a), corporatized or company-dependent/friendly labor (Jacoby, 2004; Lee, C., 1999), family-centered and/or "developmental" welfare regimes (Goodman, et al., 1998; Peng, et al., 2010; Chang, K., 2018, 2019), "education zeal" as developmental impetus (Seth, 2002; Kariya, 2013), and so forth. The international scholarly appeal of these arguments has oscillated with fluctuations in the practical performance and stability of East Asia's economies, polities, industries, labor systems, welfare regimes, and educational systems. Most recently, the gradual, yet seemingly irreversible, degeneration of Western economic, political, corporate, and social systems has increasingly led numerous Western observers to tout "East Asian alternatives" as possible universal prescriptions for new directions in socioeconomic change.

Despite these seemingly congratulatory appraisals of East Asia, each society in this region has struggled with a range of chronic contradictions between the state-organized collectivist order of political rule and civil life on the one hand and individual citizens' fundamentally atomized pursuit of material interests on the other hand (Yan, Y., 2010; Chang and

Song, 2010). Historically speaking, the frail contractual basis of the state-society (or state-citizen) relationship has plagued each country in their respective state-led and/or international order-driven transformation of national governance and political economy. Such sociopolitical defect has had to be complemented by circumstantially improvised ideologies and incentives for materially incorporating citizenry into public life.

It is in this context that East Asian societies' inventive and occasionally neotraditionalist systems of political rule, economic governance, corporate management, labor relations, social policy, and education have typically come into play. Such improvised strategies and programs often lack a fundamental philosophical-ideological ground which would allow for legitimate, consensual, and effective settlement of disputes between the state and citizenry concerning the diverse problems indicated above. Because of this fundamental historical and civilizational dilemma of East Asian societies, citizenship—as the institutional core of state-citizen relationship in modern politics—can serve as the foundation for their sociopolitical and even economic rebirth. In contrast to their common economic vitality and competitiveness, each East Asian society's political modernity has been plagued with various illiberal norms, practices, and powers that tend repeatedly to compromise or distort citizens' legitimate rights and political status to the service of oligarchic political interests. Therefore, the scrutiny of these state-society relations from the citizenship perspective can lead to a deeper and more wide-ranging structural critique of East Asian politics and society.

Broadly speaking, citizenship as a theoretical concept and an analytical perspective can present a new level of understanding even in respect to the earlier mentioned East Asian alternatives to Western modernity. Concerning "the developmental state", for instance, we need to research the specific conditions and attributes of citizenship as are shaped by the state's aggressive mobilization of national resources and authoritarian control of class relations and civil life in the overt interests of economic development (see Chapter 4 in this book). While "developmental statism" is rarely codified in terms of public and constitutional stipulations of the state-citizen relationship, the everyday content of statist political rule and social reactions to that rule mostly revolve around these very developmental issues and interests. Thus, the predominant focus on economic management in most studies on East Asia's developmental states should be critically complemented by a sociopolitical focus on the developmental enfranchisement of social classes and individual citizens often at the expense of civil, political, and social citizenship rights (see Chapter 4 in this book). Concerning family-controlled business and society, we need to question the hollowed-out nature of civil society and the national economy outside the familial boundaries that often liquidate, either legally or ideologically, the declared social rights of ordinary citizens. Concerning paternalistic management and company-dependent labor, we need to examine, on the one hand, the compromised civil and political rights of workers who are chronically subjugated to the legally unjustifiable, yet practically tolerated, absolutist labor relations and, on the other hand, the disenfranchised social rights of other citizens who are excluded from various corporate welfare benefits as a surrogate of state-organized social security (Chang, K., 2019). Concerning the family-centered and/or the developmental welfare system, we need to pay serious attention to the systematically absent social rights of those who lack adequate familial support networks or remain alienated from the developmental political economy owing to the lack of health, skill, or capital (Chang, K., 2010, 2019). Concerning the "education zeal" of East Asian families as yet another developmental impetus, we need to scrutinize the disenfranchising effect of family-financed competitive education on increasing numbers of children who have neither affluent parents nor generous support from communities, governments, or schools (see Chapter 6 in this book). Likewise, with respect to the idea of politics with "Asian values", we need to investigate thoroughly the philosophical and political parameters by which each modern state in East Asia asserts itself toward its citizenry as the supposed embodiment of sovereignty. The substantive necessity and analytical value of examining citizenship are obvious in these critical issues in contemporary East Asia. But such scholarly utilities of citizenship are yet to be realized in terms of actual research efforts, whether by East Asian scholars or by anyone interested in the region.

Aside from the general theoretical and analytical utilities of citizenship in understanding East Asian societies, citizenship as a specific social institution and/or agenda therein should be examined more systematically. It is in very recent years that such examinations are actively carried out, mostly by local scholars, in response to the changing political economic and sociocultural conditions in East Asia's own late modernity. South Korea has been particularly active in such scholarship, which in turn reflects the society's dynamic transformations that are often perceived or framed through citizenship. Such transformations include: social citizenship demands attendant upon political democratization and economic neoliberalization (see Chapter 5 in this book), promotion or propagation of multicultural citizenship in response to explosive marriage transnationalization (see Chapter 8 in this book), even human rights claims at chronically authoritarian workplaces (Kim, D., 1995), and so forth. Most of these studies are empirically oriented and have generated abundant vivid outcomes on South Korea's changing social realities in the twenty-first century. Nonetheless, this line of scholarship has been limited to a certain group of "special topics" that have also been studied in numerous other societies in similar citizenship perspectives. That is, the recently activated local scholarship on citizenship has yet to evolve into broader, hopefully inventive theoretical and analytical paradigms on society-at-large.

Such scholarly evolution cannot, of course, do without systematic readings of Western or global knowledge on citizenship. But there are two critical aspects in which (West-led) global scholarship on citizenship should be ameliorated for the sake of its East Asian, and global, utility. First, there seems to be a critical lacuna in theoretical work on the macro-historical conditions for citizenship to become a fully meaningful framework for non-Western (liberal) countries' sociopolitical order. Citizenship—citizenship rights in particular—has civilizationally traveled to formally democratic nations outside the West mainly as a *reflexive* institutional element—above all in defining citizens' legal rights and duties in their broadly West-simulative constitutions. However, such legal-institutional simulation does not necessarily ensure that either state elites or ordinary citizens will give serious moral attention and/or political commitment to citizenship, under the absence of critical historico-social processes for its formation comparable to those of "the West". Second, citizenship, mostly as forms and substances reflecting Western experiences, has recently been adopted as a conceptual-cum-analytical tool for social, cultural, and political analyses in rapidly increasing fields and bodies of research on Asian and other non-Western societies. However, partly due to the first aspect, conclusions of these studies are often based upon simplified, explicit or implicit, allusions to the distances or differences of these societies from Western societies in the extent and/or quality of citizenship. More of conceptual/theoretical and empirical work on different forms and substances of citizenship, and/or other possible types of sociopolitical belonging, in non-Western societies, should be encouraged and acknowledged in order to understand these societies in their own historical and sociopolitical terms. (This book has been prepared partly as an effort to help overcome these two critical limits of global and local scholarship on citizenship.)

In this study, as a final point, citizenship is approached simultaneously as a substantive concern, a theoretical perspective, and, finally, an analytical strategy. Concerning citizenship (or various types of citizenship) as a substantive concern, suffice it to say that, as already indicated above, citizenship in South Korea/East Asia has been somewhat neglected in the existing scholarship. This lacuna in citizenship research is of course not just a problem at the level of scholarship, but also a practical issue in East Asian political systems. Not only are East Asian societies much less progressively liberal than Western societies, but their scholars are much less sensitive to the fundamental sociopolitical components of a liberal order (including, above all, citizenship) than is the case for Western scholars. Relatedly, taking citizenship as a major theoretical perspective will automatically lead to a debunking of innumerable scholarly as well as practical issues in South Korean/East Asian politics, society, and economy. Finally, citizenship can serve as a powerful analytical strategy for researching East Asia. Citizenship studies provide detailed and systematic accounts of state-society relations and citizens' status within the national society and polity that may be readily communicated to ordinary citizens as well as experts. The language of entitlement and fairness is not inherently complex or obscure, and, in my view, it is a language shared in the public sphere by ordinary persons. In the terminology of John Rawls (2001), the academic account of citizenship rights provides a vocabulary that is well suited to establishing an overlapping consensus of fundamental beliefs in a "well-ordered decent society". I contend that the academic and practical utilities of citizenship as a substantive concern, a theoretical perspective, and an analytical strategy are clearly demonstrated in the South Korean context as shown in the subsequent chapters of this book.

4 Summary of the Chapters

This book consists of three segments, respectively entitled: Part I. Historico-Political Contours of Citizenship; Part II. Citizenship as Transformative Contributory Rights; Part III. Whither Post-Transformative Citizenship. Part I presents two chapters respectively covering broad comparative and historical contexts for modern South Koreans' sociopolitical status by focusing on the interrelationships among the state, civil society, capitalist social classes, as well as colonial/neocolonial foreign forces. These two chapters will help elucidate why and how citizenship-in-practice in postcolonial South Korea has fundamentally diverged from Western precedents and instead veered toward the particular form of transformative contributory rights as explained in Part II. The six chapters in Part II are the main outcomes of my analysis of South Koreans' transformative contributory rights in respect to national economic development, social welfare, education, population (fertility in particular), culture, and risk. Part III concludes this book with a chapter on transformative victimhood vis-à-vis transformative citizenship.

Chapter 2. State-Society Relations and Citizenship Regimes in East Asia

This chapter overviews the individual dynamics of state-civil society relations in Japan, South Korea, and China, comparatively assesses the historico-political effects of such relationships on each country's citizenship regime, and discusses major theoretical and/or analytical issues of citizenship politics particularly characteristic of East Asian countries. Wide diversities in East Asian civil societies' basic characteristics and relationship with the respective states have critical direct ramifications for the history and politics of citizenship in each country. Modernization in East Asia, as elsewhere, has been a simultaneous process of social and economic restructuring and nation-state (re)formation, so that civil society (often as communal formations) and the state in each country have intricately interacted over the allegiance of individual citizens. For instance, Japan's militarist imperial state, China's communist revolutionary state, and South Korea's Cold War state all strived to subdue or eradicate potential antithetical forces of each respective civil society, and the citizenship regimes these states promulgated for individual citizens closely reflected such political needs. These *illiberal* states coerced their citizenries to swap personal material and physical security for political freedom and ideological autonomy, thereby compromising democratic principles of modern statehood. The political liberalization under Japan's post-war democratic governments, South Korea's post-military democratic governments, and China's post-Mao pragmatist party leaderships have not fundamentally altered such anti-civil society tenet of the respective citizenship regimes.

In response, civil society actors, though in varying degrees and durations, attempted to defy the state-centered citizenship regimes and propose alternatives under which individual citizenship rights are promoted and enjoyed in such a way as to establish and fortify individual citizens' civil engagement, solidarity, and activism. The Tocquevillian ideal of political modernity has been consciously or unconsciously upheld by progressive intellectuals and likeminded grassroots in East Asia as well, so individual citizens' sociopolitical efficacy vis-à-vis the state, as embedded in and emboldened through civil society camaraderie, has been eagerly yet diversely sought as a citizenship right. Individual citizenship rights have been a highly contested terrain between the East Asian states and their respective civil societies.

Chapter 3. Political Citizenship Without Democratic Social Representation

In South Korea's sociopolitical modernization, there has been a systematic dislocation among the main societal spheres of modernity—that is, among civil society, industrial class structure, and democratic polity. Each of these spheres has gone through rather dramatic formations and transformations. The nation's independence in 1948 was a celebration of its formal political departure as a hyper-democratic institutional entity largely thanks to its wholesale adoption of the American political system. Its early economic development from the mid-1960s to the mid-1990s was characterized by a miracle-pace capitalist industrialization in which a predominantly agrarian population was socially transformed into a predominantly urban industrial population merely in a few decades. Its civil society has kept overcoming the far rightwing state's suppression, in particular, by frontally overthrowing the illegitimate political regimes in 1960, 1987, and 2017. Perhaps as South Korea's biggest dilemma in sociopolitical modernization, these enviously drastic changes in the main societal spheres of modernity have failed to structurally redress the chronic mutual dislocations among such spheres. Under such dislocations, the historically exclusionary and regionalistically entrenched groups of conservative political elites and their parties, by distorting the nation's democracy into a collusive system of self-appointment and self-reproduction, have kept reducing South Koreans' political citizenship to an empty shell. On the other hand, the nation's political modernization, including both the initial institutional setup of the national polity and the restoration of the democratic procedures after a lengthy period of military dictatorship, has failed to achieve an effective and sustained rooting of an exclusively or broadly proletarian political party. Democratic in "form" only, the formal political domain has almost completely ruled out organized labor despite its apparent presence as a strong social force (and the demographic preponderance of the urban working population), whereas unions and union-based parties have been unable to deal with this incongruous situation very effectively. The chronic limit of the nation's (demographically) largest social class in effective democratic representation in formal institutional politics, particularly in the heavily state-centered system of socioeconomic governance, has systematically disadvantaged them in the process of capitalist economic development and industrial restructuring. In fact, this dilemma of empty political citizenship has been nearly universal to all social classes at the grassroots level and thereby structurally hindered the nation's Marshallian evolution in citizenship politics. The lack of such class-based representative politics as is accommodated by the mainstream political parties through the parliament has inevitably implied that, as shown in the subsequent six chapters in Part II, South Koreans' social citizenship on all fronts has been framed and realized through the pragmatic daily interactions between the technocratic state and individual citizens.

Chapter 4. Developmental Citizenship and Its Discontents

In nations ruled by developmentalist—democratic or not—regimes, the practically observable rights and duties of citizens with regard to their state have predominantly revolved around national economic development and individualized material livelihood. What I propose to call *developmental citizenship* has served as a basic framework for state-society (citizen) relations in these nations. The state is expected to concentrate on economic development so that its citizens can *benefit as private economic players in the state-promoted market system*—be workers, industrialists or self-employed entrepreneurs. These issues have not been on the center stage of Western politics and thus are not directly codified in terms of constitutional provisions and major policy agenda, so the imported democracies in non-Western regions lack a systematic legal and/or theoretical representation of developmental politics. In these societies, the developmental politics as a mode of state governance and its citizenship ramifications mostly exist as everyday political culture.

This chapter explains how developmental citizenship in South Korea has been conceived, protracted, and habitually renewed amid the dynamic interplay between political democratization and capitalist economic development, and also analyzes what social practices have constituted such historical constructions and reconstructions of developmental citizenship. The primacy of developmental citizenship does not necessarily preclude a political commitment to social citizenship, but the former at least tends to delay the latter for the sake of maximum national economic growth, epitomized by the political slogan of "growth first, distribution later". Besides, the political pursuit of national economic development has often been accompanied by a self-serving emphasis of the state leadership on political stability, often implying serious infringements on civil and political rights.

Chapter 5. Social Citizenship Between Developmental Liberalism and Neoliberalism

The so-called development state's commitment to ordinary people's social citizenship was fairly low-keyed and, at best, bluntly conservative. Under what may be called *developmental liberalism*, the successive developmentalist administrations suppressed grassroots demands and rights concerning social citizenship and exhausted public resources to finance industrial projects and corporate assistance. In its institutional form, South Korea's modernization in social policy was modeled after the so-called Continental European "conservative" welfare state. This model, as represented by the inclusionary social insurance programs of Bismarck's Germany, had been devised in order to effectively organize society—the working class in particular—toward a politically concerted path of national capitalist development. A sort of hierarchical or segmented social citizenship has been characterizing the South Korean working population's fate under an exclusionary application of the Continental model of social welfare. In the early 1990s, on the other hand, Western neoliberalism (with its regressive social policy orientation) was formally accepted exactly at a time that when various serious policy measures were required in order to stabilize risky social conditions accumulated through decades of developmental liberalism. The tenaciously developmentalist state equated neoliberal reform with globalization in order to silence critical voices for social democratic reform. The exigency of economic globalization, especially since the national financial crisis in the late 1990s, supposedly made it inevitable to bypass grassroots demands for labor rights and redistributive benefits. South Korea's post-crisis neoliberalization, focused upon labor market flexibility, was particularly devastating due to its developmental liberal context in which stable employment had been an almost exclusive platform for grassroots livelihood and even social security guarantees.

Chapter 6. Citizenship by Education, or Education as Citizenship

South Koreans' citizenship in the nation's social institutional order, economic development, cultural life, and democratic politics has been decisively facilitated and shaped by their participation, competition, and struggle in public education. At the societal level, education, especially at higher levels, has been crucially instrumental to the nation's all fundamental transformations since its liberation from Japan, including the condensed institutional modernization into a liberal system of sociopolitical governance and economic regulation, the expeditious and extensive capitalist industrialization buttressed by human capital, the potent democratization movement propelled by the allied forces of intellectuals and workers, and the technological and cultural surge into global leadership in the new century. Whether it is the quality, the intensity, or the universality of education that has been the most decisive for education's such contributions is debatable. Nonetheless, it is beyond dispute that South Koreans' educational fervor has both bolstered and been intensified by these societal transformations. In citizenship terms, education has critically enabled South Koreans to march into modern institutional, developmental, political, and scientific/cultural citizenship. In a great paradox, however, South Koreans' access to education itself has remained quite dubious as a citizenship right. Public education has been constitutionally stipulated both as every citizen's right and duty ever since the nation's independence. The South Korean government has been consistently effective in promptly establishing public schools and mobilizing civilians to set up private schools that operate with the largely same curricula and financial rules, leaving virtually no children beyond reasonable access to universal public education. However, the same government kept balking, even until the beginning of the twenty-first century, on its legal duty to provide free public education up to the constitutionally designated level of middle school (7th to 9th grade). The virtual universalization of tertiary education at colleges and universities came about under the private payment of tuitions and other school expenses. Most adolescents attain college/university diplomas not as a citizenship right but as a parental gift. An aspect of education in which South Koreans do make a strong citizenship claim is the effective governmental regulation and management of various components of college/university entrance examinations. In presidential and parliamentary elections, the reform of *daehakipsijedo* (the system of college/university entrance examinations) is quite frequently presented as a key election pledge, while universal and excessive financial burdens for college/university education have curiously remained untouched until recently. South Koreans' apprehension about fair and transparent exams for college/university entrance sensitively reflects the instrumentality of higher education to all major components of modern citizenship. To the extent that such citizenship instrumentalities of education are conditioned upon meritocratic differentials and hierarchies, South Koreans' commonly shared anxiety about college/university exams falls short of constituting a clear sociopolitical basis of social citizenship.

Chapter 7. Reproductive Contributory Rights: From Patriarchal to Patriotic Fertility?

South Korea's demographic restructuring in a great many aspects has been no less radical than its socioeconomic transformations under compressed modernity. This is no coincidence in that individual behaviors and familial choices determining demographic parameters such as marriage, fertility, and migration have closely reflected South Koreans' intense desire and active effort to participate in their nation's literally explosive development and modernization on all fronts. In a sense, the full realization of their citizenship rights in the national socioeconomic progresses has been conditioned upon their active demographic behaviors attuned to the qualifications for and opportunities from such progresses. Likewise, the unprecedented and unparalleled drastic transitions in the rates of marriage/divorce, migration, and fertility in recent years all have mirrored the notable fulfillment, enhancement, and, most recently, erosion of various citizenship rights. Until recently, in a fundamental paradox, such demographic behaviors themselves have not been subjected to strong social demands and active political proposals for social citizenship rights. They have mostly been perceived, by both the state and citizens themselves, as private choices and responsibilities, which in turn have reflected the chronic patriarchal order in gender relations and intergenerational interactions. This does not imply that the state has not intervened in such supposedly private affairs. Its family planning program was one of the most draconian instances of governmental intervention in demographic behaviors, whereas its industrialization strategy was accompanied by a comprehensive range of urban-centered infrastructural, educational, and housing policies for accommodating the urban migration of a majority of villagers. But these policies were rarely classified or publicized in citizenship terms. In the long run, South Korea's industrialized capitalist economy and social security system have socioeconomically frustrated rapidly increasing segments and proportions of its population. Much like during the earlier period of socioeconomic progresses, the latest neoliberal era of South Koreans' massive socioeconomic disenfranchisement has been accompanied by drastic changes in demographic indicators, with which the country now appears almost scandalous—the world's lowest fertility rate, the world's third highest suicide rate (and, among aged persons, the world's highest suicide rate), a divorce rate rivaling the United States and the UK, and so forth. While these trends are sometimes reanalyzed as an outcome of defective social citizenship, the primary thrust of the public policy is placed on the long-term political and economic predicaments of a national demographic meltdown. The collectivist conception of transformative citizenship has been desperately applied to young people's marriage and fertility. The politically insinuated patriotism in young citizens' marriage and parenthood seems to have been rather counterproductive because of the thereby induced feeling that their fundamental individual(ist) rights to marriage and parenthood, as well as their possible children's future, are arbitrarily subjugated to the state's unreservedly professed technocratic necessities.

Chapter 8. Ad Hoc Cultural Citizenship: Neotraditional to Multicultural (Non)transition

South Koreans' postcolonial neotraditionalization was an epochal incident of popular cultural self-reinvention. Through this incident, grassroots South Koreans came to translate their newly won democratic citizenship into a collective historical nexus to the precolonial aristocratic Confucian system of sociocultural self-governance. None of the post-independence governments, whether conservative or progressive or whether authoritarian or liberal, have dared to deny or liquidate the ad hoc cultural self-citizenship of ordinary South Koreans. The developmentalist government under Park Chung-Hee formally ratified its citizens' neotraditional familialism while carefully moderating lavish Confucian family rituals into reasonably frugal forms and sustaining the universal familialization of its citizens' material care and support with Confucian norms. In a sense, grassroots South Koreans have traded their social citizenship for an ad hoc cultural self-citizenship. This arrangement, particularly in rural areas, was widely resented by women because of their asymmetrical sacrifices and contributions for the neotraditional social reproduction of families, most of which were even growing in size and complexity. Most of rural young women have opted to head for urban places, leaving villages devoid of women in marriageable ages. Even most of rural young men also moved to cities for work and/or education, except those few who have often reluctantly succeeded their parents' farms, risking their marriage prospect. As many of them have ended up marrying foreign brides since the mid-2000s, the South Korean state and society have coalesced to invent another ad hoc cultural citizenship of "multiculturalism". This late modern citizenship has seemingly been conferred on foreign brides in terms of various paternalistic assistances and benefits under the loud welcoming of their home-country cultural traits. The hidden desire of South Korean society, however, has consisted in its strategic cultural self-reinvention into a supposedly multicultural or cosmopolitan entity—multicultural in terms of coexistence with foreign bodies with permanently frozen and repeatedly staged ethnocultural diversities. In a great paradox, the loudly publicized notion of *multicultural citizenship* more hides than reveals most foreign brides' everyday conditions of life and work, particularly in rural families. Foreign brides usually live far more Korean (neo)traditional types of family life than their native Korean counterparts (by whom rural families have been deserted). The simple fact is that what has been mobilized from poor Asian countries is not so much the cultural attributes of foreign brides as the *material instrumentalities of their gender as women* in coping with the wide meltdown of rural families' (neotraditional) social reproduction.

Chapter 9. Risk Citizenship in Complex Risk Society

The particular manners and intensities of South Korea's compressed economic development and social change have engendered a risk society with correspondingly particular risk characteristics. South Korea can be characterized as a *complex risk society* in which various risk factors and symptoms of developed, un(der)developed, slapdash, and compressive societies are present simultaneously and interactively. It is thus necessary to adopt the notion or concept of *risk citizenship* and elaborate on its practical (and possibly theoretical) characteristics in sociopolitical and other domains if we are to understand the unique (but perhaps not unprecedented) nature of such risk-accommodative political economy. South Koreans' subjection to multifarious risks, dangers, and threats are reasonably expectable from their country's multi-front, expeditious transformations and their personal, communal, and organizational lives situated in such transformations. Unless South Korea had pursued an exceptionally risk-averse line of developmental, institutional, and civilizational progresses, its citizens would not have been exempted from normally contingent risks from all modern activities. However, a systematic probing into the structural nature of South Korea as complex risk society leads to a revelation that virtually all categories of risks have practically reflected the pragmatic, strategic, and/or urgent efforts to expedite and aggrandize developmental, institutional, and/or civilizational purposes and utilities in the nation's particular historical and international contexts. Where risks are perceived, diagnosed, commanded, praised, and rewarded in terms of their probable or supposed transformative contributory quality, they cannot simply be prevented, avoided, minimized, or hedged in personal, familial, communal, industrial, and governmental activities. Where whatever transformative contributory risks are detected or promoted, we should explore their citizenship implications.

Chapter 10. Transformative Citizenship, Transformative Victimhood

Since the mid-twentieth century, postcolonial war-devastated South Korea has kept impressing the world and even themselves by aggressively and precipitously carrying out societal transformations on all fronts and thereby becoming a paradigmatic case of compressed modernity. While each of such transformations is rather a generic experience in postcolonial societies, South Korea's impulsively proactive pursuit of them has induced the country to become a *fixatedly transformative* social entity. In this context, a distinct mode of citizenship arose in terms of *transformative contributory rights*—namely, effective and/or legitimate claims to national and social resources, opportunities, and/or respects that accrue to each citizen's contributions to the nation's or society's transformative purposes. By the early twenty-first century, it has painfully turned out that the citizenship regime of transformative contributory rights has a fatal side effect of structurally and abruptly engendering *transformative victims*, in numbers and extents that are no less conspicuous than those for transformative beneficiaries. There have been structural victims not only inherent in the substantive nature of each transformation (e.g., traditionalists and nativists in West-dependent modernization, peasants in capitalist industrialization, and local interests and communal agents in neoliberal globalization) but also embedded in the impulsive, excessive, and violent manners of pursuing the transformations (i.e., students in cramming educational institutions, workers controlled and abused by the authoritarian state and employers, women abused at home and work under patriarchalized capitalism, and foreign workers and brides maltreated respectively by opportunistic employers and in-laws). In fact, given the unevenly developmental and selectively democratic nature of South Korea's postcolonial capitalist modernization, virtually every category of transformative citizenship has been accompanied by the transformative victimhood of certain social groups.

CHAPTER 2

State-Society Relations and Citizenship Regimes in East Asia

1 Introduction: State-Society Contestation over Citizen(ship)

No other region in the world seems to have entered modernity in a more diverse way than East Asia.[1] The region gave birth to an aggressive capitalist imperial state (i.e., Japan), fervent revolutionary socialist states (i.e., China, Mongolia, North Korea, Vietnam), and dynamic late developing capitalist economies (i.e., South Korea, Taiwan, Hong Kong). Although these countries have commonly entered the late capitalist era as global neoliberal actors, their economic, political, social, and even cultural diversities are still quite remarkable.

The formation of civil society, one of the most revered elements of modernity, and its structural relationship with the state are particularly notable in such intra-regional diversity. South Korea's "contentious" civil society once attracted global attention as its organized working class often staged forceful struggles against the "strong" state and its business allies and as its activist intellectuals and students led influential political and social movements, often dwarfing the power of the ruling elite (Koo, H., 1993a). Across the DMZ (demilitarized zone), an absolutist North Korean leader and his cadre corps seemingly remind the world that totalitarianism—society being completely organized and controlled in a politico-bureaucratic framework—still operates.[2] Communist China, which once alarmed outside observers by politically mobilizing grassroots for violent attacks on the institutional apparatuses and officers of the Leninist state itself, impresses the world again by unleashing literally explosive grassroots activism—this time in private economic activities—under the so-called socialist market economy. In Japan, its civil and economic organizations still boast of (or suffer from?) the tightly meshed network with relevant bureaucratic offices in carrying out various agreed-upon social and economic functions in a much similar way to a century ago (Pekkanen, 2004). No matter how similar they may appear to outsider observers in physical look, daily life, and cultural attribute, each of the East Asian peoples associates with other citizens and deals with the state in quite a distinct way.

Such diversities in East Asian civil societies' basic characteristics and relationship with the respective states have critical direct ramifications for the history and politics of citizenship in each country. Modernization in East Asia, as elsewhere, has been a simultaneous process of social and economic restructuring and nation-state (re)formation, so that civil society (often as communal formations) and the state in each country have intricately interacted over the allegiance of individual citizens. For instance, Japan's militarist imperial state, China's communist revolutionary state, and South Korea's Cold War state all strived to subdue or eradicate potential antithetical forces of each respective civil society, and the citizenship regimes these states promulgated for individual citizens closely reflected such political needs. These *illiberal* states coerced their citizenries to swap personal material and physical security for political freedom and ideological autonomy, thereby compromising democratic principles of modern statehood. The political liberalization under Japan's post-war democratic governments, South Korea's post-military democratic governments, and China's post-Mao pragmatist party leaderships have not fundamentally altered such anti-civil society tenet of the respective citizenship regimes. In response, civil society actors, though in varying degrees and durations, have attempted to defy the state-centered citizenship regimes and propose alternatives under which individual citizenship rights are promoted and enjoyed in such a way as to establish and/or fortify individual citizens' civil engagement, solidarity, and activism. The Tocquevillian ideal of political modernity has been consciously or unconsciously upheld by progressive intellectuals and likeminded grassroots in East Asia as well, so individual citizens' political efficacy vis-à-vis the state as embedded in and emboldened through civil society camaraderie has been eagerly sought as a citizenship right.[3] Individual citizenship rights have been a highly contested terrain between the East Asian states and their respective civil societies.

This chapter overviews the individual dynamics of state-civil society relations in Japan, South Korea, and China, comparatively assesses the historico-political effects of such relationships on each country's citizenship regimes and rights, and discusses major theoretical and/or analytical issues of citizenship politics particularly characteristic of East Asian countries. In undertaking these tasks, I uphold Bryan S. Turner's (1993: 2) conception of citizenship, namely a "set of practices (juridical, political, economic and cultural) which define a person as a competent member of society, and which as a consequence shape the flow of resources to persons and social groups". This is because "[t]he word 'practices' should help us to understand the dynamic social construction of citizenship which changes historically as a consequence of political struggles" (Turner, 1993: 2).

2 STATE-SOCIETY RELATIONS IN EAST ASIA

2.1 *Japan: Symbiotic or Incestuous State-Civil Society Relations*

Thanks to the relatively decentralized feudal governance structure of premodern Japan, and the largely lenient stance of the Meiji state toward social associations and organizations, Japan was ostensibly entering a nascent stage of civil society in the modern sense toward the end of the nineteenth century. Alongside the modernizing political regime, both rural and urban communities nurtured various associations and organizations for technological learning, philanthropy, cultural and political discussion, and so forth (Garon, 2003). But the basic view of the Japanese state over civil social elements was at best instrumentalist, so that it immediately encouraged and sometimes coerced them into the state-set goals of social services and economic tasks. In the essential areas where voluntary civil initiatives were insufficient or absent, officials themselves helped to set up civil—more precisely, para-governmental—organizations and supported their budget, office, and, sometimes, personnel (Pekkanen, 2003). Needless to say, the government was most keen to assisting and utilizing industrial and commercial organizations.

In the course of politically driven catchup modernization, the proactive stance of the state even over civil society concerns was not seriously resisted by ordinary citizens. Even civil society actors cast an instrumentalist perspective upon themselves (Garon, 1997). As far as practical purposes for modernization were served, state intervention and guidance were acceptable. State dominance over civil society was not yet a consciously recognized political problem. There arose a prematurely co-opted civil society whose characteristics would survive even into the twenty-first century. Although the interwar (1918–1931) democratization process ("Taisho democracy") was accompanied by the socialist challenge of the state leadership in labor and other affairs, such challenge failed to constitute a counter-hegemonic struggle of civil society. And then came the social mobilization drive during the fifteen-year wartime when most of autonomous civil associations and organizations—not to mention para-governmental ones—had to be reborn as official arms of the militarist state. In particular, the infamous Imperial Rule Assistance Association (IRAA), established in 1940, was designed to politically control and incorporate most of the non-governmental associations and organizations for the ambitious war efforts.

Interestingly, Japan was defeated by a country which cherished its liberal civil society tradition more than anything else.[4] Autonomous civil society was considered by the US-led Allied Occupation (1945–1952) a core remedy for militarist statism and a critical basis for liberal democracy. Full-scale efforts were made to dismantle the collusive structure of Japan's state-civil society relations, involving local residential organizations, IRAA, and the masterminding Home Ministry. Many of the formerly co-opted associations reformed themselves for autonomous civil activities, whereas numerous new associations and organizations arose for civil initiatives in social, cultural, political, and international matters. However, not many of Japanese bureaucrats changed their "habits of heart" in controlling and mobilizing civil associations and organizations, and most grassroots Japanese took side with them through tacit cooperation in nullifying or resisting American orders. Persistent efforts were made to maintain and reinstate the corporatist framework for controlling civil society (Garon, 2003). Furthermore, the Cold War confrontation with Soviet Union, China, and North Korea made Allied Occupation officers in Japan increasingly intolerant of the rapidly expanding socialist influence in unions and other elements of civil society. Social and political reforms halted in a half-way manner could not induce a genuinely liberal polity and civil society.

The post-war developmental drive was backed by renewed efforts at economic and social mobilization. Seemingly, the entire Japanese nation was integrated into what may be called *developmental corporatism*. Various economic and civil associations rendered entrepreneurs, workers, women, and community volunteers enfranchised into a grand developmental coalition between the state and civil society. Whether formed voluntarily or induced administratively, these associations functioned as a transmission belt for the ambitiously interventionist state. Business associations arranged regular consultations between industrial managers and technocrats over the administrative economic targets and strategies as well as private business interests (Johnson, 1982). Company-based unions persuaded workers to peacefully yet actively cooperate with management in exchange for job security and sustained wage increases (Suzuki, 2003). Women's organizations taught women to frugally manage the household economy with a strong focus on saving and education (Garon, 2003). Semi-governmental welfare authorities mobilized partially paid grassroots volunteers to deliver social services to elderly and other needy persons at a cost far below that of an otherwise full-scale welfare state (Estevez-Abe, 2003). The successful outcome of such orchestrated efforts in terms of national economic development, corporate growth, and household income increase, in turn, reinforced the utility and legitimacy of the all-encompassing developmentalist governance.

Nevertheless, Japan was not immune to various social costs and economic instabilities attendant upon rapid industrialization and economic growth (Tsujinaka, 2003). On the one hand, Japanese citizens had to be awakened over various shocking instances of environmental hazards since the mid-1960s. It became obvious that their material attainment could easily be overshadowed by the environmentally caused deterioration of their quality of life. Led by intellectual activists, grassroots Japanese took to the street to reprimand the government and concerned businesses. Overlapping with the worldwide progressivism in the period, such social eruption (called "citizens' movements") then seemed to foretell a potential proactive civil society in Japan. However, the immediately accompanied economic crisis associated with the oil shock served a serious countervailing force as ordinary Japanese began to immerse in everyday material livelihood again (Garon, 1997). And the specter of economic depression ("bubble bursting") was long lasting until quite recently.

While civil associations and initiatives kept expanding ever since, the social dynamism of the late 1960s has not been restored. They seem to content themselves with only patchwork revisions of the tenacious developmentalist rule to which Japan's entrenched developmental bureaucracy comfortably agreed and even responded gratefully in terms of relaxed administrative regulations and increased subsidies. The 1998 Non-Profit Organization Law seems to indicate more continuity than discontinuity in the century-old developmental corporatism in Japan. The twenty-first century has not seriously changed this stalemate. In particular, fortunately or unfortunately, the social influence of global neoliberalism has been much more limited in Japan than in other Asian societies due to Japan's entrenched status in global political economy and its sociopolitical and cultural inertia.

2.2 South Korea: Hegemony Struggle Between the State and Civil Society

The making of modern civil society in Korea began very much as an international political incident. In the late nineteenth century, the ailing dynasty of Chosun finally confronted a major social revolutionary challenge from the grassroots forces organized by the semi-religious Donghak movement. The half-millennium old dynasty managed to survive the civil social challenge only by relying on the self-appointed military intervention by Japan. Imperialist Japan, however, contributed to the formation of Korean civil society in its own (unexpected) way. It replaced itself for the ailing dynasty as a new state in 1910 and staged such an oppressive political rule as to integrate Koreans under one of the most potent nationalisms in history (Shin, Y., 2001; Koo, H., 1993a). Nationalism—instead of liberalism—became the civic culture for Koreans as they confronted and resisted the relentlessly exploitative colonial state (Shin, G., 2006).[5] The defection of many former *yangban* to the colonizer's side (for preserving feudal landholdings and/or attaining new privileges) did not seriously disturb the accidental social unity but psychologically homogenized the oppressed grassroots. About a decade of colonial rule effectively transformed the Korean nation into a highly contentious and volatile civil society as evidenced by the sweeping nationwide independence movements in 1919. Ever since, not only armed struggles but also various types of social movements and campaigns were staunchly launched in order to drive away the colonial state. Colonial capitalist industrialization marked by turbulent labor relations and excessive wartime mobilization of labor, resources, and even sex significantly added to the appeal and energy of nationalist civil society.

The abrupt termination of Japan's colonial rule in 1945 was surprisingly accompanied by an instant formation of vigorous civil communities across the nation. Japan's harsh colonial suppression and capitalist exploitation for nearly four decades, in effect, served as a gestation stage for Korea's modern civil society with a strong socialist orientation. Socialism not only fortified Koreans' nationalism ideologically but also helped to organize grassroots population into effective units of self-governance (Cumings, 1981). This was far from a desirable situation in the eyes of the self-appointed American military occupation government. When it entered the Korean Peninsula in 1946, its main objective had already shifted from disarming Japanese (or liberating Koreans) to containing the Soviet influence (Cumings, 1981). Fearing that the widespread socialist influence among grassroots associations and communities could result in the formation of a unified leftwing state, the occupation force launched formidable military campaigns for disbanding grassroots organizations and hunting down progressive activists. In order to fill the thereby caused personnel and organizational vacuum, American officers did not mind rehabilitating bureaucratic, military, judiciary, and industrial collaborators during the Japanese rule (Park, T., 2008). Such human resurrection of colonial rule was accompanied by institutional reinstatement of the colonial administration, police, and education.

Paradoxically, Japan's defeat by Americans led to the diametrically contrasting occupation policies for Japanese and South Korean civil societies—nurturing autonomous civil social groups and associations and eliminating various mechanisms of state interference in Japan and repressing the former and resuscitating the latter in South Korea. Before Koreans, unlike before Japanese, American occupiers did not bother to pose themselves as sincere liberal philosophers with a deep faith in civil society.[6] If any, they installed an on-paper liberal state system and staffed it with their own collaborators (many of whom had been laundered from pro-Japan collaboration). In quite an extraordinary political experimentation, a copycat liberal democracy devoid of civil society was installed in South Korea with its instance result being a premature "aristocratization" of politics—the same trend as would distress American intellectuals and citizens half a century later. The controversial launching of a divided republic in South Korea betrayed the dominant nationalist sentiment among most intellectuals and grassroots and thereby emboldened the supposedly more nationalist North Korean regime toward a civil war for unifying the two Koreas (Park, M., 1996). During the Korean War, the uneasiness of the South Korean government (and even the allied military forces of the United States) about nationalist grassroots led to random suspicion and execution of its own people in many parts of the country (Kim, D., 2000). The North Korean military was no more merciful to those South Koreans who were suspicious by its own criteria.

After the war, with all casualties and sufferings, grassroots South Koreans had to accept an even more suppressive political rule that abused their basic civil and political rights for the sake of anti-communism (Kim, D., 2006). To the liking of the war-survived state elite, the historical legitimacy question of South Korea's illiberal (or anti-civil) democracy became critically eclipsed by the Korean Cold War imperative. In fact, the utility of democracy itself was seriously challenged by anti-communist military generals led by Park Chung-Hee when they replaced themselves for civilian political elite through successive military coups from the 1960s to the early 1980s. While the American-installed autocratic regime was expelled by civil society in a historic student-led uprising of 1960, the anti-communist military immediately replaced civil society (and a democratic government) as a new center of political hegemony and then managed to rule the country well into the mid-1980s (Kim, S., 2000).

Once in power, the military had to reinforce their rationale for state leadership. As a long-term strategy of governance, the military coerced civil society (or poor South Korean grassroots) to exchange democracy for development—or exchange politics for income and job (Chang, K., 2019). Besides, economic development was deemed an indispensable condition for successfully competing against North Korea, which by then was emerging as a highly successful case of socialist economic development (Brun and Hersh, 1976). In propaganda, a "Korean-style democracy" should go hand in hand with *bugukgangbyeong* (rich nation, strong army). The military regime initiated a sort of developmental restructuring of civil society by disbanding, co-opting, and instituting various social, cultural as well as economic organizations according to strategic economic instrumentalities.[7] Across the nation, individuals and social groups were demobilized politically and remobilized developmentally. In industrial policy, Park and his technocracy underwent a complicated sequence of trials and errors, and ultimately conjured up a remarkably successful strategy of state-led, export-oriented industrialization (Amsden, 1989; Lim, H., 1986; Chang, H., 1994; Lee, K., 2016). Under this strategy, the state as a whole posed itself as a grand industrial capitalist, exercised a sort of entrepreneurial bossism over private industrialists (often through various industrial associations) (Chang, K., 2019), and dealt with the laboring population more as its captive employees than as its political constituencies (Koo, H., 2001). (In Chapter 4 in this book, such entrepreneurially oriented relationship between the South Korean state and its grassroots constituencies is conceptualized and analyzed in terms of *developmental citizenship*.)

In proportion to the success of this entrepreneurial statism, two mutually contradictory social consequences arose. First, the sensationally rapid economic growth, accompanied by rapid job increases and average income hikes, made South Koreans favorably reassess the state leadership in terms of its instrumental utility (despite their continuing denial of its political legitimacy). Second, the exploitative labor relations and many other instances of economic injustice, as they were apparently backed by the state in the eyes of grassroots, made various pockets of disadvantaged social and economic groups consider their economic injustice as much a political question as an economic one (Chang, K., 2019; Koo, H., 1993b). As the authoritarian rule kept being extended increasingly through coercion and deception, the latter response became predominant from the mid-1970s. It was in this context that Park's assassination in late 1979 immediately led to the collapse of his political regime under the allied pressure of the intellectuals/students (demanding democracy) and industrial workers (demanding economic justice). However, Park's sudden fall did not give sufficient time for democratic forces to effectively organize a new state leadership, so military authoritarianism was briefly extended by the "new junta" (*singunbu*) of Chun Doo-Hwan and his associates. Their rule, however, was subjected to basically the same allied forces of activist intellectuals and defiant industrial workers. Then, much more systematically organized and ideologically armed in the framework of the so-called *minjung* (grassroots masses) movement, the civil social forces successfully restored the full democratic procedures in 1987 (Koo, H., 1993b).

The institutional democracy thereby restored after over two and a half decades of military authoritarianism turned out quite robust, but a new challenge awaited civil society. The democratic transition inevitably entailed the softening of state patronage and/or control of corporate and other collusive interests. While this implied potential fairness and balance in labor relations, consumer rights, social services and protections, and so forth, it also occasioned less supervision and weaker regulation of various entrenched private interests (Chang, K., 2010a, Chapter 7). In business, media, education, and even religion, decades of collaboration with the authoritarian state had allowed civilian actors to amass phenomenal wealth and power, often in illicit ways. Along the course of democratization, these oligarchies resented reduced patronage from the state especially when they had to confront social pressure on their own, but they also made full use of relaxed political and administrative supervision for entrenching their baronages in various controversial, often illicit ways (Song, W., et al., 2016; Yun, Y., 1998). Many conservative technocrats, alienated from the democratized state leadership, opted to collaborate with these oligarchies for personal interests. Also, many then-opposition politicians of the dethroned, formerly pro-military party would maintain their collusive relationship with these oligarchies as an important source of budget and influence.[8] Besides, the all-encompassing doctrine of neoliberalism—to which the democratic governments could not but be wedded in social and economic policies—presented an ideological bonanza for these cunning private forces (Chang, K., 2019, Chapter 7).

Against them, civil society rose once again. Under intellectual initiatives, such prominent groups of *siminundong* (citizens' movement) as the Citizens' Coalition for Economic Justice, the People's Solidarity for Participatory Democracy, the Korean Federation of Environmental Movements, and the Citizens' Solidarity for Media Reform (Kim, S., 2004) have staged quite extensive and effective campaigns for redressing various irregular, corrupt, and unjust practices of *chaebol* (business conglomerates), *sahak* (private education groups), *jokbeoleonlon* (clan-controlled media), and so forth. While such activities have often been identified with "New Social Movements" in the West, their political weight was much heavier. The social reforms pursued by them have spawned an inevitable political historical implication—i.e., fighting the social legacy of developmental corporatism. The developmental state, at least in its autocratic form, has declined, but its former economic and social collaborators have tried desperately to maintain and sometimes aggrandize their politically and legally controversial privileges. The social and political prominence of South Korean citizens' movements heightens in proportion to such reactionary interests.

2.3 China: Exclusionary Clientelism and Fragmented Civil Society

Traditional Chinese literati (and, for that matter, Korean literati) would argue that the sociocultural and political association among themselves constituted a legitimate public space independent of the imperial statehood. Though lacking a demarcated physical space of autonomous association like Greek polis, they nonetheless enjoyed largely free association for scholarly, social, and political discourses. Such tradition at least led to the prominence of intellectuals at critical junctures of national history including China's early modern crisis (Grieder, 1983). Unfettered civil society was what Chinese enlightenment intellectuals envisioned as a basis for China's new civilization since the late nineteenth century. Civil society was both the goal and tool of their struggle against the turbulent historical situations marred by the degenerated imperial order, colonial intervention and invasion, social dislocations, and mass impoverishment. At least as a cultural phenomenon, civil society was rapidly burgeoning in the Chinese mind, and several enlightened social movements managed to induce public interest and aspiration in modern democracy. Such grand intellectual motives, however, were outright rejected by the oligarchic leadership of the Guomindang (KMT) in its consolidation and expansion of political power in alliance with warlord-like regional elites (Eastman, 1972). In fact, this betrayal of grassroots citizens (if not civil society) has often been considered as the most critical factor for the defeat of rightwing republicanism to populist communism.

The admirable success story of a communist revolution under Mao Zedong primarily revolved around the unique pattern of the state-society relations dubbed "the mass line" (Selden, 1971). In each revolutionary base, and then in each locality of post-revolutionary system transition, the communist leadership tried to mobilize grassroots in the form of mass social participation. In this way, a sort of social mobilizational approach enabled the Communist party to achieve impressive success in their revolutionary and developmental projects. However, the rigid institutional framework of a state-socialist system dealt a critical blow to the mass participatory governance. Particularly in rural areas, the collective production system called People's Commune inevitably forced Chinese peasants to lead captive life lacking lateral relationships with other groups of grassroots. Production unit (*danwei*) replaced (civil) society. A honeycomb-like administrative structure made Chinese peasants associate only with upper-level bureaucratic authorities with whom no meaningful civil interaction was possible (Shue, V., 1988). While, in each production unit, they were encouraged to interactively participate in production and political study stimulating each other's revolutionary zeal, the economically and socially stagnant life domain could not but dispirit them (Riskin, 1987). The organizational structure of urban life was not fundamentally different although the strategic industrialization effort had the effect of rewarding industrial workers preferentially.

Intellectually, China should be recognized for the historic but costly experimentation with a Maoist version of civil society—i.e., the Cultural Revolution. According to Mao Zedong, the rigid organizational hierarchy and division and the bureaucratic attitude of cadres stifled the voluntary energy of grassroots workers and peasants. Mao prescribed a *social takeover* of the Stalinist system which would allow spontaneous association among producer classes in each work unit. Mao was a very much Habermasian (or Habermas is a Maoist?) in envisioning a genuine "public sphere" in the Chinese production unit. This radical and inevitably violent project of organizational transformation did leave fundamental ramifications for Chinese life, however, not in a direction Mao dreamed of. Both in rural and urban areas of Maoist China, clientelism in degenerated forms prevailed as local cadres with limited resources strived to simultaneously maintain their prerogatives and pacify destitute grassroots' discontent in the face-to-face context (Oi, J., 1989; Walder, 1986).

A pragmatist or materialist turn marked the state-society relations after Mao's death (and Deng Xiaoping's political ascent). Deng orchestrated rural and then urban reform mainly by revising and shedding the rigid organizational control of production and marketing by the state. Rural reform, while its courses were never clearly charted in advance (Zhou, K., 1996), began with step-by-step privatization of agricultural production and bloomed full with spontaneous rural industrialization, spawning new classes of private cultivators (using collective land) and rural entrepreneurs and employees in various ownership types of manufacturing and service enterprises (Chang, K., 1992, 1993). As a result, Chinese rural producers were very much left to themselves and consequently form an economically integrated, whether rich or poor, community in each locality. (Even the basic rural administrative framework—the villagers' committee (*cunminweiyuanhoe*)—sounds like representing an autonomous social unit.) Such economic autonomy, in turn, has engendered increasing spaces for social and cultural association. As illustrated by frequent collective revolts of peasants against local cadres and governments, autonomous association has not been infrequent even in political causes.

Despite such economic and sociopolitical changes in rural China, massive numbers of peasants, particularly from poor inland provinces, have opted to venture into urban places of various sizes and distances. It is illegal, if not illicit, to live or work in a city without the residential permit called *hukou*. Thus, these migrants are subject to various disadvantages and penalties forced by their employers as well as the local authorities (Yoon, J., 2020). Their movements are market-driven, but their inferior social status is administratively determined. Neither local urban governments nor the central government is willing to systematically deal with the social and economic problems associated with them because such action may spawn an administrative or political connotation of recognizing them as a permanent policy subject (Solinger, 1999). It is this official reluctance that drives peasant migrants into forming comprehensive communitarian networks with their hometown fellows. Major Chinese metropolises have served as the hub for region-based miniature communities that feed on the voluntary association among disenfranchised urban citizens (Jeong, J., 2011).

In contrast to the immediately successful rural reform, urban reform kept faltering and stumbling well into the 1990s. A full reform of Stalinist state enterprises in obsolete heavy industries meant their shutdown, which even the pragmatist party leadership could not afford for numerous reasons (Chang, K., 2003). Various ways of reforming urban state enterprises partially and gradually were devised, discussed, and experimented. In the mean time, specially designated coastal areas were allowed full access to foreign capital and management, as institutional (inland) islands of capitalism. Chinese workers across the nation began to be subjected to market principles which require many of them to give up their jobs and related welfare benefits. For the same reason, urban youth have had to accept their difference from elders and seniors in job attainment and welfare protection. While Chinese urban workers are now much more resembling to capitalist proletariat, they have not been able to construct such class-based civil culture as were noted by E. P. Thompson (1963) in the English context. Labor unions, still the semi-official corporatist arm of the state, do not add to anything meaningful in that regard. Instead, when turned jobless, Chinese workers suddenly form a socially identifiable mass whose protest against various relevant sections of the state is easily legitimated and patiently tolerated. Joblessness under a socialist polity tends to serve a rather unexpected ground for civil activism (Cai, Y., 2002).

Such civil activism has not been found among private urban entrepreneurs, whose number has simply exploded in post-Mao China (Solinger, 1992; Gallagher, 2004). They are rather impressively associated with one another and with the government and party organs. Most of such associations are not compulsory, at least in a legal sense. Their interrelation, however, rarely results in social contention or pressure against the public authority but instead leads to the compliance with state directives and cadre interests (of course, in exchange for preferential or, at least, fair administrative treatment). To begin with, most of Chinese private entrepreneurs (unless with powerful political backgrounds) have struggled to establish a political citizenship locally and/or nationally. Nonetheless, they were formally notified by the Communist party in the early 2000s that they are an indispensable tool for political leadership in its developmental drive.[9] Private entrepreneurs naturally (ab)use such political utility of theirs in order to gain access to preferential terms of licensing, financing, marketing, supply of raw materials, and so on. Innumerable business associations constitute a crucial basis for the state-business developmental alliance by serving a customary venue for strategic relationships and interactions with various public authorities—a phenomenon widely familiar in the neighboring economies of Japan and South Korea. It is all too early to talk about liberal bourgeoisie in a rigorous political sense.

While none of the major classes in post-Mao China seem to be constitutive of liberal civil society, this has been elevated once again as a critical intellectual agenda. On surface, contemporary China may boast of the impressive growth of civil (reads non-governmental) associations and organizations covering a wide span of issues ranging from environmental protection to legal aid for workers and migrants. Although such advocate activities are more likely to be intellectually initiated than ordinary citizen-driven, they nonetheless attest to a qualitatively different nature of Chinese society today. The Habermasian public sphere is enlarging, albeit, very gradually. Such intellectual initiatives for civil causes may be listed against the innumerable semi- or para-official associations and organizations serving politico-bureaucratic objectives and interests under the comprehensive governmental support of budget, office, and even personnel (Gallagher, 2004).[10] Political and administrative leaders have become more and more aware of the infeasibility and inefficiency of direct governmental problem-solving in an increasing range of issues (Lee, H., 1991). But, as they are still concerned about possible diminutions of their political authority and organizational mandate, they will be tempted to create more of such deceptive non-governmental organizations and associations on the one hand and to co-opt existing ones on the other. Under the blatant lack of grassroots citizen-driven civil organizations, the balance between intellectually initiated civil organizations and technocratically inserted ones is a crucial criterion in appraising the objective nature of China's nascent civil society.

3 Divergent Trajectories of Citizenship Politics

The above overview of the diverse historical trajectories and current states of state-society relations in Japan, Korea, and China critically challenges any conception or impression about East Asia as a homogenous social entity. To begin with, the driving forces behind state (re)formation and social reconstruction since the late nineteenth century have fundamentally differed among the three countries, so have the structural patterns of state-civil society relations. Such diverse state-society relations, in turn, have brought about mutually distinct citizenship regimes. Citizenship, as juridical, political, economic, and cultural "practices" (Turner, 1993) for defining a person's competent membership in society (and the nation-state), has been dynamically constructed and reconstructed under the intense political struggles between the state and social forces in each country.

In Japan's Meiji revolution, the political project of creating a bureaucratically integrated nation-state did not frontally assail local social organizations and communal associations of the feudal past but carefully incorporated and reinvented them as sociopolitical instruments for state-led modernization and, ultimately, for militarist imperialism. After defeating Japan in the Pacific War, the American military occupation authority seriously, yet not quite successfully, attempted to upend the asymmetrical state-society relations and instead promote American-style liberal democracy championed by civil autonomy and activism. The Cold War, under which the United States came to collude with Japan's political "old boys" in containing leftist influences through illiberal political measures, allowed political and bureaucratic elites to regain the firm upper hand over civil society. Furthermore, the renewed mercantile nationalist drive for capitalist industrialization induced Japan's developmental state to aggressively mobilize civil organizations, resources, and aspirations in a prototypical corporatist framework justified in terms of national and individual material gains.

In Japan's modern political history, individual citizens' national allegiance and identity cannot be comprehended without fully taking into account engagement in local communal activities and organizations (including communally behaving companies), through which their aspirations and resources have been channeled into state-directed developmental and other national goals in exchange for public, communal, or, not least importantly, corporate deliveries of individual opportunities and services. In this way, individuals' political and social rights have been conceived and materialized in a much *depoliticized* manner, allowing national politics to single-mindedly focus on rightwing developmentalism. The once seemingly permanent rule by the (illiberal) Liberal Democratic Party, as coupled with constantly increasing jobs and rising incomes for virtually all Japanese citizens, was thereby made possible and has recently been reinstated after a brief rule by non-LDP political leaders. (This is not fundamentally different from Park Chung-Hee's nearly two-decade developmentalist rule, which I analyze in terms of *developmental citizenship* in Chapter 4 of this volume.)

South Korea's sociopolitical landscape, while it would increasingly resemble that of Japan in the post-war period, has been much more complex, turbulent, and even tattered. Ever since Koreans' autonomous early modern (or late feudal) attempts at social revolution (i.e., the Donghak revolution) or political rebuilding (the Daehanjeguk, or Great Korea Empire) were thwarted by internal resistance and external intervention, state power and civil society have fiercely struggled against each other in order to establish the hegemonic status over the other. Korean political history is full of the confrontational pairs: the Japanese colonial state versus (ethno)nationalist civil society, the American occupation authority versus leftist local communities, Syngman Rhee's anti-communist dictatorial rule versus liberal civil society, the military's developmental (and anti-communist) authoritarian rule versus pro-democracy civil alliance (ideologically spearheaded by the *minjung* movement), and, even in the post-democratic era, the radically neoliberal (yet supposedly developmental) administrations versus new (or progressive) social movement forces. As a latest manifestation of the confrontational relationship, South Korean civil society at the national level erupted again in 2016. In the name of "candlelight revolution", students, salary workers, and even parents with accompanying children staged spontaneously organized protests across the nation to oust the then president, Park Geun-Hye, after the shocking revelation of her involvement in a series of corruption scandals. The current state leadership under Moon Jae-In very much boasts its supposed allegiance to civil society in spite of conservative political attacks on its internal power blocs.

The seemingly permanent struggle between the successive intrusive political regimes and resolutely defiant civil society tends to chronically impede satisfactory political institutionalization of the state-society relations, for instance, through formal party politics and parliamentary representation. The remarkable improvement in most people's educational and occupational status, income, and health accompanying decades of miraculously rapid economic growth used to be regarded by the authoritarian state leadership as realization of its version of citizenship as "practice"— i.e., *developmental citizenship* (see Chapter 4 for details). However, the main political parties and the parliament they have constituted have rarely envisioned or promoted comprehensive social citizenship. In fact, the so-called "growth first, distribution later" doctrine and, more recently, the "save the economy first" doctrine have made developmental and social citizenship structurally incompatible. Such incompatibility between economic and social goals has often induced the crude denial of civil and, sometime, human rights as the fervent protests of exploited workers, impoverished urbanites and peasants, and angered students have often been quelled down by indiscriminate arrests, brutal crackdowns, and/or political procedural irregularities. On ordinary public mind, the protection of civil and political rights has more often been perceived more as the political mission of civil society than as the legal duty of the state. Against this illiberal political situation, civil activism has always involved discussion of a fundamental reworking of the state system (e.g., *minjung* democracy).

As compared to the Japanese and South Korean situations, China's sociopolitical landscape has been characterized by much more dialectical (or transformative) interactions between the state and society. The success of the communist revolution under Mao Zedong is understood primarily as the outcome of (peasant) society-centered political rebuilding of the ailing continental nation. (Conversely, the failure of the republican reconstruction of China is usually understood as the result of retrogressively asocial assertion and exercise of state power by the KMT (Guomindang) and its feudal class allies.) Upon the communist revolution, however, the leftist state immediately began to transform people (*renmin*) and their communities and production systems in a much superimposing manner, that is, according to unilaterally state-set goals, rules, and tactics for the socialist systemic transition. This basically bureaucratic—albeit camouflaged through social mobilizational campaigns—usurpation of social life not only estranged and angered numerous grassroots communities but also distressed Mao Zedong himself, an oddly liberal philosopher-politician, about the ideal sociopolitical nature of a communist China. The Cultural Revolution—grassroots groups capsizing bureaucratized state power for the sake of truly *voluntaristic* rule by the mass—did not remain Mao's thought experimentation but broke out as an extremely complex sociopolitical manifestation of post-revolutionary China's state-socialist order. Mao's death amid the sociopolitical pandemonium of the Cultural Revolution, matched with the structural economic problems attending on China's Stalinist command economy, was inevitably followed by the ascendance of pragmatist leader Deng Xiaoping, who in turn strived to promote grassroots activism in economic, but not sociopolitical, affairs. Despite the unexpectedly remarkable success of economic reform, the utmost difficulty of containing grassroots freedom and desire within the economic sphere has politically haunted the Communist party-state. A range of sociopolitical measures for preempting, threatening, co-opting, or para-governmentalizing present and potential elements of autonomous class power and civil society have been devised and implemented in recent years.

In spite of its vastly different sociopolitical history from those of Japan and South Korea, China is currently under a state leadership which purports to rule its people in a way highly reminiscent of the Japanese and South Korean practices—that is, *developmental citizenship*, albeit, of a market socialist variety. However, modern China's weighty historical experience of society-in-command political transformations is not likely to be easily erased out in public and intellectual memory since the entrenched dictatorial political system is yet to envision or concede people's civil and political rights. In particular, unlike their counterparts in Japan and South Korea, China's rural and urban producer classes (i.e., peasants and workers) once functioned as a fundamental material basis for revolutionary political change and have been politically (or, at least, in propaganda) espoused as the sovereign source of state power. Their class membership, according to the very ideological nature of a socialist system, automatically constitutes the exclusive political rights.[11] Besides, the

Maoist liberal legacy has spawned a popular political culture of cherishing (Chinese-style or latent) civil rights as illustrated in explosively increasing networks, associations, action groups, cafes, media, web forums, and even square-gatherings for discussing communal, administrative, and sometimes political issues. In today's China, not only the party-state leadership but also its political constituencies (i.e., Chinese people) are fundamentally pragmatist. Thus, the current state of developmental dictatorship (or the political rule through developmental citizenship) will last within the foreseeable future as far as economic growth (along with complementary social policy measures) continues to generate tangible material benefits for a majority of Chinese people.[12] Besides, the political engineering of a flamboyant nationalist sentiment against both the West and its East Asian neighbors may help buy political time. With all these economic and political ingredients, the popular demand for a new citizenship regime as well as a viable democratic political system can critically intensify for myriads of known and unknown reasons.

4 Shared Particularities in Citizenship Politics

Traditional China, Korea, and Japan closely interacted and assimilated for such a long period, but the way they entered modernity (or the way they initiated the modern state and civil society) was incomparably disparate. Those historical conditions reverberate now in terms of the mutually distinct regimes of citizenship. However, such societal and historical distinctions should not mislead us to ignore or neglect many sociopolitical elements and dimensions they have been commonly subjected to. The following seven issues are particularly significant because they make an integrative view of East Asian citizenship regimes still an indispensable intellectual tool.

Democracy, civil society, citizenship Ironically, South Korean democracy was initially institutionalized after its (nationalist) civil society was completely subdued. The ensuing aristocratization of democracy endowed civil society with a moral upper hand, and democratization has always been identified with the rise of civil society (Kim, S., 2000). In post-Mao China, the dictatorial Communist party has tried to reinforce its revolutionary political legitimacy with an instrumentalist turn (i.e., material improvement, or *xiaogang* in Chinese), which in turn has engendered various non-state social groups and spaces with varying degrees of political autonomy. If these new elements constitute a civil society in China, will it be compatible with the Communist party-state's continuing political dictatorship? The South Korean experience answers with a clear "no", but what about Japanese experience? Can Chinese communist elite replicate a Japan-like political construct—i.e., a seemingly permanent one-party domination (despite occasional interruptions) under formal institutional democracy along with a docile or cooperative civil society? What do these complex equations involving democracy and civil society imply for East Asians' civil and political citizenship? In South Korea, and increasingly in Japan and China, the tenaciously illiberal nature of state power has induced people to conceive their civil and even political rights as contingent upon or even embedded in the critical, if not always militant, supervisory function of civil society over the state (Kim, D., 2006; Kim, S., 2000). In this regard, the sociopolitical role of (progressively) liberal intellectuals as uncorrupted representative of civil society and thus as de facto guardian of civil and political rights continues to be popularly acknowledged and politically harassed.

Developmental corporatism and citizenship Developmental corporatism as a unique social governance system of the so-called developmental state has been most durable in Japan, lasted more than two decades in South Korea, and is now apparently in its operation in post-Mao China. In these societies, the corporatist control over classes, industries, regions, and various social associational groups has been firmly yet dynamically founded upon developmental goals and interests (Johnson, 1982; Riskin, 1987; Chang, K., 2019). Because the basic nature of the political regimes adopting it and the historical contexts and sociopolitical conditions surrounding it are very diverse, it is a very intriguing question whether and how much developmental corporatism assimilates East Asian civil societies. In a nutshell, however, the *practical* (rather than legal) logic of developmental citizenship has often enabled the developmentalist (and often illiberal) political regimes to authoritatively demand pragmatic material collaboration or collusion to various social groups and economic actors and thereby override latent sociopolitical and legal challenges to such illiberal governance. To the extent that the recent rapid spread of neoliberal economic policies and practices in South Korea, Japan, and even China structurally destabilizes developmental citizenship for staggering proportions of each respective population, the political viability of developmental corporatism is brought under question and the pragmatically framed compromise of civil and political rights becomes untenable. Paradoxically, the neoliberal destabilization of developmental governance has required the East Asian governments to devise and implement the so-called social safety net measures, which have somewhat helped assuage the grossly underprovided social rights in the region. But even this corrective effect has to be gauged against the social security losses accruing to those unemployed and underemployed people under East Asia's conservative (i.e., *regular* employment-based) welfare systems.

Illiberal bourgeoisie, corporatized proletariat, citizenship In all three countries, rapid economic development has not been accompanied by the rise of liberal bourgeoisie autonomous from the state and active in civil society. To varying extents, Japanese and South Korean bourgeoisie have been installed and/or reshaped by the respective state which has often suppressed civil society to its client bourgeoisie's benefit (Johnson, 1982; Chang, K., 2019). The post-Mao state in China increasingly shares such trait, though much more implicitly. On the other hand, a societal integration of labor activism and advocacy in the three countries has been commonly hindered by the company-based segmentation of labor interests—in particular, company-based unionization. While the political origin of Chinese unions basically as a para-state organization is not shared by Japanese and South Korean unions, the three countries' common lack of labor hegemony in civil society or in state leadership may not be unrelated with such corporatized labor unionism. State-dependent bourgeois interests and company-contained labor activism fundamentally dissociate East Asia from West Europe with regard to the class foundations of democracy and citizenship politics. Civil and political rights in West Europe were initially secured on the demand of bourgeoisie for establishing and maintaining liberal political order and economic freedom. Before long, organized proletariat jointly advocated civil and political rights in order to protect their social and material interests and, eventually, to take over state power through democratic elections. The actual and potential political ascendance of organized proletariat became the critical historical basis for the rise of the European welfare states with comprehensive social citizenship schemes. In East Asia's apparent historical void or deficiency of such class foundations of civil, political, and social rights, citizenship politics has often involved direct confrontations and compromises between the bureaucratic state and assertive civil society through election votes, street rallies, media tactics, civil litigations, NGO lobbies, and/or even outright rebellions. South Korea's civil activism in national politics is particularly noticeable, whereas Japan's civil activism is more focused upon local ecological, cultural, material, and technocratic issues (Kim, S., 2000; Garon, 1997). China's civil activism is also burgeoning, however, within the intricate sociopolitical parameters set by the party-state (Sautman, 1992). Within state offices, paradoxically, the lack or weakness of class-based political causes for social rights often requires social policy ministries to take on an opposition party-like position in advocating progressive or corrective welfare programs, usually with references to welfare state policies in the West, against the dominant developmentalist ministries (see Chang, K., 2019, Chapter 2). The same goes with ecological, cultural, and other non-material or post-material affairs.

Referential communities and citizenship As evinced in French intellectual Alexis de Tocqueville's (1988) classic observation of America in the nineteenth century, the freely associative nature of American people and communities was highly impressive even to (continental) Europeans. In a social ecological perspective, much of such impression may have derived from the inherent nature of aged historical societies—i.e., social relationships are usually saturated with pre-established norms, hierarchies, and networks. Associative life itself is nothing novel, but people usually associate not as free subjects but as what I suggest to call *referential* subjects. Before establishing interrelationships, people are consciously and unconsciously burdened (or endowed) with predetermined positions in hierarchy, network, or any other forms of shared collectivity.[13] In fact, if possible at all, it is their "habit of heart" to try to limit their association to such referential persons or at least dig out such referential information once they are associated.[14] This may have been even more strongly the case in pre-modern East Asian societies. Moreover, even contemporary East Asians are suspected to have failed to cleanse themselves of such traditional social trait, and in some cases to have neotraditionalized social relationships (e.g., Walder, 1986). Even through full-scale urbanization (relocating people from face-to-face villages to impersonal urban districts), East Asians tend to show the "urban villager" characteristics by identifying themselves with families, clans, places, cultures, and even schools of their origin and expanding social networks on the basis of such criteria. At critical junctures, such referential associations or interactions have afforded many East Asians a highly useful organizational basis for collective social actions against the autocratic state or other abusive powers, complementing the underinstitutionalized or underprotected political rights.[15] Also, such collective actions often include communitarian provision of material, social, and cultural resources (in terms of extended kin support, familialist corporate welfare, regionalist favoritism in business and administration, and so forth), complementing East Asians' weak social citizenship (Chang, K., 2019). However, the same complementary functions of referential communities are sometimes abused by political rulers in their attempt at nullifying civil and political rights through the divide-and-rule strategy (particularly in South Korea) and minimizing social rights through the familial and communal self-help ideology. Furthermore, the rigid hierarchical orders within referential communities often involve the culturally framed sacrifice or abuse of various rights of minor groups such as women and youth. State supervision or intervention in these social practices usually remains minimal.

Citizenship ramifications of Confucianism(s) In spite of protracted cultural and ideological controversies over the possible Confucian nature of East Asian capitalism, politics, and modernity in general, there is no denying that Confucianism has been a sort of epistemological air East Asians have been breathing since antiquity. Thus, the critical issue is not whether there exist Confucian cultural, social, and political heritages in East Asian societies, but how Confucian civilizational elements have been resented, rethought, reasserted, reprocessed, and reinvented in their arduous and disparate encounters with (West-derived) modernity.[16] Even as to the pre-modern era, Confucianism should not be taken as a holistically homogenizing force across East Asia, but as cultural and ideological ingredients jumbled up with each country's distinct political (or political economic) system and everyday organization of social relations. In practice, therefore, there have always been multiple Confucianisms, not one Confucianism, in East Asia.[17] (In a latest illustrative development, the post-Mao Chinese leadership is now globally promoting a communist-friendly version of Confucius heritages through hundreds of "Confucius Institutes" (Kongzixueyuan) across the world.) Among other classic components of Confucianism, nevertheless, the hierarchical conception of state-society relations and the primacy of (patriarchal) kin relations in private life have exerted particularly significant effects on contemporary East Asians' political and social life (Chang, K., 2018, Chapter 3). The authoritarian or authoritative states in Japan, South (and North) Korea, as well as China have often mobilized Confucian or pseudo-Confucian conceptions of state-society relations (under which loyalty to the state is supposedly the prime virtue of citizenry), and sometimes have even asserted parent-like positions (under which the state or its head is supposed to be revered and served by citizenry in a mood of filial piety).[18] These practices have been critically obstructive to the politico-cultural establishment of liberalism as the basis for democratic governance and civil and political citizenship rights. The primacy of kin relations in private social order and personal livelihood, often framed in reasserted or reinvented patriarchal patterns of inter-gender and intergenerational relations, has entailed two critical ramifications for contemporary state-society relations and citizenship practices. First, the discriminatory social practices against women and youth have too often been ignored or tolerated by the East Asian states (including the communist state of China), so their civil, political, and/or social rights have been critically compromised. Second, as briefly alluded to in the above discussion on referential communities, people's livelihood has continued to be conceived as a private or familial affair in spite of breathtakingly fast national economic transformations often on the basis of state-orchestrated production activities, so that state protection of social citizenship rights has usually been minimalized (under the rubric of "family-centered" welfare system in the cases of Japan and South Korea).[19]

Nationalism, state-society relations, citizenship Nationalism in East Asia, as elsewhere, is often condemned as a dishonest tool for distracting or oppressing civil social contentions against state leadership. However, the renowned morality and dynamism of South Korean civil society originated very much as an (ethno)nationalist cause (Shin, Y., 2001). The frequent reliance of autocratic state leaders on anti-Japanese and/or mercantilist nationalism did not tarnish such civil social prominence of grassroots nationalism. In fact, political reliance on nationalism is a very risky option in South Korea because it can easily be overturned into a social basis for anti-state contention. In Japan, however, state-initiated mercantilist nationalism has served as the core ideology of modern nationhood which civil society actors have not been able to challenge significantly (Garon, 1997). Even its wartime degeneration into totalitarian chauvinism did not result in political demise. The Chinese revolution was as much (ethno)nationalist as communist, but is this history instrumental to the social appeal of the Communist party's increasing reliance on mercantilist nationalist discourse in the twenty-first century, an era marked by aggressive global economic integration? While nationalism has facilitated the pragmatist (or developmentalist) reformulation of modern politics in each East Asian society, its broad popular appeal falls short of engendering a systematic social system or ideology for nurturing citizenship rights beyond Western models.[20] With bitter memories of imperialist encroachment or war defeat still being reverberated in political discourses and imaginations, the international political sovereignty and dignity of their nations are still among the most cherished political values of East Asians. Instead, such collective political culture has tended to be exploited by the state (often against the resistance or criticism of liberal civil society actors) as an excuse for neglecting, suspending or distorting various citizenship rights of individuals—a common practice shared by South Korea's military juntas, Japan's rightwing political factions, and China's postsocialist leaderships. These sociopolitical costs of nationalism tend to be confused or blurred by the occasionally burst anti-American and anti-East Asian neighbor sentiments of East Asian citizenries (accompanied by the shrewdly neutral position of the respective states).

The Cold War, American influence, citizenship The United States often boasts of its supposedly progressive engagement earlier in Asia against civil society-suppressive, illiberal political regimes, whether military-nationalist (Japan) or communist (North Korea, China). In immediate post-World War II years, however, the American military occupiers initiated diametrically different policies over Japanese and Korean civil society—promoting autonomy and activism of civil society actors in Japan and deracinating (mostly left-bent) civil society groups in South Korea (Cumings, 1981; Kim, D., 2000). (Even in Japan, the pro-civil society policy of the United States would soon fade away as it began to collude with Japan's rightwing politicians and bureaucrats amid the abruptly intensifying Cold War with the USSR and the PRC.) In South Korea—and, to a less extent, in Japan—America's tacit or open support for the illiberal yet rightwing political regimes made itself a historical enemy to civil society and an accomplice in the abuse of civil and political rights.[21] Yet it is also undeniable that the American democratic system and ideology—once the political model even for European countries with regard to advanced civil and political rights—were authoritatively recommended to Japan and

South Korea in their critical historical junctures of political restructuring or modernization, thereby radically "disembedding" Japanese and South Koreans from abundant feudal sociopolitical habits and relationships.[22] On the other hand, the United States, as a general civilizational reference as well as a strategic supporter for national development, has critically circumscribed East Asian mind concerning the ideal system of political economy and social welfare, making Japan and South Korea eager followers of the American doctrine, "market freedom instead of social citizenship". Since the late twentieth century, ironically, the former Cold War foe China has apparently been pursuing the same economy-lopsided liberal doctrine in spite of the tenacious American criticism of China's human rights and democracy issues.

5 Conclusion and Prospect

"One bed, different dreams" is a Chinese (or East Asian?) proverb, meaning that mutually different ideals or goals are pursued by individuals under a common situation or context. East Asia's variegated politics of citizenship as critically molded by the complex and dynamic state-society relations in China, Japan, and South Korea may be much more aptly described in terms of "different beds, one dream" (*isangdongmong* in Korean). Having entered modernity in starkly different ways—i.e., class revolution and socialist system transition (China), top-down political rebuilding and imperialist expansion (Japan), and successive colonizations and dependent development (South Korea)—the three countries have engendered mutually distinct patterns of state-society relations and citizenship regimes. Nevertheless, the state in each country is commonly under mounting pressure from civil society to devise and implement a comprehensive set of modern citizenship rights despite or at par with the remarkable pace of national economic development. It is perhaps through this citizenship perspective that the current state and future aims of national progress in each country can be most meaningfully appraised. The globally popularized discourse on "the East Asian era" may have to be critically reappraised by carefully reflecting the limits, dilemmas, and requisites of East Asians' citizenship rights in practice. The decline and destabilization of Western political economies (and, concomitantly, Western citizenship regimes) may not only spotlight the relative current stability and progress of East Asian political economies, but also necessitate East Asian states and peoples to more autonomously explore—instead of mechanically drawing on Western experiences—viable alternatives in theories, models, and programs of citizenship. This necessity, however, should not lead East Asians to deny the historical progress and present utility they have garnered from Western experiences in citizenship politics.

CHAPTER 3

Political Citizenship Without Democratic Social Representation

1 Introduction

South Korea's swift capitalist industrialization, at least until the mid-1990s, was accompanied by the correspondently rapid formation of a working-class population. An overwhelming majority of South Koreans had been socially transformed from family farmers to various types of urban wage workers and self-employees (most of whom alternate to wage labor) merely over a few decades since the early 1960s (Chang, K., 2010a, Chapter 5). After having played a decisive sociopolitical role in the nation's democratic restoration in the late 1980s, these present and former proletarian citizens were expected to decisively change the substantive nature of national politics so that their material needs and interests would be legitimately accommodated in the public work of the state.

This would become possible either by the existing political parties' adaptation or reform for reflecting the fundamentally restructured social (class) composition of the population or by the formation of new political parties that would advance the working population's material betterment as their core public aim. The first possibility has never taken place meaningfully to date in spite of the almost universally pronounced propaganda on their supposed political commitment to the work and livelihood of *seomin* (humble people).[1] If any, virtually all the governments formed legitimately by the existing major parties—under the habitually and frequently changed names—have apparently repeated or even copied the authoritarian military government's developmentalist politics in the 1960s to the mid-1980s. That is, despite democratization (or democratic revival), formal politics has not meaningfully changed so as to systematically incorporate sovereign citizens' class values and interests in their own terms (Chang, K., 1999; Mobrand, 2019). In fact, in the worst instance, Kim Young-Sam's *munminjeongbu* (civilian government) ended up pushing the nation into an unprecedented financial crisis—the so-called IMF crisis—after mimicking the Park Chung-Hee- style developmental drive on the basis of massive unscrupulous foreign borrowings by domestic banks and industries (Chang, K., 2019).

The second possibility did materialize, however, with badly frustrating outcomes. Since the early 1990s, there arose a series of sociopolitical attempts at organizing political parties that would mainly represent the class interests and identities of workers along with peasants, urban self-employees, etc. Such attempts sequentially included an intellectually driven ethnonationalist-cum-populist-cum-proletarian political party (i.e., Minjungdang, or People Party, 1990–1992), a proletarian political party based on national trade union organizations (i.e., Minjunodongdang, or Democratic Labor Party, 2000–2011), a progressive ethnonationalist-cum-socialist political party with sectarian labor representation (i.e., Tonghapjinbodang, or Integrated Progressive Party, 2011–2014), and a broad proletarian political party with a pragmatic social democratic policy line (i.e., Jeonguidang, or Justice Party, 2012–present). None of these partially or mainly proletarian parties have been able to establish themselves as a major force in the nation's formal political arena, so their respectively short existence has only symbolically referred to the constitutional possibility that proletarian class interests and identities can be politically represented in principle. In social reality, most of South Korea's current, former, and even prospective members of the working class have supported and voted for either of the two dominant parties which are ideologically ambiguous yet nepotistically influential.

Nonetheless, when South Korea entered full-fledged democratization in the late 1980s, its labor organizations also turned from "government pawn" to "democratic trade union movement". Thereafter, trade unions began to display a clear sociopolitical autonomy from the state and a strong capacity for mobilizing proletarian class interests "from below" (Roh, J., 2012). They have even helped accelerate the general democratization process by strategically allying with civil society organizations and activists. Organizationally, the formation of Minjunochong (the Korean Confederation of Trade Unions; KCTU) in 1995 was a watershed event as this progressive national umbrella organization began to mobilize and represent various industrial and corporate unions in the national arena of economic, social, and political competition. The KCTU boasted an impressive capacity for strong internal mobilization and broad societal influence—particularly in view of its modest status in promoting and sustaining the general unionization rate of the entire workforce. Such capacity was evidently manifested in late 1996 and early 1997 when the Kim Young-Sam government's attempt at a neoliberal revision of labor law was badly frustrated by the KCTU's effective struggle amidst the general public's support, even drawing worldwide attention (Moody, 1997; Koo, H., 2001). While such instant heydays of proletarian sociopolitical activism did not last long, South Korea's organized labor in national, industrial, and corporate unions has continued to exercise visible force to reckon with whenever their serious material interests are at stake (Roh, J., 2012).

Contrary to organized labor's display of strong social power, the status of the political parties representing the working class has been incongruously weak in formal institutional politics (Choi, J., 1992).[2] A series of attempts to establish an effective working-class party have been made, however, without any initially distinct and/or lastingly significant impacts in the nation's formal political domain. The most memorable moment in this regard was the 2002 presidential election in which the KCTU-backed Democratic Labor Party's candidate, Kwon Yung-Ghil, was able to elicit a nationwide popularity even though his final tally of received votes amounted only to 3.9%—a third place far behind the candidates of the two major parties claiming 48.9% and 46.6%, respectively. Afterward, this party had to even relinquish its formal name, explicitly identified with the working class. In short, the status and influence of the explicitly or broadly proletarian parties have been so minimal in the formal political domain as to be virtually inconsequential.

In South Korea's sociopolitical modernization, there has been a systematic dislocation among the main societal spheres of modernity—that is, among civil society, industrial class structure, and democratic polity. Each of these spheres has gone through rather dramatic formations and transformations (Chang, K., 1999). The nation's independence in 1948 was a celebration of its formal political departure as a hyperdemocratic institutional entity largely thanks to its wholesale adoption of the American political system. Its early economic development from the mid-1960s to the mid-1990s was characterized by a miracle-pace capitalist industrialization in which a predominantly agrarian population was socially transformed into a predominantly urban industrial population merely in a few decades. Its civil society has kept overcoming the far rightwing state's suppression, in particular, by frontally overthrowing the illegitimate political regimes in 1960, 1987, and 2007. Perhaps as South Korea's biggest dilemma in sociopolitical modernization, these enviously drastic changes in the main societal spheres of modernity have failed to structurally redress the chronic mutual dislocations among these spheres.

Such dislocations, as analyzed in this chapter, have been particularly distressful to industrial workers as social and political citizens. The nation's political modernization, including both the initial institutional setup of the national polity and the restoration of the democratic procedures after a lengthy period of military dictatorship, has failed to achieve an effective and sustained rooting of an exclusively or broadly proletarian political party. Democratic in "form" only, the formal political domain has almost completely ruled out organized labor despite the latter's apparent presence as a strong social force. Unions and union-based parties have been unable to deal with this incongruous situation very effectively. Their lack of effective representation in formal institutional politics, particularly under the heavily state-centered system of socioeconomic governance, has systematically disadvantaged them in the process of capitalist national development. Labor's weak representation in formal democratic politics has made it difficult for civil society to rectify the exclusionary and self-serving nature of the formal political domain. The practical void in the class-based political citizenship of proletariat, as the nation's demographically largest occupation, has rendered their (and all other South Koreans') social citizenship on all fronts to be framed and managed through the pragmatic daily interactions between the technocratic state and individual citizens (as to be analyzed the six chapters in Part II). If ordinary individual citizens see the conservative developmentalist state keep neglecting and sacrificing their social citizenship, they would ferociously turn to individual civil rights in aggressively and loudly staging their socioeconomic causes (instead of begging the aristocratized political parties for help). In order to explain these inter-sphere dislocations and their impacts on workers' political (and other) citizenship, various complex historical conditions for South Korea's postcolonial modernization and development—particularly, the Cold War at both the national and the international levels—should be examined carefully.

2 POLITICAL MODERNIZATION UNDER THE COLD WAR

In a liberal democratic polity, formal political parties are supposedly composed of forces constructed through a variety of ideologies and interests in civil society. That is, they should reflect and represent civil society. In South Korea, however, the relationship between civil society and the formal political domain seems to have existed contrary to that premise. Not only has formal institutional politics lacked a rational and firm basis in civil society since its birth, but also in fact it was created, and has been maintained, by systematically subduing and excluding civil society. This paradox, above all, is a result of the Cold War. It is well known that, on liberation from Japan, the immediate construction and maintenance of the two ideological rival states on the Korean peninsula were undertaken as the military outposts of the US-Soviet Cold War. Important here is the fact that when leftwing and rightwing forces in North and South Korea seized state power as agents or proxies of the Cold War, any opposing ideas and forces that existed in civil society were mercilessly removed (Kim, D., 2000, 2006). Consequently, various elements of civil society still in the early stages of their formation were suddenly liquidated. This situation caused a lot of public confusion, especially in South Korea, because the frontlines of (ethno)nationalist resistance to Japan's colonial capitalist exploitation, as in other colonial societies, had been substantially tinged with socialist goals and ideologies (Cumings, 1981).

In South Korea's modern history, there are three critical occasions by which the formal political domain has been constructed and reinforced through the coercive exclusion of civil society. First, Koreans' aspiration for autonomously establishing a modern democratic state in the immediate post-liberation period was frustrated by a series of political incidents and decisions driven by the United States. In a paradoxical outcome of the Japanese colonial state's ruthless rule, Koreans as a whole had ended up being reborn into a sort of (ethno)nationalist civil society, which, on liberation, would lead to the political surfacing of all kinds of organized social forces such as the National Founding Preparation Committee (Geongukjunbiwiwonhoe, or Geonjun), People's Committees (Inminwiwonhoe), and national organizations of labor unions and peasants (Cumings, 1981).[3] However, the American military occupation authority allied with local rightwing factions in violently rooting out suspected socialist political influences and sympathetic grassroots sentiments from society. At the toll of hundreds of thousands of innocent lives, a hard-line rightwing government of Syngman Rhee was installed under America's tacit tutelage. Secondly, the Korean War, a total civil war with Communist North Korea, wrecked South Korea's civil society in two ways.[4] On the one hand, it severely disrupted the grassroots communities as the foundation of civil society since mass casualties and demographic dislocations unsettled regional communities as basic units of social order.[5] On the other hand, the occupation of South and North Korea respectively by the opponents' armies fomented suspicion and alarm between neighbors and friends in the process of tracking down and punishing supposed traitors. Also, in South Korea, the war politically strengthened anti-communist ideology and brought about its routine internalization as a public ethos. Finally, the military's takeover of state power 1961 became the third occasion for civil society's exclusion in the formal establishment of a supposedly democratic polity. The April 19th uprising in 1960, by which Syngman Rhee was deposed from autocratic presidency, reflected signs that a civil society could be formed on the central basis of urban intellectuals and students (Kim, S., 2000). But this possibility suddenly evaporated with a military coup led by Park Chung-Hee in 1961. A similar situation was repeated in the 1980s when broad social demands for democratic rights and procedures on Park Chung-Hee's sudden assassination were mercilessly suppressed by yet another military coup, led by Chun Doo-Hwan.

South Korea's neocolonial subjection to American influences and the Cold War system led to its formal political domain's formation through the removal of civil society. Not only was its beginning paradoxical, but also such conditions made civil society's exclusion from formal institutional politics chronically elongated even into the twenty-first century. The nation's controversial division and total civil war with communist North Korea and the concomitant military-led political regimes brought about an excessive expansion of state apparatuses and bureaucratic forces. Amid intense class conflicts and revolts after the liberation, the state apparatuses grew bloated under the attempts of the U.S. military occupation authority and the Syngman Rhee government to control, exclude, and, if necessary, quell civil society, and this tendency was further strengthened through the civil war with North Korea (Kim, D., 1997). Subsequently, the condensed industrialization often dubbed "the South Korean miracle" was not initiated by any civilian economic classes (for instance, indigenous bourgeoisie), but reflected a political economic model of development led by the state bureaucracy preoccupied with competition with North Korea. That is, virtually all authoritarian state leaderships, from the Syngman Rhee government to the military governments under Park Chung-Hee and his supposed successors, managed socioeconomic governance and, in fact, politics itself in a systematically exclusionary manner—overriding civil society's values and demands by absolute executive commands and technocratic prerogatives. The political parties and politicians who gained (nominal) power by collaborating to exclude civil society had to agree to the hegemony of state bureaucratic offices that, in turn, have been exclusively accountable to each authoritarian state leader.

Nevertheless, the basic reason for (at least nominally) adopting and maintaining a system of representative democratic politics centered on formal political parties lies in the historical fact that the postcolonial model for South Korea's formal political modernization was transplanted from the U.S. The pro-American political line paired with the anti-communist ideology based its legitimacy in the supposed superiority of American democracy, as compared to both the traditional sociopolitical order and the communist system. Various pro-American intellectuals quickly emerged to support it. That is, the hitherto existing modern political domain in South Korea was not discovered amid the free citizens' struggle to achieve a democratic system, but began as a top-down, externally given form of democratic political system (Park, M., 1998). After liberation, the Cold War that continually constrained South Korean society and its multi-faceted dependency on the U.S. spawned the paradoxical result of removing the seed of modern civil society while at the same time also transplanting, at least in form, an advanced democratic political system. Eventually, this historical situation resulted in a systematic dislocation among the main societal spheres of modernity—that is, among civil society, industrial class structure, and democratic polity.

In these circumstances, South Korean politicians' foundation has not been civil society but the political system itself. Most of the major political parties have lacked a sustained social base in terms of systematic social identities and interests. They have been organized not "from below" but "from above", oftentimes according to the strategic need of those already in control of state power. The goals of such political parties and their member politicians simply lay in individual acquisition of parliamentary seats, and sometimes accessorial administrative appointments, that have often been allocated by the authoritarian state leaders themselves. Some studies, having tried to extract social class and civil society foundations for these parties and politicians, reached the common conclusion that the basis of their existence is not a footing in social classes or civil society but the self-reproducing mechanism of the political parties themselves.[6] Even when dealing with some urgent issues to social classes or civil society, they have rarely spoken for or mobilized for action the relevant social groups. The decisive factor has always been the exclusionary political domain's own logic of self-reproduction, which, in turn, is reinforced by the structurally embedded interests of its personal incumbents. Ultimately, such politicians take on a trait of political aristocracy that focuses on "institutional parasitism" (Chang, K., 1999).[7] They do not practice formal institutional politics on behalf of civil society, but nominate themselves to their positions through a prematurely aristocratized political domain, thoroughly and consistently carrying out their self-serving political aims (Chang, K., 1999; Mobrand, 2019).

3 INDUSTRIALIZATION AND DEMOCRATIZATION

3.1 Rapid Industrialization and the Growth of the Working Class and Civil Society

As a result of its unprecedentedly rapid industrialization and economic growth since the 1960s, South Korea transformed from a typical agricultural society to an industrial society within a few decades. In 1963, at the onset of full-fledged industrialization, the proportion of individuals employed in agriculture (including forestry) was 63.0%, but this figure fell to 48.2% in 1971, marking the nonagricultural sectors' surpassing of agriculture for the first time in history. It plunged to slightly less than one-fifth (19.6%) in 1989, and shrank still further to just over one-tenth (11.0%) in 1997, the year of the so-called IMF economic crisis, (*The Fifty Years of Socioeconomic Changes in the Republic of Korea as Seen through Statistics*, p. 98). During this period, employment in manufacturing increased rapidly, reaching its highest level of 28.5% in 1988 (as compared to just 8.7% in 1963). Employment in services remained at 28.3% in 1963 but came to exceed a half of the total for the first time in 1985 at 56.0% and reached 67.6% in 1997, heralding a new service economy era. Such rapid economic restructuring was accompanied by an explosive migration from rural to urban areas. Of a total population of 24,990,000 in 1960, city residents amounted to just 28.0%; town (*eup*) residents, 9.0%; and township (*myeon*) residents, 63.0%. By 1980, the total population had grown to 37,440,000, with city residents now 57.3%, town residents 12.1%, and township residents 30.6%. In 2000, out of a total population of 47,270,000, city residents comprised 79.7% and rural (towns and townships) residents 20.3%, manifesting a typical urban industrial society (*Korea Seen through Statistics*, p. 41).

Rapid class restructuring was inevitable in such compressed processes of industrialization and urbanization. A large majority of female workers, the backbone of labor-intensive sweatshop industrialization until the 1970s, were poorly educated women in their teens and twenties, mostly recruited from rural areas. By contrast, from the mid-1970s, workers employed in heavy industrial cities, concentrated in the so-called Yeongnam belt (Ulsan, Changwon, and so forth), were mostly men. The 1980s saw an end to the "unlimited supplies of labor" from the countryside (cf. Lewis, 1954), and the 1.5th and 2nd generations of proletariat with familial backgrounds in the working class formed the core of the nation's labor force. Workers' education level rose consistently, and heavy industry workers in particular were highly educated (Koo, H., 2001). The working class consolidated its social identity, performed increasingly skilled labor in large-scale worksites, formed a culture of mutual support in cramped quarters, and emerged as the core force of the nation's new industrial social order. All of a sudden, these proletarian women and men acquired the social capacity to promote their class interests through organized collective actions, if necessary, even by confronting the state and capital (Koo, H., 2001).

Within a very short period, South Korea's working class had become socially and politically consolidated, increasingly resembling its counterparts in the earlier industrialized West. According to Hyman (1998), the traditional image of working-class life during the heydays of Western labor movements was characterized by group labor in large factories, living in the same quarters, relatively stable employment, male wageworkers as breadwinners, and so forth. While some of these characteristics were also shared by South Korea's unmarried female workers from rural areas in the early industrialization period and functioned as the basic foundation for their labor movements (Koo, H., 2001), the shift to male workers in the core industrial labor force under the heavy and chemical industrialization drive rapidly assimilated South Korea to advanced industrial societies in the West in the social configuration and class struggle potential of industrial proletariat. As laboring in large-scale heavy industrial factories, long-term stable employment, residence in special housing quarters, as well as high level of education increasingly characterized the core group of South Korea's industrial proletariat, their capacity for autonomous labor movements was swiftly augmented.

At the same time, the civil society domain also began to grow rapidly. South Korea's industrialization expanded not only the traditional working class in the industrial sphere but also a well-educated and increasingly awakened middle class, and both groups took a highly critical position to the military's political domination that persisted into the 1980s (Han, S., 1991). With regard to the development of civil society, two points are in order. One is the rapid rise in South Korean citizens' education level. In 1966, the overwhelming majority (79.6%) of South Koreans over age 25 had not completed an elementary school education, while in 1995, more than a half of them (57.7%) had a high school education or above, with a fifth (19.7%) holding a college degree or more (Department of Statistics, 1998). With this rapid proliferation of modern education, many South Koreans quickly escaped from old social values and gained a social identity as a modern citizen (see Chapter 6 in this book). The other is the alliance in civil society between the middle and working classes. This alliance was rooted in two factors. First, the authoritarian military regime openly oppressed both the middle and working classes, inducing unintentionally the two classes to share the same political goal of democratization (Han, S., 1991). Second, the nation's rapid industrialization in the early stage was largely based in labor exploitation—e.g., low wages, long working hours, risky working conditions, and so forth—so that, in order to improve workers' living and working conditions and sociopolitical rights, progressive intellectuals and students began to ally themselves with workers and directly engage in pro-labor activism at industrial workplaces (Koo, H., 2001; Eun, S., 2006). Due to these factors, the working and middle classes formed close ideological, political, and even personal interrelationships, and thereby formed united class fronts in advancing civil society.

During the 1970s and 1980s, industrial labor and civil society were not only aggrandized in size but also politicized in quality. The sociopolitical growth of grassroots forces based on class ideologies and interests was apparent by then, but the path for incorporating such forces into the institutional political world remained structurally and chronically blocked.

This condition, in turn, led to the strengthening of an unprecedented alliance between intellectuals, middle class, and working class. On this basis, labor movements in the industrial domain took on a markedly political trait (Koo, H., 2001). The June civil uprising in 1987—a nationwide sociopolitical upheaval triggered unintendedly by the "New Military" government's attempt to extend its autocratic rule—became a historical venue for the explosive manifestation of the quantitative and qualitative advancement of civil society and industrial labor movement (Yoon, S., 1997). This incident may be characterized as a civil society struggle to regain the long denied civil and political rights, whereas the Great Labor Struggle in the months of July to September in 1987 represented a political self-establishment of the working class that had arisen as the key force in the industrial arena. Thereafter, civil society advanced in line with its ordinary basic configuration composed of various social identities and interests, and the labor movement, as described below, was on its path to stable growth and organization.

3.2 The Renewed Dislocation of Institutional Polity In/Despite Democratic Restoration

Despite these activations of the industrial working class and civil society, the self-nominating, self-serving behaviors of the formal political domain's entrenched elites did not disappear. Party politics in South Korea had deteriorated considerably under Park Chung-Hee's Yusin reform staged in 1972 and the New Military's coup in 1980. Various constitutional functions of the National Assembly were severely constrained and distorted, and the political activities of many civilian politicians were obstructed and suppressed. The presence of opposition parties, a minimal condition for the supposedly liberal political system's legitimacy, merely allowed the junta dictatorship to maintain a veneer of propriety. Many opposition party politicians "migrated" to the ruling bloc and covertly or openly served the autocracy. The political parties, organized "from above", merely served as a means to receive and distribute top positions in the state apparatuses (Yoon, S., 1997; Mobrand, 2019). The New Korea Democratic Party (Shinhanminjudang) founded in 1985, nonetheless, announced a return to the "traditional orthodox opposition"—traditional not only in the sense that it would be faithful to the functions of an opposition party as a counterforce to the ruling party, but also in its implicit seeking to revive the personal composition of the parties before the Yusin system. In effect, it was a return to the party politicians of the 1950s and 60s who reproduced themselves at a remove from civil society. The main opposition party, the biggest beneficiary of the June civil uprising in 1987, had its roots in the self-serving party politics of an earlier time and reproduced it in the era of democratization.

Yet, the 1987 situation did differ from the 1950s and 1960s in that an explicit pledge was made by politicians from all wings to reconstruct formal institutional politics in line with the needs and pressures from civil society. The formal political domain, despite such inclusionary gesture, continued to operate largely apart from civil society. After all, politicians from the old military governments continued to play a leading role in formal institutional politics with the presidential election of Roh Tae-Woo in 1987. Roh was part of the ruling military bloc at the time, but held on to power by winning the free presidential election after the June civil uprising.[8] The uprising led to the "June 29th declaration", personally read by Roh, in which the military junta announced a return to free democratic procedures.

Even the traditional opposition party resurrected at this time was not meaningfully anchored in civil society. When normal democratic party politics was suspended during the 1970s and early 1980s, the opposition party politicians ejected from the formal political domain had chimed in with conscientious intellectuals' political resistance and voiced strong support for civil society forces. However, the basis of their political existence continued to be the protection of exclusionary vested interests within the formal political domain itself. As emphasized by Cumings (1997), the lineage of the opposition parties led by Kim Young-Sam and Kim Dae-Jung (who would become presidents in turn after Roh)dates back to the Korea Democratic Party (Hangukminjudang, or Hanmindang in abbreviation) of the 1950s. It was a hurriedly formed party that represented the allied interests of rightwing politicians and landlords without any significant basis in ordinary masses. In other words, the exclusionary nature of formal institutional politics had been in operation continually since the 1950s (Chang, K., 1999).

In this sense, even after 1987, the main opposition parties not only lacked an organic social foundation in civil society, but, as compellingly argued by Lim, Y. (1997), was basically indifferent to it. Negotiations conducted after 29 June 1987 to discuss reform of the political system and national power structure were attended by the sitting military government and main opposition party leaders, who together colluded to exclude democracy movement forces in civil society—i.e., the very historical agency that had forced the military government's political surrender. In the analysis by Yoon, S. (1997: 199), "civilian party politicians feared that a union of the opposition party establishment and civil society's democracy movement forces might over time lead to a strategic war with the latter, and that its political influence on civil society might be reduced significantly". The political result was essentially a compromise between the presently vested interests of the sitting military government and the aged interests of the opposition party leaders, taking on a deliberately anti-civil society character (Yoon, S., 1997; Choi, J., 2002).

Against this backdrop, the two opposition leaders Kim Young-Sam and Kim Dae-Jung parted ways, consequently helping former general, Roh Tae-Woo to win the presidential election in late 1987. The restoration of democracy epitomized by the direct presidential election was seen by the opposition party politicians as a recovery of their own long-forfeited political rights. Despite protests by civil society in reaction to this perception, the two opposition leaders proceeded with their respective election campaigns. The opposition Unification Democratic Party (Tongilminjudang) which had split from the New Korea Democratic Party (Shinhanminjudang) in April 1984, leaving only a minority of members behind, was divided again by Kim Dae-Jung's departure with the Peace Democratic Party (Pyeonghwaminjudang), in anticipation of the upcoming presidential election. These two parties were essentially the private political instruments of Kim Young-Sam and Kim Dae-Jung. In Kim Young-Sam's view, of course, Kim Dae-Jung's strategic choice to create a new party and separately run for presidency was an act of great political betrayal. But Kim Young-Sam's credentials to run for presidency were themselves far from grounded in the fundamental needs of civil society as a whole.

3.3 *The Formation and Reproduction of Social Cleavages by Aristocratized Political Blocs: The Political Order of Regionalist Rivalism*

Defeat in the 1987 presidential election did not become a thrust for the opposition party politicians to realize their fundamental political accountability to civil society. It instead resulted in a distortion of the party organizations for their own personal political survival, above all, by inventing regional political rivalry. Many historical prejudices operated as the background of this political culture, including a long history of traditional political regionalisms, Park Chung-Hee's regionally biased industrialization strategy (in favor of Gyeongsang Provinces), and the 1980 Gwangju incident. But it solidified into a routine political culture, paradoxically, with the restoration of a democratic political order in 1987 and the subsequent processes of elitist political competition. Many experts agree that the origin of regionalist voting as a broad tendency dates back to the 1960s, but after 1987 this tendency rapidly and structurally intensified as the popular support bases for the main political parties became regionalized (Cho, K., 2000; Lee, K., 1998).

Judging from the situation in 1987 alone, the military government's strategy to overcome its political crisis by relying on the "foreseen split" between the two opposition leaders, with some supposedly rivaling bases of regional support, proved successful. Even so, these civilian politicians' reliance on—or arguable invention of—interregional political rivalry could not be justified ethically. From 1987 on, regionalist voting and region-based party politics took decisive root, engendering an additional critical factor for the dislocation between civil society and formal institutional politics. According to Yoon, S. (1997: 198), "whereas the institutional opposition parties in the past joined with social movements, allowing them to more broadly mobilize civil society's masses (the middle class), they are at present cut off from social movements and are very good at strategies for directly mobilizing the public by regionalist tactics". In conditions of procedural democratization, the political parties must seriously demarcate their social bases, but politicians who have grown comfortable with (protecting their) exclusionary vested interests through "institutional parasitism" and "rent-seeking" would not try to open up the formal political domain to potential political forces from civil society (Mobrand, 2019). Under these circumstances, entrenched political leaders exploited regionalist sentiments and tendencies in order to carry out populist mobilizations aimed at the regionally configured constituents of exclusive political support.[9] In the assessment by Choi, J. (2002: 107), "South Korea's regionalist political party system, unlike what is typically found in other countries, does not mobilize the masses according to interests or divisions by class, profession, or sector, serving to maximize political struggle on a national scale. Instead, it vertically divides up the regions using the existing frame of the old political party system to mobilize the masses according to the localized axes of conflict". Thus, regionalism has not been configured on the basis of social interests and identities but constructed and mobilized in keeping with the practical needs of exclusive political elites within the formal political domain.

But even though this regionalist political rivalry, as an artificially created construct, has instilled a sense of political futility in the ordinary citizenry, it has also gained a sort of self-fulfilling force through several decades of its political effectuation. Under regionalist prejudice and hatred fomented between the supposedly rivaling regions, political office-seekers could monopolize votes in their respective regional constituencies and exercise their earned power to the exclusion and discrimination, in both politics and daily life, against people, places, and industries from or in certain regions, and thereby help to form collective interests by people within or by a region as a whole. The sociopolitical importance of such regionalized interests may be weak relative to that of capitalist class relations, interests, and conflicts in the whole nation, but it is nevertheless a very real problem for many people, organizations, and areas. After the inauguration of the Kim Dae-Jung government, alleged political preferences and policy priorities for Jeolla provinces and their citizens, to the supposed exclusion and disadvantage of Gyeongsang provinces and their citizens, were widely seen as retribution.[10] Many who allegedly suffered as a result began to recognize their own regionalized collective interests and thereby internalize regionalist political views and attitudes, intensifying regional rivalry politics.

The strengthening of regionalist political strategies further distorted the internal organization and order of each party. That order, based in vassal relationships between party bosses and their underlings, was certainly nothing new to South Korean society. The personal incarnation of political regionalism by the key leaders decidedly intensified their dominance within each regionalist political bloc. In all elections, whether presidential or parliamentary, the political tactics to elicit regionalist votes prevailed. Main political parties crucially stood on the foundations of respective regionalist support, with each party head reigning as the modern-day political monarch in his favored region. Regionalist votes constituted the act of political support for a party boss who symbolically represented the region, rather than a real political choice for a party. Accordingly, each party became the political property of a single party boss, so other politicians acted in loyalty to his absolute authority. Otherwise, they would not be able to enter politics itself. A politician's success in politics was not determined by any will or ability to represent civil society, but by an expressed loyalty to each key leader of regionalist politics, or by his/her recognized usefulness to such leaders.

On the other hand, the self-centered interests of these political bosses caused their parties to incessantly divide, dissolve, form, and unite under the disguised pretext of political conflict and struggle— a phenomenon dubbed in media *jeonggyejaepyeon* (restructuring of the political world). The most dramatic incident was the uniting of the three regionalist parties—Kim Young-Sam's United Democratic Party (Tongilminjudang), Kim Jong-Pil's New Democratic Republican Party (Sinminjugonghwadang), and Roh Taw-Woo's Democratic Justice Party (Minjujeonguidang)—to form the Democratic Liberal Party (Minjujayudang) in 1990. Although civil society's support for the opposition party leaders was squarely based in an anti-military government stance, Kim Young-Sam decided to strategically merge his party with the military-led ruling party in order to decisively augment his prospect for presidency. He actually became the next president that way. His presidency, in no surprise, was driven more by conservative developmentalist ambitions (favored by state and business elites) than by progressive sociopolitical reforms (yearned by ordinary members of civil society).

4 Political Institutional Frustration of the Working Class

4.1 *The Establishment of Proletarian Political Parties*

The first social attempt after 1987 to establish a political party based on a sociopolitically strengthened labor class in the industrial economy and civil society resulted in the Grassroots Party (Minjungdang) in the early 1990s. At the time of the party's founding, about one-quarter of its approximately 2,000 members were activist workers in the labor movement, and the National Steering Committee of Workers for the Founding of the Grassroots Party played a key role in its creation. The Korea Workers Party (Hanguknodongjadang), which merged with the Grassroots Party just prior to the 1992 general election, was even more deeply rooted in the labor movement, and most of its members were labor activists (Kim, Y., 1999). Yet, it is debatable whether the Grassroots Party had the genuine traits of a working-class party truly representative of the laborers. It instead reflected the strategic attempt of progressive intellectuals and activists in civil society to vigorously politicize themselves by augmenting their social base across the workers' organizations in the industrial sphere.

However, those active in the Grassroots Party were generally more intellectual than blue-collar in character. In fact, most of the party's "worker" members were not workers per se but the so-called *hakchul*, i.e., college students who had come from the universities to strategically enter the industrial factories as camouflaged workers with the sociopolitical goal of helping to organize the labor movement (Koo, H., 2001; Eun, S., 2006). As for its leadership, the so-called *jaeyaundongga* (at-field or extra-institutional activists) gave the party an even more strongly intellectual slant. A majority of the party's members were socialist or liberal intellectuals, and, while active in the labor movement, were far closer to radically leaning "labor activists". In sum, the party was more a party of progressive intellectuals than an ordinary working-class party. Regardless of the makeup of the party's membership, had the party actually elicited mass support, it might have strengthened its actual role centered in a pro-working class ideology comparable to that of European social democratic parties. However, the party failed to gain even a single seat in the national parliamentary election of March 1992, winning only 1.5% of the votes nationally (NEC, 2020). Unable to fulfill the legal requirement for a political party's formal continuance, it had to be dissolved after the election. A large number of the party's active members, hardly identifiable as workers per se, incited treacherous disputes by joining the mainstream conservative political parties and exploring opportunistic political careers therein.[11]

In its political nature and effect, the Grassroots Party significantly resembled the intellectually driven progressive parties in earlier decades—namely, Cho Bong-Am's Progressive Party (Jinbodang) in the 1950s and Kim Chul's Social Party (Sahoedang) in the 1980s. They were, in a sense, political survivors from the post-liberation civil society that had virtually been eliminated under the US-backed rightwing offenses and the Korean War (Jung, Y., 1995). They personally faced all manners of oppression, and their parties failed to establish in the mainstream domain of formal politics. During their political times, while civil society had critically been dismantled, the industrial working class had yet to grow in size and get socially organized. Under such circumstances, these progressive parties had to depend unilaterally on the *reflexive* intellectual movements attuned to West European experiences and ideologies in social democracy. Thus Kim Chul (2000) argued "unlike other (reads Western) countries,

South Korea's reform parties could not base themselves in the organized workers" but instead in "thick layers of intellectuals". By contrast, the Grassroots Party in the early 1990s did find a strong social class basis in the enlarged and organized industrial labor, but its ambiguous vision and limited organizational capacity fell short of effectively incorporating them into a solid working-class party.

In this respect, the real institutional history of working-class politics began with the Democratic Labor Party (DLP, Minjunodongdang) that was conceived by the KCTU (Minjunochong) shortly before the national financial crisis and kicked off immediately after it. The KCTU's formal decision to set up a political party was made at a meeting of its representatives in March 1997 as follows: "The Korea Confederation of Trade Unions... will provide a base for a new party to realize democratic reform in our society and speak soundly for the best interests and needs of the workers" (Jung, B., 2016: 87). Its goal was to launch the party in 1998 or 1999, but a sort of pilot political mobilization was attempted in anticipation of the 1997 presidential election. That is, the People's Victory 21 (Gukminseungri 21) was instantly launched as a sort of provisional party and formed broad coalitions with various political initiatives and movements from civil society such as the National Alliance (Jeongukyeonhap), the Political Solidarity (Jeongchiyeondae), and the Progressive Political Alliance (Jinbojeongchiyeonhap). The man chosen as the party's presidential candidate was KCTU chairman Kwon Young-Gil.

Although Kwon was able to elicit congenial popular responses to his friendly campaigns on essential socioeconomic issues, he received only 1.2% of the total votes, or slightly more than 300,000 votes, which at best accounted for only half the total of the KCTU's 600,000 members. In fact, some sample surveys conducted by the KCTU showed that, in the 1997 presidential election, only 21.0% of trade union members voted for Kwon. Such outcome was somewhat disappointing if it is considered that there had been a great surge in the KCTU's internal solidarity and social influence owing to the highly successful general strike of 1996–1997. Nonetheless, the KCTU subsequently launched the Democratic Labor Party (DLP), an explicitly labor-based party, at a special temporary meeting of its representatives in May 1998. Its official registration with the state authority regulating political parties was undertaken in January 2000 in time for an approaching national parliamentary election. Various progressive organizations and movements from civil society were incorporated in the DLP in conjunction with this political move.[12]

Looking at the relationship between the KCTU and the DLP, the latter was routinely and heavily dependent on the former in its operation. As seen in Table 1, as of late June 2002, half of DLP members were trade union members, a great majority of whom belonged to KCTU-affiliated unions. From its founding until its dissolving, the proportion of union members remained steady at approximately 50%. The proportion of union members among the party's leadership was about 40 to 50%. The party's official rules stipulated that workers must constitute about 20% of the representative body. Because the party's social base decisively consisted in the KCTU, participation by labor movement affiliates was conspicuously high. Such dependence was also made clear by the roster of 21 DLP candidates for the 2000 national parliamentary election, of whom 10 (48%) had been recommended by the KCTU.

The DLP's practical dependence on the KCTU was much heavier than displayed in formal statistics on its membership. This was because, as a party yet without a seat in the National Assembly, the DLP's propaganda, organization and public relations were managed with the routine support of the KCTU's organizational lines.[13] For instance, concerning the chapters in DLP districts where KCTU chapters also existed, the latter practically functioned as the former's operational platform. Indeed, it was these overlapping chapters that most actively and effectively carried out political activities. The KCTU also assisted the DLP through a series of supportive activities such as the printing and distribution of propaganda pamphlets targeting union members, the hosting of political debates and

Table 1 Rate of overlap between DLP and KCTU union members (as of June 2002)

	DLP (Democratic Labor Party)	KCTU (Korea Confederation of Trade Unions)
Total number of members	21,958	602,339
Number of members belonging to both DLP and KCTU	10,474	
Proportion of DLP-KCTU overlap members	47.7%	1.7%

Source Reconstructed from "Data on Current Party Members" (DLP, July 2002) and "Organizations during the First Half of 2002" (KCTU, July 2002)

roundtables for trade unions under their umbrella, and so forth (Jung, B., 2016).

As a result, the DLP became literally a workers' party (that is, a political party formed by organized labor) rather than a party of top-down ideology or abstract intellectualism. In the particular historical situation of Cold War-dominated South Korean politics, the spectrum of viable political ideologies was very limited and the formal institutional establishment of ideologically progressive political forces was extremely difficult. In a related foreign example, Germany's Social Democratic Party was outlawed under Bismarck for 12 years by an anti-socialist ordinance, but in the election immediately following the lifting of the ban, the socialists received 20% of the total vote. South Korea's Cold War order did not simply suppress and outlaw particular ideologies in the formal political domain, but also decisively hampered the autonomous political activation of civil society itself. Conventional political parties, paradoxically, had been established and perpetuated in the process of civil society's breakdown and deterioration, playing a central role in solidifying the dislocation of formal institutional politics from civil society (Chang, K., 1999; Mobrand, 2019). In this historical context, the DLP, as a genuine workers' party, was not born through a political conjunction of civil society's democratic initiative with organized labor's political proactivism, but arose as the latter's political self-help in the rigid polity inundated by extreme anti-proletarian sentiments and policies.

4.2 The Frustrated Entry of the Working Class into Mainstream Party Politics

Despite the DLP's huge symbolic as well as practical significance in South Korea's modern political history, its attempts to effectively establish itself in the formal political domain remained largely unfruitful, or unsatisfactory at least among those enthusiastically engaged in promoting the party's causes. In the general election of 2000, vying for seats in the National Assembly, the DLP saw very poor rates of support nationally at just 1.2% in the all electoral districts, and could not win even a single seat (NEC, 2020). It could not win a single proportional representation seat, either. This was certainly a very frustrating outcome, even much worse than the performance of the British Labour Party's first election precisely a century before. Even though DLP candidates were absent in so many electoral districts, this was nearly as poor a showing as the Grassroots

Table 2 The first election results of the British Labour Party and the Democratic Labor Party in South Korea

	British Labour Party (founded in 1900)	Democratic Labor Party (founded in 2000)
Election year	1900	2000
Candidates running	15	21
Candidates recommended by trade unions	5 (33% of candidates running)	10 (48% of candidates running)
No of election winners	2 (0.2% of total 670 seats)	0
Average votes for candidates running	35%	13%

Source Data on the British Labour Party from Ko, S. (1999)

Party in the early 1990s. Nonetheless, the average percentage of votes for DLP candidates was 13.1%, amounting to a small consolidation (see Table 2). As with the Grassroots Party in 1992, the DLP was also legally forced to dissolve and had to be re-registered for a formal return to politics.

Nonetheless, unlike the Grassroots Party, the DLP had a strong organizational base of the KCTU and therefore managed to survive many more years. In the presidential election of 2002, Kwon Young-Gil, as the DLP's candidate, was ranked at the third by winning 3.9% of votes nationally (NEC, 2020). In the general election of 2004, the DLP won two electoral district (*jiyeokgu*) seats (out of 243 seats) and claimed eight proportional representation (*biryedaepyo*) seats (out of 56 seats) by acquiring 13.0% of the party-based votes nationally (NEC, 2020). With these outcomes, the DLP established itself as the third biggest party, albeit, far behind the two consistently dominant parties. In the presidential election of 2007, Kwon Young-Gil ran for the third time, representing the working class, but had to see some ceiling to his or his party's political influence revealed in terms of only 3.0% of votes won nationally (NEC, 2020). Such political ceiling to the DLP was even lowered in the general election of 2008, in which the DLP's proportional representation seats were reduced to three (by 5.68% of the party-based votes nationally) while its electoral district seats remained unchanged at two (NEC, 2020). With five national congress members, the DLP was demoted to the fourth rank. With its national political influence stagnating at popularly negligible levels, the DLP was subjected to serious internal conflicts between different lines of political activism and fell apart before the next general and presidential elections of 2012. This implied that national politics would indefinitely be operating without an integrative working class party wholly assisted by organized labor. The North Korean politics under the virtual totalitarian dictatorship of a nominally proletarian party does not seem to have served its working class any better.

Various analyses have been undertaken on the labor-based political parties' failure to get a politically sustainable constituency in citizenry (e.g., Chang, S., 1999; Cho, H., 1995; Choi, J., 1992; Jung, B., 2016; Kim, D., 1991; Kim, D., 1993; Kim, Y., 1999; Lim, Y., 1997a, 1997b; Park, Y., 2000). External factors discussed include hostile state pressure, conservative ideological environment, regionalist political rivalism, and so forth, while internal problems noticed include difficulty in elevating class-based political awareness due to the decentralized labor union system, divisions and conflicts within the labor movement, and so forth. The external factors should be explained in more concrete terms. First, because the entire labor movement remained the tacit target of government suppression even after democratization, it was hard pressed even in maintaining its most basic organizational footings. It had no leisure to think about formal political empowerment as a mainstream force (Choi, J., 1994). Furthermore, while state policies were relatively lenient to labor's economic demands, the same was not the case with respect to its political demands. Above all, until the 1998 reforms to the Labor Law, political activities by the trade unions had been legally forbidden. Second, the biggest ideological hurdle was "red complex". While it was also true of labor movements generally, the professed joining of labor movements with formal politics evoked communism, a forbidden ideology in the everlasting Cold War context. Such ideological association served as a justifying mechanism for the government's suppression of organized labor's political attempts amid the rekindled red complex among the general populace, including industrial workers themselves (Roh, J., 1995).

Still, the biggest practical barrier to the organized labor's establishment in the formal political domain was the general electorate's regionalist voting behaviors. Since the presidential election of 1987 in which "votes according to one's native region were so dominant that nearly every eligible voter voted for their own region's candidate" (Choi, J., 1994), regionalist tendencies in nearly all political elections have frustrated the entry of labor-based candidates and parties into formal institutional politics. Even most industrial workers themselves tended to vote regionalistically, rather than by their class-based identities and interests, as a critical sign of their fragile class consciousness (Jung, Y., 1995). It is argued that despite labor organizations' strong influence at workshops on the basis of mostly company-based trade unions, ordinary workers had few opportunities to develop political consciousness (Kim, D., 1995).

It must be noted that the main reason that a majority of KCTU-affiliated union members did not vote for the DLP was not that they supported other political parties but that they were wary of the formal institutional domain of politics as a whole. According to *Report on Surveys about the Living Circumstances and Awareness of Union Members*, a survey report issued by the KCTU for 1999 and 2001, the surveyed union workers' support rates for the DLP in the concerned years were 25.7% and 23.1% respectively. These numbers were rather much larger than their support rates for other major parties (remaining at less than 10%). Their dominant response was "no support for any party", exceeding a half of all responses (at 57.4% in 1999 and 54.5% in 2001). These results were not unique to the members of labor unions, or limited to those of KCTU-affiliated unions. Basically similar responses have been revealed in numerous surveys on general public opinions since the 1990s. The specific rankings of political parties in popular support may have varied over time, but those indicating "no support for any party" have always remained at incomparable levels.

Such results have usually been expressed as "the lack of trust in political authority". To surmise the cause of this lack, it is necessary to trace events back to the critical period right after 1987 when free civil society was restored. In surveys on political attitudes during 1989–1992, the political necessity of a labor-representative party drew an overwhelming support of 80%—a result not limited to organized industrial workers but relevant to the general populace as a whole (Lim, Y., 1997a). The experimental Grassroots Party (Minjungdang) rode on the wave of such drastic changes in the citizens' political opinion (Kim, Y., 1999). However, when it came to actual politics, the same citizenry was either indifferent or cold to the new initiative in progressive politics. Such chilly responses were paradoxically caused by the fact that it was promoting an institutionally correct politics on the basis of specific class interest and ideology, which remained simply alien to the general populace on the irregionalistically behaving voting days. In a sense, South Korean voters' thin trust in political authority has substantially reflected their own political self-contradiction. Their political apathy has been most critically caused by interregional political rivalism, but they have also helped to politically buttress such condemned political order by casting their votes according to regionalistic identifies and considerations.

4.3 The Entrenched Order of Institutional Politics and the Political Exclusion of the Working Class

The practical mode of South Koreans' political participation has not had much to do with class interests and identities as systematically articulated by formal political parties. The ironic, or tragic, outcome of the seemingly successful society-wide struggle for democratization in 1987 was a reiteration of the socially exclusionary mode of formal institutional politics that had been witnessed chronically from the very first days of the Republic of Korea. The dictatorial state leaders from military did not seem to feel too sorry about their aggressive stoppage of such type of formal politics and instead tried to appeal to the populace through a kind of developmental populism (as detailed in Chapter 4). While Park Chung-Hee and Chun Doo-Hwan—as well as Syngman Rhee to some extent—were to blame for their brutal denial of political rights and democratic procedures, even the so-called civilian politicians, mostly as opposition party members, more helped to sustain than reform the socially exclusionary political domain.

It was under this context that the nation's restored democracy got instantly degenerated into a regionalist politics in which both key civilian politicians leading the main opposition parties and military-turned politicians in state power practically colluded in order to enjoy and perpetuate regionally grounded political bossism. Such political regression caused popular suspicion and lack of trust to spread rapidly among all citizenry. When progressive intellectuals and labor leaders tried to establish a labor-based political party and represent grassroots class interests, most citizens remained indifferent or pessimistic to such political cause, sadly due to their resigned perception about conventional institutional politics. Yet, when an election time rolls around, the attitude of the absolute majority of voters turns compliant, casting their votes for political forces that divisively manipulate, not democratically represent, people and society. In other words, those sociopolitical attempts to rationally and justly represent workers and other sovereign citizens through genuinely democratic parties have been doubly sacrificed by the (mostly two) main political parties entrenched in regional rivalry politics.

This dilemma was most evidently illustrated in the presidential election of 2002. Given some favorable conditions including the DLP's better-than-expected performance in the latest local governmental and parliamentary elections, some sympathetic media's supportive coverage, and civil society groups' enthusiastic advocacy, the DLP candidate Kwon Young-Gil was popularly recognized as a significant contender against the candidates of the two dominant parties, Roh Moo-Hyun of the New Millennium Democratic Party (Saecheonnyeonminjudang) and Lee Hoi-Chang of the One Nation Party (Hannaradang). He was duly given the opportunity to join Roh and Lee in a series of nationally televised official debates, in which he would be popularly praised as the only candidate focusing his arguments on relevant public objectives and state policies as well as advancing a political line representative of certain legitimately identifiable groups of citizens (Justice Policy Institute, 2015). By contrast, Roh and Lee mostly argued over political problems "between them" such as calls for clarifying their personal ideologies, accusations of alleged corruption, and regionalist negations or attacks. In fact, it was apparent that Roh and Lee were tacitly colluding to sideline Kwon from the debates whenever possible. While Kwon thereby received the most positive reviews from many citizens, he was nearly abandoned in the actual election with his votes well below the popular support levels during the campaign period. The political framework set up by the two conventionally dominant parties, both being conservative despite minor and/or occasional differences, led to an almost automatic alienation of the political force that tried to most sincerely represent the interests and values of sovereign citizens within certain legitimate confines.

In sum, the chief difficulty the labor-based parties have faced in mainstreaming into the formal political domain has not been an insufficient recognition or lack of moral support by industrial workers and the general public; rather, it has instead been the chronic structural dislocation of formal politics perpetuated by the dominant parties and entrenched politicians. Among other exclusionary mechanisms, the persistence of regional rivalry politics—in spite of its subjection to harsh public criticism as well as politicians' repeated self-critique—has been most detrimental to those political parties and candidates that would pursue politics differently. Under this "nation-destroying political order" (*manggukjeokjeongchijilseo*), the firmly region-entrenched parties and politicians have sit on a sort of *prearranged internal voting blocs* (Lee, K., 1998) that enable them to automatically claim overwhelming shares of parliamentary seats both at the national and the local levels. Such voting blocs, as maintained by the two main parties' in-effect "election alliance" (*seongeoyonhap*), have operated as a fundamental barrier to the labor-based parties, among other society-representative parties, in breaking into the exclusionary domain of formal institutional politics. It has been argued that voters fall into a kind of "prisoner's dilemma" under their mutually hostile regionalist rivalism because they are led to think that they cannot afford to support a more sympathizable new or minor party due to the possibility of their favored region's election defeat. In other words, when most citizens have acted on the assumption that the supposed rival region's people would give an overwhelming support for their own favored party, those (minor) parties and politicians in pursuit of "correct" political goals and policies have been left out in the cold.

Besides regionalist voting blocs, the entrenched parties and politicians have also (ab)used various legal instruments to perpetuate new and/or minor parties' exclusion in the formal political domain. As a key component of South Korea's political affairs law, there have been explicit stipulations to ensure "prevention of the scrambling by minor parties" (*gunsojeongdang nanlip bangji*), which practically discourage and hamper the entrance of any new political forces (Park, D., 1995). For instance, unless a party is able to win a certain (significant) percentage of votes or at least one parliamentary seat, its formal political status is automatically canceled and cannot lawfully operate its political activities anymore. In South Korea's Cold War political history, such discriminatory law used to function as a political mechanism for preventing or destroying political elements with revolutionary and/or leftist causes. In fact, the Grassroots Party (Minjungdang) had to be dissolved precisely due to this viciously intended law, and the DLP had to similarly go through dissolving and reestablishing.

In addition, the two core elements of the parliamentary election law— i.e., the single member electorate system (*soseongeoguje*) and the very limited proportional representation system for party-based parliamentary seats—have systematically discriminated new and/or minor parties and politicians. These two elements of the election system may be disadvantageous to such parties in any society, but South Korea's extremely regionalist structure of voting blocs has made such disadvantages fatally decisive. Under the single member electorate system, the two main parties have virtually monopolized National Assembly seats allocated to their respective fiefdom-like regions (i.e., Yeongnam and Honam), which account for larger populations than other regions except the national capital region of Seoul and its vicinities.[14] Such regionalist division of votes has also taken place, albeit less decisively, in the national capital region according to each electorate's demographic composition of regional migrants. For the same reason, a few electorates constituted within newly constructed industrial cities and thus inhabited predominantly by industrial workers and their family members, most of whom are on the one hand migrants from across the nation and on the other hand union members and their dependants, have been exceptional to such regionalist determination of votes.[15] The two dominantly entrenched parties have also colluded to refuse reforms to the highly limited proportional representation system for parliamentary seats. The DLP and its subsequently successive parties have kept trying hard, but unsuccessfully, to pressurize the two dominant parties to accept reforms to these discriminatory components of the election system.[16]

5 Conclusion: Political Citizenship Without Democratic Social Representation

Compressed modernity, a characteristic distinguishing modern South Korean history, not only indicates the country's extremely swift development and modernization, but has also involved an uneven time zone between different societal domains, correspondent to what Ernst Bloch (1991) dubbed "a simultaneity of non-simultaneous matters". One of the most critical results in the latter aspect has been a structural separation, or dislocation, of the formal political domain from civil society and industrial class structure. Viewed historically, the most influential factor was the Cold War system which married anti-communism to pro-Americanism. To begin with, the Cold War system yielded a paradox in which the formal political domain has not only lacked a proper base in civil society, but in fact was born by violently removing it. Major historical occasions in this regard included the arrival of the American military occupation force and its promotion of a rightwing South Korean government contingent upon the national division, a civil war with North Korea, and the military coups in 1961 and 1980. Furthermore, the state's extremely coercive anti-communism under the Cold War severely narrowed civil society's ideological spectrum, and the total civilizational and political dependence on the U.S. caused the absolutization of liberal democratic ideals and institutions brought in all at once from the American system. Established by means of an alien system and without a proper base in civil society, South Korea's political elites have been, from the very beginning, inherently parasitic, self-serving, and exclusionary. South Korea was able to adopt an advanced democratic political system literally overnight, but the political incumbents formed to rule that system did not meaningfully differ from those dignitary figures in the traditional polity characterized by exclusionary self-appointment and self-reproduction. South Koreans' political citizenship in a sort of *cuttage-planted democracy* (Chang, K., 2022) was instantly degenerated into the prematurely entrenched political elites' self-awarded prize in political power.

Another fundamental aspect of compressed modernity has been an unprecedentedly and incomparably rapid growth of the capitalist industrial economy and class structure. South Korea's "economic miracle" required and facilitated the rapid formation of working and middle classes, which in turn helped to critically revitalize civil society. Conversely, progressive intellectuals, who had become the kernel of civil society through staunch democratization struggles, actively supported wage workers and their labor organizations in the industrial world. It was 1987 when these crucial changes intersected, bringing about explosive political and social reforms. Not only the dictatorial military had to agree to the immediate restoration of the democratic political procedures, but also civil society and organized labor claimed the center stage in steering the nation's sociopolitical and economic reforms. Politically, however, the ultimate result was a resurrection of an exclusionary political domain collusively occupied by authoritarian state elites and their supposedly opposition rivals—a self-nominating and self-serving political structure dating back to the 1950s, a period that had become very vague in public memory thanks to the military's total sabotage of democratic procedures since the 1960s. With all remarkable growth in industrial workers' organized struggles and civil society's intellectually driven activism, the formal political domain remained impervious to reform pressures for democratic social representation. By distorting the nation's democracy into the collusively exclusionary system of self-appointment and self-reproduction, the entrenched political elites and their parties have kept reducing South Koreans' political citizenship to an empty shell.

Various attempts to politically empower the working class were undertaken under such conditions. South Korea's literally explosive capitalist industrialization led to a correspondingly rapid formation of the modern working class, and the critical support of activist civil society in labor affairs enabled industrial workers to be effectively organized at the corporate, industrial, and national levels. On the part of civil society, the Cold War's political culture and law were chronically inhibitive to its promotion of a progressive (i.e., socialist or social democratic) political party that could organize and mobilize citizens for reformist, if not revolutionary, ideals. The existence of highly prominent intellectual politicians with popular respect and even international recognition (such as Cho Bong-Am and Kim Chul) was not a sufficient condition. This essential project in South Korea's political modernization began to be conceived as organized labor's historical task on the basis of working class interests and identities. The experimental, and unsuccessful, Grassroots Party represented an attempt with mixed targets and characteristics between intellectualist civil society's political initiative and organized labor's political activism. It was instead the Democratic Labor Party that fully represented the formal political rise of the working class on the strong organizational basis of trade unions.

So far, however, even the robustly organized working class has failed to break down the staunch wall of the exclusionary political domain in any meaningful sense. Upon their political resurrection thanks to the democratization pressure of civil society and organized labor, the entrenched "civilian" politicians resumed their business-as-usual kind of political monopoly. They even went on to collude with the ex-military politicians in distorting the restored democracy into a regionalist political rivalism that would allow them to perpetuate their partaken shares in political influence. Correspondingly, their insistence on maintaining the single member electorate system and the highly limited proportional representation system in the parliamentary election has been criticized as a coward act for collusively monopolizing the formal political domain. Virtually all of new and/or minor parties pursuing different (legitimate?) lines of politics, including the DLP as the supposed political representative of the nation's largest social class, have been discriminated and frustrated by such exclusionary power and practice of the two entrenched political parties and their members. South Koreans' arduously restored democracy has thereby brought about a political citizenship devoid of proper or legitimate social representation.

What about the democratic citizenship of rural people, most of whom are immediate family members of urban workers? South Korea's immediate developmental success in the early stage of labor-intensive industrialization was a great deal due to the proactive contributions of peasant families in eagerly sending motivated and educated youth for urban industrial work and strategically supporting them as a new basis of (extended) familial economic progress and status advancement. Consequently, village-remaining parents used to be more concerned about their urban-based children's long-term socioeconomic success than their own immediate conditions of agrarian livelihood—a phenomenon I earlier conceptualized as *indirect exit* from rural life (cf. Hirschman, 1970).[17] Such attitude has been fundamentally inhibitive to the effective consolidation of peasants' collective class interest in social struggle and political contestation against the dominant forces of the developmentally allied state and industrial capital. They may have been even less efficacious sociopolitically than those European peasants ridiculed by Karl Marx (1951) as "a sack of potatoes". Furthermore, the rapid demographic tapering of rural population has additionally weakened their national political influence. A typical extended family in South Korea composed of village-remaining peasant parents and urban-based proletarian children, no matter whether or how it has successfully gained from the multi-regional and multi-sectoral diversification of familial resources and aspirations, has not been able to meaningfully promote either of its agrarian or proletarian class interests through institutional democratic politics.

On the other hand, there were attempts by *chaebol*, South Korea's industrial conglomerates, to formally enter national politics. Chung Ju Young, Hyundai Group's founder, formed the National Party (Gukmindang) and ran for presidency in 1991, whereas his son Chung Mong Jun, the president of Hyundai Heavy Industries Group, founded the National Integration 21 (Gukmintonghap 21) to run for presidency. Neither of them was successful in winning the respective presidential election, but they did draw intense media publicity and wide popular attention. However, such public influence of the politically ambitious bourgeoisie was in no sense welcomed by the institutionally entrenched political elites in spite of their tacit collusion with *chaebol* in developmentalist national governance as well as individual corruption network (*Maeil Economic Daily*, 4 April 1995; https://www.mk.co.kr/news/home/view/1995/04/14987/). An interesting reaction from established politicians was to criticize these industrialists' supposed greed of "unduly seeking both political power and wealth", implying the unwillingness to share their monopolistic status in institutional politics. In a sense, the baffled attempts at political institutional participation by organized workers and industrial capitalists were the two sides of a coin.

In sum, South Korea's political modernization, including both the initial institutional setup of the national polity and the restoration of the democratic procedures after a lengthy period of military dictatorship, has failed to achieve an effective and sustained rooting of a class-based political party that represents wage workers as the nation's largest occupation. The historically exclusionary and regionalistically entrenched groups of conservative political elites and their parties, by distorting the nation's democracy into a collusive system of self-appointment and self-reproduction, have kept reducing South Koreans' political citizenship to an empty shell. Democratic in "form" only, the formal political domain has almost completely ruled out organized labor despite its apparent presence as a strong social force (and the demographic preponderance of the urban working population), whereas unions and union-based parties have been unable to deal with this incongruous situation very effectively. The chronic limit of the working class in effective democratic representation in formal institutional politics, particularly in the heavily state-centered system of socioeconomic governance, has systematically disadvantaged them in capitalist economic development and industrial restructuring as well as in public social protection. In fact, this dilemma of empty political citizenship has been nearly universal to all social classes at the grassroots level, and thereby structurally obstructed the nation's Marshallian evolution in citizenship politics (Marshall, 1964). The lack of such class-based representative politics as can be accommodated by the mainstream political parties through the parliament has inevitably implied that, as shown in the subsequent six chapters in Part II, South Koreans' social citizenship on all fronts has been framed and managed through the pragmatic daily interactions between the technocratic state and individual citizens. As ordinary individual citizens have found their social citizenship neglected and sacrificed by the inherently conservative state with a long developmentalist legacy, they have vigorously turned to individual civil rights in aggressively and loudly staging their socioeconomic causes (instead of begging the aristocratized political parties for reasonable justice).

PART II

Citizenship as Transformative Contributory Rights

CHAPTER 4

Developmental Citizenship and Its Discontents

1 Introduction: Citizenship in Comparative Historical Perspective

In one of the earliest critiques of T. H. Marshall's theory of citizenship, Michael Mann charged him for being Anglocentric and evolutionist. Michael Mann (1987: 339) instead proposed a comparative historical understanding of diverse strategies for "the institutionalization of class conflict" (of which citizenship is a political manifestation)—namely, "liberal, reformist, authoritarian monarchist, Fascist, and authoritarian socialist". For these varied types of sociopolitical formations, Mann highlighted the decisive role of ruling classes and *ancien regimes* (vis-à-vis bourgeoisie and proletariat) and the overruling influence of geopolitical events (vis-à-vis the internal efficiency of the above sociopolitical formations).[1] While Mann's alternative categories of sociopolitical formations do not properly cover the historical situations of many non-Western countries, his emphasis on the importance of dominant conservative forces and international political conditions for the emergence and transformation of various sociopolitical formations (or citizenship regimes) is irrefutable. As to be shown in this chapter, the South Korean case is particularly instructive.

The democratic form of modern statehood, no matter how much variegated and/or distorted its actual conditions are, has become prevalent across the world more as a result of the coercive civilizational incorporation of non-Western regions by Western powers than as an evolutionary achievement of individual national polities. When the modern state was "imported" (Badie, 2000), democracy, usually in terms of sheer political vocabulary, came along together. The elections as liberal institutional arrangements for political contract between the state and its legal constituencies (i.e., citizens) are supposed to be respected as an institutional minimum of democracy. But even this very basic tenet of democracy has not been consciously and voluntarily accommodated in too many countries, so that political procedural irregularities are still rampant in today's all too common democratic polities around the globe.

The profound acumen of Marshall (1964) consists in the understanding that democracy evolves (or deepens) along different sequential sets of citizenship rights. Indeed, such evolution has been commonly observable at least within European industrial democracies. In most of the imported democracies of non-Western regions, however, the historical process of political evolution or democratic deepening could not be imported as well. Specifically, unlike the civil and political rights of citizens (which are usually considered as the definitional components of democracy), social rights have rarely been systematically incorporated into the political ideology and administrative goal of the ruling governments.[2] In reality, the predominant concern of both the state elite and grassroots citizens rests with economic development and material livelihood. What is often dubbed "developmental politics" takes precedence in the everyday political process of most of non-Western, late developing nations.[3] Furthermore, the exigency of (rapid) national economic development is often considered to legitimate the distortion or stoppage of democracy. This phenomenon of developmental authoritarianism has not only been a widespread historical reality but also given birth to an influential functionalist theory on authoritarian politics in Third World countries (Huntington, 1968).

In nations ruled by developmentalist—democratic or not—regimes, the practically observable rights and duties of citizens with regard to their state have predominantly revolved around national economic development and individualized material livelihood. What I propose to call *developmental citizenship* has served as a basic framework for state-society (citizen) relations in these nations. The state is expected to concentrate on economic development so that its citizens can *benefit as private economic players in the state-promoted market system*—be workers, industrialists, or self-employed entrepreneurs. These issues have not been on the center stage of Western politics and thus are not directly codified in terms of constitutional provisions and major policy agenda, so the imported democracies in non-Western regions lack a systematic legal and/or theoretical representation of developmental politics. In these societies, the developmental politics as a mode of state governance and its citizenship ramifications mostly exist as everyday political culture. Most countries asserting a supposedly distinct political paradigm centered on national development have failed to sustain it as legitimate and viable in the long-term institutional consolidation of their formally democratic polities.

In comparison with such conventional (Western) categories of citizenship as suggested, above all, by T. H. Marshall (1964), developmental citizenship in its socioeconomic outcomes to citizens may fall on social citizenship in a broadest possible definition. At the same time, to the extent that the developmentalist state's promotion of *national* economic development is a political act relying regularly on political measures, the publicly assured participation of all motivated able citizens in such national(ist) development—that is, developmental citizenship—reflects a spirit of political citizenship. On the other hand, to the extent that a developmental citizen, in principle, is not immune to various socioeconomic inequalities and risks of a capitalist market economy, developmental citizenship can potentially be reduced to a simple economic denizenship.[4] With all such properties combined, developmental citizenship may be categorized as a kind of political economic citizenship.

A brief conceptual note is in order. I follow Bryan Turner's (1993: 2) definition of citizenship, namely "[a] set of practices (juridical, political, economic and cultural)" which allows us "to avoid a state and juridical definition of citizenship as merely a collection of rights and obligations" and "to understand the dynamic social construction of citizenship which changes historically as a consequence of political struggles". On my part, I have attempted here and in other works to explain how citizenship—developmental citizenship in particular—in South Korea has been conceived, protracted, and habitually renewed amid the dynamic interplay between political democratization and capitalist economic development and what social practices have constituted such historical constructions and reconstructions of (developmental) citizenship. More specifically, I suggest developmental citizenship as a mode of political culture which forcefully shapes the nature of state-citizen relations.

2 DEVELOPMENTAL POLITICS AND CITIZENSHIP IN SOUTH KOREA

[T]he rapid pace of economic development has not been matched by efforts to guarantee economic, social and cultural rights... [I]n such a situation, some rights or the rights of some groups are being sacrificed for the sake of economic recovery and market competitiveness.

[T]he "economy-first" approach adopted by the State party has resulted in a low priority placed on the protection of economic, social and cultural rights. This has led to the marginalization of certain groups in society in such matters as housing, social welfare, and health care.

[T]he State party did not take into account its Covenant obligations when negotiating with international financial institutions to overcome its financial crisis and restructure its economy... [T]here have been large-scale employee dismissals and layoffs, the significant deterioration in employment stability, growing income inequalities, an increasing number of broken families and marginalization of a large number of persons.

The above are part of the official observation made by the Committee on Economic, Social and Cultural Rights (under the U.N. Economic and Social Council) in 2001, after scrutinizing South Korea's social and economic situation under a U.N. covenant. According to this report, the country remained as a country in which even the international covenant on the most basic social rights had not been satisfactorily respected. While the U.N. committee was particularly concerned about the post-crisis economic management and social decay, it traced the root cause back to the earlier developmental statist era in South Korea. This meant that at times of both rapid economic growth and economic crisis, ordinary South Koreans had to do without reasonable social citizenship rights.

In the period of early industrialization, such sacrifice of basic social rights was politically buttressed by the authoritarian rule of the military-dominated government. The revival of democracy since the late 1980s, however, did not necessarily lead to a rise of a serious social policy state for which the protection of social rights would be a prime political objective. In fact, none of the main political parties tried to centrally identify themselves with such task (see Table 1 for comparison of the election campaign pledges of major presidential candidates in the 1950s through the 1980s). This implies that a majority of South Korean citizens have

4 DEVELOPMENTAL CITIZENSHIP AND ITS DISCONTENTS   93

Table 1 Main election pledges of presidential candidates in the authoritarian political era

Election order & date	Candidate name	Party name	Political	Diplomatic & defense	Admiration	Economic	Social	Cultural	Total
2nd 2 Aug 52	Rhee S M	Liberal	2	1	1	1	3		8
	Lee S H	Independ	3	4	3	8	4		22
	Cho B A	Independ	1	2	4	1	1		10
3rd 15 May 56	Rhee S M	Liberal	2	4		6	2		12
	Shin I H	Democrat			2	4	9	4	17
	Cho B A	Progressive	2	3		11			19
4th 15 Mar 60	Rhee S M	Liberal	3	7	1	31	4	1	47
	Cho B W	Democrat	1	1	1	4			7
5th 15 Oct 63	Park C H	Republic	4	2		4	1		11
	Yoon B S	Dem Polit	5		5				10
6th 3 May 67	Park C H	Republic		3		7	3		12
	Yoon B S	New Democ	1	5		1	1	1	8
7th 27 Apr 71	Park C H	Republic	4	6	2	22	17		51
	Kim D J	New Democ	38	40	10	34	26	5	119
13th 16 Dec 87	Roh T W	Dem Justice	25	39	49	143	147	18	421
	Kim Y S	Uni Democ	42	42	33	133	75	17	342
	Kim D J	Commoner	21	31	1	73	45	1	171

Source Constructed from data in *Monthly Report on Legislation, Republic of Korea* (in Korean), August 1992, p. 163

not expected the protection of social rights to be responsibly undertaken by the popular political parties or the governments they may form. What then is the central issue of politics? What kind of citizenship do South Koreans hope to see evolve under their arduously won democracy? In a short answer, democratization has not fundamentally altered the developmental focus of national politics, so that the "economy-first" approach has been shared by the democratically formed civilian governments. What are the citizenship implications of such protracted developmental politics?

In classifying contemporary nations according to social policy characteristics—in particular, the contents and strengths of their welfare systems—West European social democracies have been considered distinctive in terms of the protection of comprehensive social citizenship (cf. Esping-Andersen, 1990). According to the same classification, South Korea is often seen as a "welfare laggard" in which the level of social citizenship is conspicuously low vis-à-vis its miraculous achievement of economic development. In many studies on the South Korean social policy regime, the country has been described as an unsystematic institutional mixture of conservative and liberal characteristics with a remarkably limited public financial commitment (Kim and Seong, 1993). Such West-centered classification of the South Korean situation may be valid if the ultimate goal of national development is conceived as the establishment of a Western-style welfare state, or if the long-term direction of sociopolitical progress is set in terms of an evolutionary expansion of social citizenship in accordance with the Western experiences. Indeed, the normative appeal of such West-centered diagnosis is apparent in the reformist, if not revolutionary, efforts of various social and political groups (including social democratic parties, progressive intellectuals and NGOs, and labor organizations). However, the dominant political parties, state elite, business oligarchies, and even most of grassroots citizens seem to have only a very modest and vague sense of social citizenship as a key political objective.

There are many historical factors for the reality that the establishment of comprehensive social citizenship is not placed on the center stage of political development. First, the establishment (or importation) of the modern political system in South Korea was modeled after and supervised by the United States, which represents an extreme case of liberal political order. In the United States, the overpowering class interests of industrial, commercial, and financial entrepreneurs (i.e., bourgeoisie) have prevented the state and civil society from staging serious social democratic, if not socialist, reforms of the liberal capitalist system, whereas, in Western European countries, social citizenship kept expanding as the condition and consequence of the sociopolitical compromise between labor and capital.[5] The American military occupation of post-liberation South Korea, its direct intervention in the politico-legal formation of the republic, and the prolonged dependence of post-independence South Korea on the United States in political, economic, and social management came to impose an epistemological limit on South Koreans with regard to civilizational goals and options.[6] The protracted political indifference of both political elite and ordinary citizens to social citizenship is substantially derived from such epistemological limit. In the 1990s, the deepening of democratic politics led South Koreans to rapidly expand their political and intellectual interest in the West European (social democratic) models of state development. However, it was precisely at that time that the Anglo-American neoliberalism was seemingly spreading into Continental Europe, allowing the conservative factions in South Korean technocracy, academia, and media to loudly justify the passive stance of the state concerning social citizenship.[7]

Second, the ruthless control of labor by the authoritarian state in the process of state-led capitalist industrialization and the prohibition of political and ideological critique on capitalism under the (national and international) Cold War made it impossible for an organized working class to politically initiate socialist or social democratic alterations of the capitalist system as has been observed in many West European societies (Chang and Chang, 2002). In a society where the Cold War became the pretext for violently removing socialist political forces, even the social democratic cause as intellectual initiative or social movement was difficult to sustain. If any, part of the social democratic social policies has been accommodated by the state technocracy as a means for stabilizing the capitalist system. Thereby arose the Bismarckian nature of the social policy regime in South Korea, albeit with an extremely limited financial commitment of the state to social wage.[8] The democratic transition since the late 1980s gradually enabled the working class to organize itself in the institutional political arena, but its negligible political weight (in terms of political popularity and parliamentary seats) has implied the continuing marginal location of social democratic agendas in national politics (Chang and Chang, 2002). Furthermore, ever since the organized labor naively agreed with the state and business to neoliberal restructuring, focused on labor reshuffling, as a supposedly concerted effort to overcome the national economic crisis of 1997–1998, the guiding or reform of national politics by the working class has become a political impossibility (Chang, K., 2019; also see Chapters 3 and 5 in this book).

Lyric of "Let's Live Affluently" by Han Un-Sa
(translated from Korean)

Let's live affluently. Let's live affluently. We once, let's live affluently.
Adorning silk-embroidered rivers and mountains and the beautiful country with one mind,
Fun of frugal livelihood is automatic, wealth and prosperity ours.
Let's live affluently. Let's live affluently. We once live affluently.
Let's live affluently.

Let's work. Let's work. We once, let's work.
Rich countries over the sun were not created overnight.
Amassed dusts making a huge mountain, we would not reserve our blood and sweat.
Let's work. Let's work. We once work.
Let's work.

Let's run. Let's run. We once run.
Open wide the heavily closed windows of the country to the world,
Learn all good things. Shall we lag behind. Let's run.
Let's run. Let's run. We once, let's run.
Let's run.

Third, the main driving force behind the full-scale socioeconomic modernization since the 1960s and the establishment of a mammoth industrial capitalist system today has derived, on the one hand, from the mercantilist developmental politics by the (military-led) state and, on the other hand, from the material achievement desire of industrialists and workers who intensely engaged themselves in the economic process accompanying such developmental politics. Under the entrepreneurial alliance between the government and business elite (often dubbed *jeonggyeongyuchak*, that is political-economic collusion) and the enthusiastic participation in industrial labor by abundant young workers supplied from villages, the economic development-centered governance of the military regime was elevated to a status of pan-national endeavor, under the rubric of "national regeneration" (*minjokjungheung*). The capitalist class interest was identified with the corporate growth and profit increase accompanying national economic growth, whereas that of the working class was equated with the employment growth and income improvement similarly accompanying national economic growth. In pursuing national economic growth as fast as possible, the developmentalist military regime not only damaged full political citizenship but also downplayed the need to build up decent social citizenship. Instead, under the slogan of "Let us once live affluently!", the state demanded all citizenry to devote their resources, energy, and motivation to the economy-centered national politics (see the politically popularized lyric of "Let's Live Affluently" in the above Box). The pursuit of individual material interests through national economic development became a de facto political contract between citizenry and the state. The assurance of what may be called *developmental citizenship* became the main basis for the political legitimacy of the authoritarian military regime. And, the astonishingly rapid and sustained growth of the national economy made it possible to firmly ingrain the politics of developmental citizenship in South Korean society.

The primacy of developmental citizenship did not imply that South Koreans were indifferent to their political citizenship rights. In fact, their sociopolitical struggle for rehabilitating the democratic procedures and recovering civil rights was no less staunch than their economic endeavor. It was their own strenuous revolts that finally brought an end to the military dictatorship and recovered democracy into civic life and state governance. However, democratization did not seriously destabilize or reform the primacy of developmental politics. Even the democratically elected administrations have been expected by citizens to prioritize economic development, and actually have done so.

The democratically elected administration of ex-general Roh Taw-Woo briefly discussed "the establishment of the welfare state" in order to pacify the controversy over his political legitimacy (see Chapter 5). But Roh was succeeded by three democracy fighter-turned presidents who tried to emulate Park Chung-Hee during their respective presidency. While their reign itself represented the revival of South Koreans' political citizenship, they consciously attempted to evince their capacity for sustaining South Korea's developmental progress. That is, Kim Young-Sam's "civilian government" tried to reproduce the Park-style rapid-growth political economy under the slogan of "the New Economy."[9] Kim Dae-Jung's "prepared government", inaugurated amid "the IMF economic crisis", exerted all efforts in order to bring about an instant recovery of the national economy at the systematic sacrifice of labor and future generations, whereas Roh Moo-Hyun's "participatory government" launched an interregionally redistributive developmental policy involving relocation of the administrative capital and major public enterprises and promotion of regional infrastructural development projects (Cho, 2007). Such sequential (quasi-)developmental administrations, however, failed to relieve the destabilizing employment conditions and deteriorating livelihood of most grassroots South Koreans. The political response of the disappointed South Koreans was not to seek an alternative political force that would establish comprehensive social citizenship, but to give another definite try to developmental politics by electing Lee Myung-Bak, a famous construction CEO during the Park's developmentalist era, into presidency (see Photo 1 for a scene of his flamboyant "747" election campaign, playing a sort of developmental populism with the promises of "*seven* percent annual national economic growth, *forty* thousand dollar per capita income, and the world's *seventh* biggest national economy").

As surveyed above, mercantilist developmentalism has been rooted in South Korea as the dominant political ideology since the military rule. The arrival of the democratic era has not resulted in its termination but its reproduction, albeit in different forms. The practical content of citizenship in South Korea, as a definition of state-society (or state-citizen) relations in a liberal polity, seems to have consisted more crucially in

Photo 1 Presidential candidate Lee Myung-Bak addressing the Republic of Korea 747 Supporters Association, 7 August 2000 (*Source* Lee Myung Bak's presidential election campaign homepage)

the developmental obligations and rights (summarizable in terms of the collective pursuit of national economic development and the indiscriminate enjoyment of the concomitant market-based benefits), than in the constitutionally stipulated civil, political, and social rights. Such political order (or political culture) has resulted in the assimilation of all (dictatorial and democratic) administrations into a pseudo-Park Chung-Hee regime. Under this circumstance, main political parties, which are not only incapable of developing autonomous ideologies and policy paradigms but also unable to systematically comprehend the Western ideologies and policy paradigms they openly attempt to replicate, have remained chronically dependent upon government technocracy. For the same reason, the so-called developmental bureaucrats (*gaebalgwanlyo*—technocrats in charge of economic developmental affairs) have inundated main political parties and parliamentary seats, in place of ordinary politicians who are supposed to have built up their political status through struggles for representing the values and interests of ordinary citizens.

3 Developmental Citizenship: Sociopolitical Traits and Limits

Since developmental citizenship is not a legally codified set of rights and duties but a political culture of practical governance and support, its substances and characteristics are beyond any easy clarification. Besides, developmental citizenship is not a highly unique phenomenon confined to the South Korean experience, so that wide national variations of its forms and contents are duly expected. Thus, what are presented below as the sociopolitical characteristics of developmental citizenship in the South Korean context do not necessarily constitute a generalizable theory or description of developmental citizenship.

First, developmental citizenship was not constructed interactively between the state and citizenry, but superimposed from above by the state onto citizenry. The national exigencies of rapid economic recovery and social integration after the Korean War made it indispensable for the state to authoritatively mobilize and regiment populace for various developmental projects. In addition, the continuing confrontation with North Korea accompanied by the global Cold War urgently required South Korea to build up its economic and military capacity as rapidly as possible (under the slogan of "rick country, strong army", or *bugukgangbyeong* in Korean). These historical conditions induced the state to focus on economic development as a state responsibility and to oblige all citizens to cooperate and participate in economic activities as a kind of civic duty.[10]

Second, developmental citizenship has been intricately enmeshed with both autocracy and democracy whereas its relationship with the constitutionally prescribed citizenship rights such as civil, political, and social rights is quite amorphous. The successive reign of the autocratic regimes from the 1950s to the mid-1980s entailed protracted and recurrent infringements of civil and political rights. The circumscription of civil and political rights, in turn, was inhibitive to the establishment of a progressive political regime that would have actively promoted comprehensive social rights (Kim, D., 2006). In a political context where the legally declared citizenship rights were practically nullified or neglected, the actual political relationship between the state and citizenry was substantiated mainly in terms of developmental expectations and performances. The sustained rapid growth of the South Korean economy helped to buttress the political utility of developmental citizenship well after democratization (Chang, K., 2012a). The continuing utility of developmental citizenship in the democratic era implies that even the democratically elected governments have tried to concentrate their political energy on economic development, not on social welfare (or social citizenship). The interrelationship between developmental citizenship and other more conventional components of citizenship is not chartable according to any evolutionary schema.

The Court Indictment on the Doosan Group (*chaebol*) Case and the Comment by the Chief of Justice

Indictment: "That the accused damaged the value of the firms by using corporate properties like private properties, that they embezzled the huge sum of about 28.6 billion won (note: about 30 million US dollars) in ten years, and that they severely weakened the corporate creditability and the reliability of the national economy through make-up accounting [in the sum of 300 million US dollars] are unfavorable factors for weighing the offense; but that part of the secret funds were contributed to improving the corporate financial structure and that all of the embezzled sum was paid back, and that the accused served economic and social development and contributed to national interests have been taken into account as favorable factors."

(*Source* Translated from *Financial News*, 21 July 2006)

> **Comment by the Chief of Justice**: "It was an opportunity to recover the reliability of the judicature, but I regret that did not happen... There may be no judge who would not sentence a prison term to one that entered another's house and stole things worth a hundred million won (note: about a hundred and five thousand US dollars)... Then, if probation is allowed to the accused that embezzled twenty to thirty billion won, how would citizens understand?".
> (*Source* Translated from *Money Today*, 17 February 2006)

Third, to the extent that the state-led capitalist industrialization implicates a merge of the class interest and ideology of bourgeoisie with the political objective and interest of the state, developmental citizenship involves fundamental asymmetries of rights between bourgeoisie and proletariat.[11] *Chaebol*, the business conglomerates (in)famous for their complicated nexus with the state, came into existence when the state had to distribute the "enemy assets" (Japan-left industrial facilities) to private entrepreneurs and additionally support them with preferential loans, exclusive import licenses, and other privileges, for a sustained operation of the concerned industries.[12] In the thought of developmental technocracy, *chaebol* have been an inseparable arm of the state and their corporate success (particularly in terms of export figures) is as much a political duty as a private achievement. Such thought has been shared even by courts in which big business criminals are conventionally subjected to special treatment thanks to their supposed "contribution to national economic development" (see Table 2 for offense assessment factors for chaebol's business crimes). Of course, this judiciary practice has often ignited serious public as well as legal controversies, leading to a self-critical confession by a chief justice (see the above Box).[13] In this milieu, South Korean business seems to have been influenced by a highly unique type of corporate citizenship—namely, *developmental corporate citizenship*.[14] As compared to corporate social responsibility (CSR) which is demanded of transnational (foreign-invested) corporations in many rapidly globalizing economies, it may be rephrased as *corporate developmental responsibility* (Chang, K., 2019, 2020b; Moon, W., 2020).[15]

The same state-business alliance has entailed a diametrically opposite impact on labor. The authoritarian developmental state used to deal

Table 2 Offense assessment factors for business crimes committed by ruling shareholder families and professional managers of business conglomerates (*chaebol*)

Offense assessment factors	All accused (239)		Ruling shareholder (chongsu) and family members (118)			Professional managers (121)		
	Cases	% (A)	Cases	% (B)	B–A	Cases	% (C)	C–A
Social service and economic contribution	43	18.0	37	31.4	13.4	6	5.0	△13.0
Crime record	119	49.8	52	44.1	△5.7	67	55.4	5.6
Age, health	16	6.7	16	13.6	6.9	0	0.0	△6.7
Protest by professional managers	81	33.9	7	5.9	△28.0	74	61.2	27.3
No personal gains	135	56.5	55	46.6	△9.9	80	66.1	9.6
Customary practice of the time, or special situation like the IMF crisis	20	8.4	20	16.9	8.5	0	0.0	△8.4
Paid back the damaged sum	151	63.2	102	86.4	23.2	49	40.5	△22.7
May lose property, managerial control or position	41	17.2	34	28.8	11.6	7	5.8	△11.4
Confessed crime, self-surrendered	34	14.2	20	16.9	2.7	14	11.6	△2.6
Punishment not wanted by complainant	28	11.7	17	14.4	2.7	11	9.1	△2.6

Source Translated from Solidarity for Economic Reform (2007), "Analysis of the Factors for Offense Assessment concerning White Collar Crimes in the Courts of Our Country: Under What Reasons Convicted White Collar Criminals Are Released" (*Economic Reform Report* 2007–2009), 28 August 2007 with labor just like its own class enemy, regardless of the business-labor confrontation (Chang, D., 2009). The developmental state's self-identification as a national general bourgeoisie has induced its direct, and inherently anti-proletarian, involvement in industrial labor relations (Chang, K., 2019). The anti-communist stance of the South Korean state under the Cold War (with North Korea and its patron countries, namely China and Soviet Union) added to its hostility to labor. Developmental citizenship for ordinary laborers has consisted of docile hard work in exchange for sustained income growth, whereas the reciprocal developmental duty of the state was to maintain rapid economic growth and nearly full employment.

Finally, developmental citizenship has an inherent problem of disenfranchising those citizens without productive assets and capabilities—i.e., elderly, children, youth, handicapped, and so forth. Under an economic development-focused polity, these dependent social groups cannot be meaningfully incorporated into the national community, not to mention the national economy.[16] The developmental(ist) state tends to organize even the minimal public measures for social security in tight conjunction with the developmental contribution of each would-be beneficiary group—an extremist application of the regular employment-based Bismarckian social security system. Therefore, many supposedly social democratic institutions in South Korea have rather exaggerated the existing market-linked inequalities. The concentration of poverty among (current) elderly and handicapped has been particularly serious because they have simply been left out of both developmental and social citizenship. In the post-IMF crisis era, the social security-based exaggeration of inequalities encompasses an increasing number of people *with* laboring capacities (Chang, K., 2019). The devastating economic crisis and the unreserved neoliberal measures to its tackling have made South Korea an economy recovering without significantly more and better jobs.[17] Unemployment and underemployment have engulfed South Korean workers to alarming extents, and those unemployed or underemployed have been doubly disadvantaged due to their frequent exclusion from social insurances and services (that are attached to regular employment under the Continental European welfare state framework). The severest injury in this regard has been experienced by youth, who have arduously prepared their human capital through the world's most competitive education system.[18] If developmental citizenship is very narrowly defined in terms of access to a stable job and its concomitant social security benefits, it has become a rare aristocratic privilege enjoyed by a constantly dwindling number of regularly employed workers in public sectors, heavy and high-tech industries, and so forth.[19]

4 Developmental Citizenship in the Post-Park Era: Democratization and the Neoliberal Reproduction of Developmental Politics

In his *Democracy after Democratization* (2002), South Korean political scientist, Choi Jang-Jip incisively argues that democratization has failed to bring about the deepening of citizenship toward comprehensive social rights. Regardless of democratization, as briefly pointed about above, developmental politics has continued to shape the basic framework of the state-society (or state-citizen) relationship. Every democratically elected government has tried to verify its direct capacity for delivering better economic opportunities for individual citizens or rescuing the national economy from the unprecedented crisis and its aftermaths. Under such *democratic succession of developmental politics*, the long delay in the installment of comprehensive social citizenship has not been meaningfully corrected. Instead, developmental citizenship still pervades the political epistemology of both state elite and grassroots citizens.

Historically speaking, the failure of the democratically elected governments in seriously advancing social rights is not surprising. The two main parties dividing most of the popular votes in presidential and congressional elections—as of 2020, the Future Integration Party (Miraetonghapdang) and the Together Democratic Party (Deobuleominjudang)—respectively succeed the authoritarian developmental regimes from the 1960s to the mid-1980s (under Generals Park Chung-Hee and Chun Doo-Hwan) and the conservative coalition party of landed interests and colonial collaborator elite formed in the late 1940s (i.e., the Hanmindang). Since the early 1960s, the latter's strong congressional influence was abruptly halted and then coercively checked by the former, which interestingly helped to establish a strong political legitimacy for the latter. Despite their differences in political origin and policy orientation, neither of the two main political parties can be considered as a genuine promoter of social citizenship. Besides, the democratic transition in the late 1980s did not thoroughly dissolve the authoritarian developmental alliance composed of economic technocracy, big capital (*chaebol*), conservative media, and legal elite (judges and prosecutors). The departure of the military-based executive power, in fact, hardened the political affinity among these remaining components of authoritarian developmental politics because of their commonly threatened material and political interests.[20] Their concerted and persistent influence on state policy and public opinion has forcefully engulfed even the democratic governments under the relatively progressive leaders, so that conservative developmentalism would remain as the centerpiece of national politics (Lim and Jang, 2006). Unfortunately, this did not mean that such prolonged developmental politics actually brought about desirable economic results for South Koreans (or enhanced the developmental citizenship of South Koreans).

The resuscitation of conservative developmental politics (and the resistance to progressive reforms for advancing social rights) was facilitated by the international political economic environment as well. The neoliberal offensive against labor and welfare, that had first been staged in the United States and the UK and then propagated globally through the IMF and other political economic arms of the West, was all the more welcome by the South Korean developmental technocracy and business at a time of great labor upheaval and social demands (see Chapter 5 in this book). Furthermore, neoliberalism helped to arbitrarily redefine economic development mainly as corporate freedom and expansion. An unfortunate result of such corporate liberalization was the unmonitored and unchecked financial bloating of major business groups (*chaebol*), which in turn drove the entire national economy into financial insolvency.

Ironically, the unprecedented national economic crisis of 1997–1998 paved the way for another round of developmental politics under Kim Dae-Jung. "Rescuing the economy" became the supreme goal of state governance. Even the militant labor organizations were politically exhorted to cooperate in pursuing this goal through neoliberal and/or developmental policies (including labor reshuffling and flexibilization), whereas numerous industrial and financial firms were authoritatively reorganized and recombined (usually with generous public financial support) for the sake of financial security and international competitiveness (Chang, K., 2019, Ch. 3). The massive layoffs signaled a sudden denial of developmental citizenship for a huge number of South Korean citizens, whereas the economy-wide pervasion of non-regular employment implied the erosion of even the minimal social citizenship that had been arduously established in conjunction with formal employment (Yoon, et al., 2005).

The breathtaking corporate restructuring involved, among others, the tax money-based bailout of numerous insolvent industrial and financial firms and the foreign takeover of many (potentially) lucrative enterprises. While the former was a rather familiar practice of the South Korean developmental state, the latter brought about an unprecedented situation in which foreign capital became a major player in South Korea's developmental political economy. Can foreign capital be expected to respect the above-indicated developmental corporate citizenship? Should foreign capital be offered benefits and privileges designed to promote national economic development?

Roh Moo-Hyun, Kim Dae-Jung's successor in presidency, could not but inherit the neoliberalized developmental policy, but he felt a strong ideological disgust about what was in fact his own practice. In such context, Roh staged an apologetic ideological campaign on the web (i.e., through the homepage of the Blue House, the presidential office) to advocate various progressive causes, at least in propaganda. As the painful costs of the neoliberal economic and social policies felt by grassroots were not meaningfully relieved despite Roh's progressive ideological propaganda, a crucial epistemological obfuscation came to pervade the political mind of South Koreans (Chang, K., 2012b). By the end of Roh's presidency, the progressive ideologies and policies as a whole lost their appeal to troubled South Korean citizens because they had been unexpectedly induced to associate their destitute livelihood and unstable work with the supposedly progressive causes. In the next presidential election, Lee Myung-Bak, the main conservative candidate with colorful propagandas for what could be summarized as *developmental renewal*, almost freely charged in. In a huge political paradox, South Korean voters' "path-dependent" or conservative choice of developmental citizenship was critically facilitated by Roh's apologetic progressivism.

5 Comparative Implications: Developmental Citizenship in Post-Socialist Transition Societies

The founding and reproduction of developmental politics (and, concomitantly, developmental citizenship) have been a predominant reality of most non-Western regions since the mid-twentieth century. Its visibility and viability have been most conspicuously detected in East Asia where developmental politics has been most successfully substantiated in terms of rapid economic development and related social change.[21] No doubt South Korea has been a paradigmatic case in point.

What constitutes developmental citizenship—or its South Korean model—may not have been systematically theorized and widely studied in social sciences, but its practical utility seems to have been popularly acknowledged in the international political arena. Just as the South Korean economy has frequently been considered as a (potential) model of Third World development, its mode of political rule has attracted serious international attention. In particular, a particular group of post-socialist transition nations in Asia have tried to observe the South Korean experience as a viable mode of rapid economic development in combination with authoritarian political rule (Chang, K., 2020a). Implicated herein is a viable alternative model of citizenship.

Since the late twentieth century, many of the former socialist countries have tried to thoroughly remold (or marketize) the socialist system of work and distribution for the sake of economic recovery and development. Under the supposed exigency of rapid economic development, citizens in these transition economies have been asked to trade their socialist entitlement to work and distribution for individualized economic opportunities and risks—i.e., a transition from socialist citizenship to (market-based) developmental citizenship. In some transition countries, developmental citizenship is also a pretext for refusing civil and political rights by the communist dictatorial regimes (Chang, K., 2020b). In China and Vietnam, among others, the Communist party-states still reign despite the rapid system transition away from socialism into an externally open market economy. Such system transition, dubbed reform or reconstruction, has been pursued by the Communist party-states themselves because they have judged that sustained economic development is more important than socialist ideological principles in sustaining their political rule. In accommodating ideologically regressive policies and institutions required by the market system, the communist regimes have had to legitimate their continuing dictatorial power through clear developmental performance. That is, an instrumental legitimacy (based upon rapid economic development) began to be desperately sought in order to replace the increasingly thinning historical-ideological legitimacy amid the ever-worsening economic structural crisis. If the immediate rapid development of the national economy requires serious systemic revisions, including marketization and privatization, the party-state should not hesitate trying them out and people should appreciate and participate in them. Improving people's material livelihood through increased jobs and incomes has become the raison-d'etre of the post-socialist dictatorial politics (Gu, S., 2012). This implies that another version of developmental citizenship has been evolving in these transition economies under the continuing communist dictatorship.[22]

Therefore, it was not coincidental that both China and Vietnam began to show intense interest in the South Korean developmental experience (particularly of the Park Chung-Hee era). Delegations from various levels and sections of the two party-states kept flooding the counterpart units in South Korea. Although the motive for learning the political art of sustaining an authoritarian rule through state-led economic development was not expressed directly, it was merely an open secret. Some intellectuals in China, directly and indirectly involved with the community party-state, even staged a neo-authoritarianism debate, implicitly advocating a South Korea-like authoritarian state rule for the sake of rapid national economic development (Sautman, 1992). By the same token, the US-published Park Chung-Hee biography (by Peter Hyun) became more popular in China than in the United States or South Korea (*Yonhapnews*, 24 July 2004). Both the pragmatist party-state and its civil (if not legal) constituencies commonly displayed their serious interest in the life of a man whose authoritarian rule led South Korea into an industrial power and made South Koreans an eager subject of developmental citizenship.

6 Conclusion

Seemingly, South Korea is placed in a historical situation that is highly reminiscent of the early years of European social democracies in terms of both socioeconomic and political conditions. However, its democracy, now institutionally robust after a few decades of political retrieval, has not progressed along the evolutionary trajectory suggested by T. H. Marshall. That is, the accumulation of civil and political citizenship has not been followed by a systematic initiation of full social citizenship. This political impasse used to worry even the international political and intellectual communities as strong concerns were openly expressed on the basic social rights of South Koreans. South Koreans themselves, however, tend to think otherwise. There is every indication that they have yearned for a revival of what I propose here to call developmental citizenship. They have expected the state to concentrate on economic development— and, more recently, economic revitalization—so that they can benefit as private economic players—be workers, industrialists, or self-employed entrepreneurs—in the market system.

The South Korean experience of citizenship politics presents several significant theoretical implications for international scholarship in citizenship studies. First, the conceptual boundary of citizenship needs to be extended in order to reflect the political situation of many late developing societies in which *de facto* citizenship rights in everyday real politics fundamentally diverge from *de jury* citizenship rights emulating Western models. Most of the "imported states" (Badie, 2000) in the non-Western world, including South Korea, have tried to justify their historical position in terms of national economic development under an assumption that such development will enable their political constituencies to win the supposedly most important public service, that is, material wellbeing. The developmental formulation of state-citizen relationship (i.e., developmental citizenship) has been substantiated not in terms of legal rights to specified benefits and services but in terms of political pledges or ideological exhortations for hard work-based material gains. Hence, developmental citizenship is more a political culture, with its socioeconomic substances variably enforced, than an institutionalized status. In order to reflect this historical reality of most non-Western societies, a conceptual reformation of citizenship is indispensable.

Second, and relatedly, various citizenship implications of the predominant developmental politics in non-Western societies need to be explored both empirically and theoretically. The citizenship regime under developmental politics is in fact a new frontier for citizenship studies. South Korea is certainly a paradigmatic case followed by an overwhelming majority of late developing capitalist societies. The primacy of developmental citizenship does not necessarily preclude a political commitment to social citizenship, but the former at least delays the latter for the sake of maximum economic growth. This is epitomized by the South Korean political slogan during the Park Chung-Hee era, "growth first, distribution later".[23] Besides, the political pursuit of national economic development has often been accompanied by a self-serving emphasis of the state leadership on political stability, often implying serious infringements on civil and political rights. Recently, many of the former socialist countries have joined suit as they have tried to thoroughly recast (or marketize) the socialist system of work and distribution for the sake of rapid economic development. In this process, citizens in the transition economies are being asked to swap their socialist entitlement to work and distribution for individualized economic opportunities and risks. In so-called gradual reform economies (e.g., China, Vietnam, and so forth), developmental citizenship is also a pretext for the refusal of civil and political rights by the communist dictatorial regimes.

Third, democratization does not necessarily facilitate the substantive enhancement of citizenship—i.e., the expansion of citizenship rights to economic, social, and cultural resources. South Korean democratization has proceeded without a comparable deepening of institutionalized class politics. In particular, the political parties representing working-class interests (and thus expected to lead the political struggle for social citizenship) are so young and weak that they have made little political impact on the citizenship regime yet. The post-democratic failure in politically articulating class interests into meaningful social citizenship has been accompanied by a political retreat to developmental politics and developmental citizenship in a path-dependent manner. Since the late 1980s, a series of *democratic developmental regimes* have governed South Korea, spawning much political confusion about their ideological identities.

Fourth, neoliberalism has intensified the developmentalist suppression of social citizenship rights. Neoliberalism, while it condemns developmental state intervention in private economic activities, shares the anti-social democratic orientation with developmental statism. The spreading of neoliberalism to South Korea and other societies under developmentalist political rule took place at a time when progressive reforms in social policy were anticipated by citizenry after decades of welfare-suppressive economic development. Particularly for South Koreans, their arduously won democracy was certainly expected to bring about more and better rights to economic, social, and cultural resources. In such context, neoliberalism was gladly embraced by conservative developmental technocracy and its social and economic allies as a useful counter ideology.

CHAPTER 5

Social Citizenship Between Developmental Liberalism and Neoliberalism

1 INTRODUCTION

"Economic miracle" in South Korea did not take place without equally consequential social costs. The so-called development state under Park Chung-Hee and his military successors was renowned for their intrusive entrepreneurial role in industrialization and export promotion, but its commitment to ordinary people's social citizenship was fairly low-keyed and, at best, bluntly conservative. Under what may be called *developmental liberalism*, the successive administrations suppressed grassroots demands and rights concerning social citizenship and exhausted public resources to finance industrial projects and corporate assistance (Chang, K., 2019). South Korean citizens had been identified, approached, and persuaded as *developmental citizens* (see Chapter 4) by the developmentalist state, so its social policy liberalism was not entirely unpopular. As illustrated by the slogan of "growth first, distribution later" (*seonseong-jang hubunbae*), the national developmental project of catching up with Western countries and Japan in economic strength supposedly necessitated deferred gratification. Inevitably, various risky social conditions in welfare, environment, safety, health, education, and other social matters accumulated behind the eye-catching process of unprecedented rapid economic growth.

© The Author(s), under exclusive license to Springer Nature Switzerland AG 2022
Chang K-S, *Transformative Citizenship in South Korea*, International Political Economy Series,
https://doi.org/10.1007/978-3-030-87690-6_5

Developmental liberalism as an actually practiced regime of social governance did not necessarily define the formal institutional configuration of social policy. Broadly speaking, South Korea's institutional modernization in social policy was modeled after the so-called Continental European "conservative" welfare state (Esping-Andersen, 1990). This model, as represented by the inclusionary social insurance programs of Bismarck's Germany, had been devised in order to effectively organize society—the working class in particular—toward a politically concerted path of national(ist) capitalist development. The military-led government of Park Chung-Hee initially tried to co-opt civil service, educators, as well as military through exclusive social insurance benefits in the 1960s (Kim and Seong, 1993). These benefits began to be further applied to privileged civilians employed in *chaebol*-dominant major industries and public corporations only from the 1980s, but have never become universalized to date, primarily due to the radical economic disenfranchisement of wage workers during and after the national financial crisis in the late 1990s and the continuous presence of the heavily bloated informal tertiary sectors (Chang, K., 2019, Ch. 4). A sort of *hierarchical or segmented social citizenship* has been characterizing the working population's fate under an exclusionary application of the Continental model of social welfare.

In the early 1990s, Western neoliberalism (with its regressive social policy orientation) was formally accepted exactly at a time when various serious policy measures were required to stabilize risky situations in the social, cultural, and ecological aspects of grassroots life. Even after three decades of splendid economic development, South Korean officials, industrialists, and journalists colluded to *invent an economic crisis* into public mind and adopted Western neoliberalism as a supposed remedy, thereby intensifying the pro-business doctrine of the state (Chang, K., 2006). This was a special historical period of intense democratic pressure on *chaebol* and their politico-administrative patrons and of a high popular hope for the social democratic transition. In this context, the supposed economic crisis was coined as a counter-democratic measure of political diversion, and neoliberalism was presented as a counter-democratic policy alternative to the welfare state.[1] The succession of catchup politics by crisis politics and its ideological legitimation by neoliberalism generated a crucial obstacle to the establishment of a serious social policy regime as the key foundation of social citizenship in this tenaciously developmentalist nation.

Neoliberalism, an outcome of Westerners' conservative reflection on their social democratic past, turned out recklessly counter-reflective in the South Korean context. During the initial years of neoliberal reform in the early to mid-1990s, among others, pervasive urban poverty, chronic housing shortage, environmental and safety disasters, and education burdens kept inflicting most ordinary citizens. To make matters much worse, the prime beneficiary of neoliberalism—i.e., *chaebol*—drove the country into national bankruptcy after several years of suicidal expansionist drive using short-term foreign loans as well as government-underwritten policy loans.

The state technocracy equated neoliberal reform with globalization in order to silence critical voices concerning grassroots socioeconomic conditions (Chang, K., 2006). In their preaching, the exigency of economic globalization, especially since the national financial crisis in the late 1990s, supposedly made it inevitable to ignore grassroots demands for labor rights and redistributive benefits. They tried to reinvent themselves as the crusaders for global standards and practices. In this way, the administrative technocracy successfully sustained their dominating position in national politics with full support from the democratically elected civilian presidents. However, their cause did not constitute anything global but led to an uncritical acceptance of Western neoliberal agendas and policies. This was how neoliberalism, a flatly irrelevant line of ideology in the South Korean context, came to exert such power as to override the intense demand for meaningful social citizenship by grassroots citizens and intellectuals. In fact, South Korea's abrupt neoliberalization even stunned many international observers who had considered and/or analyzed the country as a prototypical case of (counter-liberal) statism in development (e.g., Cumings, 1998; Wade, 1998).

The post-crisis measures of emergency reform undertaken by the administration of Kim Dae-Jung widely shared the neoliberal doctrine with the US-controlled IMF and seemed to produce some market-disciplinary pressure on lax industrialists.[2] However, their dysfunctional impacts on the labor market and social security concerns brewed potentially explosive social conditions. The radical reshuffling of industrial labor put an end to millions of workers' *developmental citizenship*, whereas the concomitant liquidation of social security guarantees to those workers already discharged from regular employment or prospectively subjected to unstable employment and unemployment derailed the existing social welfare system as the main platform for social citizenship (Chang, K.,

2019, Ch. 4). This led to a situation of double jeopardy to young people because they found their risk of un(der)employment was critically aggravated by an accompanying fate of automatic exclusion from public social security. As far as grassroots social conditions were concerned, Kim's neoliberal strategy of crisis management was destined to become a grave failure not only as a social policy of enhancing grassroots livelihood but also as a political project of strengthening social citizenship. South Korea's post-crisis neoliberalization was particularly devastating due to its developmental liberal context in which stable employment had been an almost exclusive platform for grassroots livelihood and even social security guarantees, though confined to some privileged categories of workers, had been contingent upon stable regular employment (Chang, K., 2019, 2012b).

During the presidency of Roh Moo-Hyun—Kim's successor from the basically same political faction—the supposedly provisional conditions created under Kim's emergency neoliberal reform became congealed into a permanent structure in itself. Furthermore, the indiscriminate liberalization of domestic consumer finance in all categories induced crisis-hit households and individuals to massively turn to borrowings for immediate livelihood. Young citizens who had heavily voted for Roh turned particularly frustrated and angered, and thus strongly supported a conservative neo-developmentalist politician, Lee Myung-Bak, into the next presidency (see Chapter 4 in this book). However, Lee's devastating failure in national developmental regeneration only revealed the cold reality that the developmental substitution of social citizenship was not a practical option anymore. In an interesting political twist, Park Geun-Hye—Park Chung-Hee's daughter—capitalized on this reality by successfully leading the welfare state campaign in the next presidential election (Chang, K., 2019, Ch. 7). During her actual presidency, to her citizens' dismay, Park simply idled on work while leaving government matters in the hands of her secret cronies. The consecutive reigns of two supposedly developmentalist presidents, Lee and Park, only intensified various neoliberal havocs on social citizenship.

Although the vicissitudes of social citizenship under developmental liberalism and its neoliberal degeneration are presented here on the basis of South Korean experiences, a majority of national political economies governed by effective or ineffective developmental states may have confronted similar trends. Outside the Western families of social democratic and liberal welfare states (in Europe, North America, and Oceania), the conventional categories of welfare state regimes such as those of Esping-Andersen (1990) are hardly applicable either as direct indications or reflexive references. By contrast, the developmental orientation of the ruling governments and their political constituencies, whether successful or not, is an almost universal phenomenon outside the West. Accordingly, developmental liberalism in social policy, with variant forms and contents, and its prohibitive or constraining effects on social citizenship may have been quite a widespread phenomenon. Besides, the social, political as well as economic predicaments of the neoliberal transitions in such societies and the concomitant deformations of citizenship rights have to be appraised precisely in the post-developmental liberal context.

2 Economic Catchup, Developmental Liberalism, and Social Citizenship

Like other aspects of South Korean society, public welfare (or, more broadly, social policy) has been shaped by the interplay of long historical traditions and various external influences. In every dynastic state since almost two millennia ago, various public relief programs for poor and starving people and those afflicted by natural disaster, epidemic, and war were implemented as a core mechanism for political rule.[3] Even land tenure was basically an entitlement system designed to satisfy grassroots subsistence needs in an egalitarian manner.[4] In grassroots communities, various forms of mutual support and relief have been found in every historical period including the present day. On the other hand, after Koreans' own effort at national transition to modernity had been frustrated by internal political conflict and foreign interference, the Japanese colonial government instituted the first modern form of public welfare (Nam and Cho, 1995). This was designed to legitimate the Japanese imperial rule, prevent Koreans' anti-Japanese rebellion, and transform Koreans adaptable to colonial capitalism. Another line of foreign influence was exercised by the United States when war-torn South Koreans had to turn to American foreign aid and missionary charity and social work in the post-Korean War period.[5] An additional critical role played by the United States was land reform across South Korea, which was initially proposed by the American occupation authority and urged to be carried out by the reluctant South Korean government under Syngman Rhee. With about 90% of the population residing in rural areas, their socioeconomic (re)stabilization through equal familial landholding was tantamount to a form of universal social citizenship that helped complete the very basic platform of social rights along with the new developments of full political suffrage and universal primary public education. Nonetheless, as state-provided welfare was extremely limited in the colonial and the immediate post-war periods, grassroots people relied frequently and heavily on communal mutual assistance and extended family support (Chang, K., 2018).

The Rhee government itself was a multi-faceted fiasco to the newly independent (old) nation and its citizenry because South Koreans were forced to sacrifice their civil and political rights and endure chronic material destitute. Rhee was ousted by a student uprising in 1960 and administratively replaced by a democratic government of Chang Myun, which in turn was coercively abolished due to Park Chung-Hee's military coup in 1961. Park's dictatorship differed from Rhee's in that he asked South Koreans to swap their civil and political rights for developmental opportunities and benefits that could supposedly be realized if following Park's authoritarian developmental leadership (see Chapter 4). In launching an ambitious national industrialization project, Park's military regime had two mutually contradictory goals concerning public welfare (Nam and Cho, 1995: Kim and Sung, 1993). On the one hand, Park had to mobilize political support from various social groups (including civil service and military in particular) by providing some social security benefits. On the other hand, the exigency of catchup industrialization necessitated minimal state spending on public welfare. This contradiction was resolved in a deceptive manner. A comprehensive range of social security laws and regulations were instituted in the 1960s and 1970s, however, with extremely limited benefits provided in practice. Actual state expenditure on public welfare, in terms of budget proportion, remained stagnant. Welfare and health expenditure merely fluctuated around six percent of the state budget for two and a half decades since the early 1960s. Comparatively, South Korea remained a country where the government spent amply on economic affairs vis-à-vis welfare matters. In this way, there emerged an on-paper social policy state having some elementary forms of social insurance, poverty relief, and welfare service (Nam and Cho, 1995: 92–94). Since both Park and his citizenry felt that the *raison d'être* of his administration was rapid industrialization and economic growth, such intentional hiatus in social welfare did not lead to a wide social discontent (Chang, K., 2019, Ch. 2; also see Chapter 4 in this book).

While the developmental state under Park and his successors has been well known for its comprehensively organized and aggressively implemented policies for late capitalist industrialization, its social policy orientation has often been simplified as one of brutal conservatism against those in need—be they workers, women, poor or a host of other disadvantaged and alienated social categories. Such appraisal may have some validity, but there is a pressing academic as well as practical need to more systematically analyze the structural relationship between national economic developmentalism and social policies and programs, instead of dwelling on a supposed zero-sum relationship between them. Above all, the extent of such zero-sum relationship itself has varied over time. Even concerning the suppressing or sacrificing of social rights, the motivations, conditions, manners, and outcomes of such actions should be systematically documented in order to explore any possibility that they are *developmentally liberal*—as opposed to being *liberally liberal* (like in the United States). A simplified comparison of the two systems of political economy and social policy, about social spending as an example, is as follows: in a liberally liberal society, bourgeoisie as the dominant class will insist on minimal social spending in order to minimize its financial burden of tax; whereas in a developmental liberal society, the developmental state will try to minimize social spending in order to maximize economic investment within a given state budget (see Table 1). In the following, drawn from my previous work, *Developmental Liberalism in South Korea* (2019), several detailed characteristics of developmental liberalism, that were sustained until the eve of the national financial crisis but now exist in variously degenerated conditions, are summarized:

Depoliticization/technocratization/developmental obfuscation of social policy State autonomy has been a key issue in research on the developmental states in East Asia and elsewhere. In South Korea's development,

Table 1 Social expenditure trend in South Korea vs OECD average (% GDP)

	1990	1995	2000	2005	2010	2015	2016	2017	2018
South Korea	2.7	3.1	4.5	6.1	8.2	10.2	10.5	10.6	11.1
OECD average	16.4	18.0	17.4	18.2	20.6	19.0	20.5	20.2	20.1

Source Constructed from "OECD Data: Social Expenditure – Aggregated Data" (https://stats.oecd.org/Index.aspx?DataSetCode=SOCX_AGG)

it was achieved mainly through depoliticization of administrative work. The government bureaucracy as a whole was a developmental institution, and its collective performance was measured in terms of growth rates of export, national income, and so forth. Generally speaking, officials and offices in charge of social policy concerns were not allowed to envisage or emphasize the importance of their duties as differentiated from economic development. Even such officials' personal ambitions often lay in a transfer to economic policy units. In fact, those ministers formally in charge of welfare, health, labor, education, environment, and other social affairs were often required to attend the regular "meeting of economic ministers" (*gyeongjejanggwanhoeui*) and present measures to (ab)use or even compromise social policy for economic development. Social policy was mostly a purely technocratic and, for that matter, technical matter whose efficiency was to be appraised in terms of its contribution to improved economic indicators.

Developmental cooptation of social policy constituencies The emergence of a developmentalist political regime in the 1960s led South Korea to seriously depart from her earlier duplication of the American approach to social policy. As widely known, the nation's initial industrial miracle was primarily based upon abundant and talented human resources. The preparation, mobilization, and organizing of South Koreans for industrial production were of course as much a social as an economic policy concern. Nonetheless, the basic aim of such social policy was not social protection of citizenry per se but economic utilization of population. A social policy regime in the direct service of national economic development was gradually forged and would survive into the twenty-first century. Ordinary citizens were not necessarily against such economic developmental subordination of social policy. Even lacking an elementary notion of social citizenship—despite its nominal promulgation in the Constitution and other declarative state documents—they rarely conceived themselves as serious constituencies of social policy. Instead, they related their citizenship status to fair economic (and educational) opportunities as expanded and improved by the successive developmentalist governments—a phenomenon explained as *developmental citizenship* (see Chapter 4). Most political leaders and technocrats welcomed such economic, or developmental, orientation of the otherwise burdensome constituencies of social policy and, more fundamentally, of social citizenship. A kind of developmental cooptation of citizenry was pursued without any serious social resistance. The successful developmental cooptation of social policy constituencies—and, for that matter, the suppression or postponement of earnest social citizenship politics—made South Korea fundamentally diverge from the West European path of social democratic reforms to industrial capitalism. On the other hand, the Park Chung-Hee government initially attempted to co-opt civil service, educators, as well as military through exclusive social insurance benefits from the 1960s. Similar benefits began to be applied to privileged civilians employed in *chaebol*-dominant major industries and public sectors only from the 1980s, but have never become universalized to date.

State-business entrepreneurial merge and direct state engagement in labor relations While international scholarship on the developmental state has mainly focused on the unique developmental nature and collaborative interaction patterns of the state-business relationship, the formation of such industrial corporate entities as would be strategically suitable for the national targets of industrial and trade growth was often considered as the mission of the developmental state itself.[6] Private (and public) enterprises the developmental state thereby helped create were treated as dear instruments for national economic development, and their corporate business interests were often protected as if they belonged to the state. It was in this political economic context that the labor policy in South Korea began to assume an inherently anti-proletarian stance. In the early stage of export-oriented industrialization, wage suppression and abusive working conditions in sweatshop factories were practically considered as indispensable conditions of international competitiveness. Thus any organized resistances to such corporate practices were often directly quelled by the state—in practice, by riot police.[7] In this aspect, *riot police served as an industrial policy instrument of the developmental state*. Even state regulations for protecting the health, safety, and basic human rights of workers were arbitrarily distorted or neglected by employers under the tacit support of the government.[8] Such asymmetrical labor politics of the developmental state was upheld into more mature stages of economic development, but the oppressed class would grow in its organized power and social influence so as to gradually, if not fully, counterbalance the anti-labor developmental coalition between the state and business.

Familial reconstitution of social citizenship No matter how successfully the economy-centered developmental policy functions, a society cannot operate without proper institutional arrangements for meeting various material, physical, and cultural requirements of the so-called social reproduction.[9] Social policy, if defined as public means, programs, and regulations for stable social reproduction of individual citizens and, ultimately, of the nation, is not an optional function of the modern state but its most essential and universal requirement. Therefore, even when citizenry is willingly incorporated into development-centered politics and remains content primarily with the economic performance of the state, its operation still needs to be complemented by various public means, programs, and regulations for stable social reproduction. For a welfare state, social policy is the core political objective; for a developmental state, it is at least a complementary yet indispensable technocratic instrument. In its actual administrative practice, however, the developmental state did everything to redefine social policy—or, for that matter, social citizenship—as private responsibilities for mutual support and protection. Families were summoned so as to meet various public necessities in social reproduction. The developmental state somehow resembled the early modern liberal state of the West in articulating various social problems accompanying industrial capitalism as individual and familial responsibilities and in morally regimenting individuals and families to cultivate human qualities and attitudes suitable for capitalist industrial work and life (Donzelot, 1979). In so doing, the South Korean state was blessed with its citizens' strong Confucian familialism in which moral duties for familial support and protection are considered as a prerequisite for all other human activities.

Welfare pluralism and demobilization of civil society Family welfare, whether codified culturally or obliged politically, is basically a self-contradictory doctrine. The core function of social protection is expected of least capable social groups (i.e., families in destitute). This implies that, in a capitalist society where the self-protection of families and individuals is politically emphasized, various types of actors and institutions need to step in to make up for the structural deficit in responsible agencies of social protection. Thus, welfare pluralism (in terms of social diversity of welfare providers) has been a common attribute in liberal societies—including developmental liberal and neoliberal ones. In South Korea, the mobilization of every thinkable type of (non-state) welfare provider has consistently been an important policy of the developmental liberal state. Such complementary agencies in welfare provision would take on diverse ideological and organizational characteristics that result from their various social and political origins, but a paternalistic attribute has been shared among most of them. That is, they have posed themselves as a kind of surrogate families that take the place of the moral duty of private families, not the political duty of the state for protecting sovereign citizens' basic social rights. In South Korea, private philanthropy, religious social work, corporate welfare, welfare NPOs, nepotistic support networks, and even media-based fundraising for emergency relief have usually been deployed in pseudo-familial ideological and/or organizational frameworks. These diverse welfare institutions and activities tend to induce welfare-receiving disadvantaged groups to become clients of narrow paternalism, and thereby turn them into hostage to divisive or sectarian interests of welfare providers and intermediaries (e.g., religious affiliation or conversion, divisive corporate loyalty, politico-ideological mobilization, and so forth).[10] Besides, much like the developmental state's role of helping to form the industrial entrepreneurial class for national economic development, the developmental (liberal) state, under the absence of sufficient non-state welfare providers, has helped form civilian actors and organizations in welfare provision. Of these state-dependent welfare entities, many have *behaved entrepreneurially* as if in profit sectors under a tacit endorsement of the budget-conscious state technocracy. On the other hand, a dominant majority of actors and organizations engaged in these welfare activities have been keen to keep distance from those progressive political lines and voices that advocate civil activism and citizenship rights. Since welfare provision has been conceived not as an active expression of civil social solidarity but usually as a clientelistic benefaction for narrowly targeted groups, it has paradoxically contributed to segmenting and demobilizing civil society.[11]

Developmental liberalism generated multi-faceted influences on South Koreans' citizenship rights. They were asked or forced to choose developmental citizenship (as explained in Chapter 4) at the cost of various civil and social rights and, ultimately, even the basic political citizenship of freely choosing a government. Broadly speaking, developmental citizenship may be considered as a variant of social citizenship, however, under such conditions as are extremely difficult to uphold or realize. For instance, if the pledge of "growth first, distribution later" was to be realized, Park Chung-Hee would have to remain in power at least a few decades. Even after holding on to the nation's presidency in several arbitrarily extended terms, Park died (by assassination) without fulfilling this key pledge. On the other hand, the pro-business state's brutal crackdowns on even shop floor-level worker resistances—a sort of *in-effect industrial policy*—implied that its developmental policy prioritization was inhibitive to even basic civil rights. Besides, the wide familialization of welfare needs and the indiscriminate pluralization of welfare services critically dampened the political recognition and social enhancement of social citizenship.

3 Democratization, Social Activism, and Neoliberalism

It should be noted that the need for redistribution and balanced development was acknowledged as early as in the 1970s as the government (led by Park Chung-Hee) changed its five-year economic development plan into a five-year economic *and* social development plan (Nam and Cho, 1995). But no serious action was actually taken for the supposed policy transition during Park's rule. Chun Doo-Hwan, a self-appointed successor to Park in the military's political rule, did not differ initially. However, the Chun regime could not rely on economic development alone in politically justifying his unlawful state leadership and thus sought other complementary legitimation mechanisms. In this context, laws were made and revised in order to expand welfare benefits for labor and needy social groups (such as children, elderly, and the handicapped). However, under Chun's continuous subscription to developmental liberalism, social welfare was still considered as a negative element to economic development and thus minimized whenever possible. Moreover, since Chun relied much more on physical coercion than on material concession, a serious social policy state had yet to be established.

It was during another ex-general, Roh Tae-Woo's presidency that more progressive slogans were pronounced and more active programs were pursued in social welfare (Nam and Cho, 1995). His administration, set up by the (re)normalized democratic procedure of direct presidential election in 1987, was much softer politically and relied more on material concessionary policies. When political democracy was recovered, problems chronically accumulated in the areas of welfare, labor, environment, safety, health, education, and culture would not be tolerated by most citizens indefinitely. South Koreans were no more content with modicum income increases in exchange for political oppression and social alienation. They also learned that they should—and could—express anger and launch resistance when their life was affected by unjust policies and actions by the ruling bloc. In particular, the political strengthening of organized labor exerted remarkable pressure for an immediate improvement in social welfare. Under democracy, South Koreans used their recovered political citizenship in order to enhance social citizenship. In the late 1980s, the powerful sociopolitical challenge from labor unions and progressive civil groups forced the still conservative government to pay serious attention to social affairs and rights (Roh, J., 2012). For the first time in history, the establishment of a welfare state was formally declared as a central political goal of the nation. New and revised laws were prepared to expand the range of social groups under welfare protection and stabilize grassroots living conditions through social insurance and pension programs.

Ironically, it was at this moment that neoliberalism began to influence South Korea's politicians, technocrats as well as businessmen as a sort of counter-ideology. The big and/or interventionist state was condemned as something critically harmful to sustained economic development. The main objective was to liberalize and reduce the economic role of the state, but a suspicious and pessimist view spread concerning social welfare as well (Chang, K., 2006). Despite slight increases in the proportion of welfare expenditure, the general neglect of social policy was maintained by the still developmental liberal state. However, the political upsurge of organized labor led to a situation where the government had to shift gradually to a neutral position in labor-capital conflict. In a sense, the government was dumping social burdens to individual companies, only a handful of which were actually able to provide corporate welfare and other social benefits to workers (Song, H., 1995). Nonetheless, increasing numbers of workers were able to win higher wages and better welfare benefits from their employers. Another significant social change consisted of citizens' rapidly enlarging awareness and demand about non-material interests, such as environment, health, education, and culture (Lim, et al., 1998). With state elites remaining passive and narrow-sighted, their chronic distance from vibrant civil society concerning social policy issues became increasingly problematic.

The dysfunctional outcomes of neoliberalism grew full scale during the rule of a civilian president, Kim Young-Sam. His administration pursued the *Singyeongje* (New Economy) policy intended to boost the already overheated economy. Concerning social policy, even the previously instituted policies and programs were scaled down whereas the substitutive roles of market, families, private organizations, and local governments were emphasized under what was above explained as *welfare pluralism*

(Nam and Cho, 1995: 97; Chang, K., 2019, Ch. 2). In particular, the privatization of welfare services and social insurance programs was strongly recommended as an alternative welfare strategy (Social Welfare Policy Appraisal Committee, 1994). In the latter half of Kim Young-Sam's presidency, some of his aides proposed what was called "the globalization of the quality of life" (The ROK National Welfare Planning Commission, 1995). But most of the governmental and political elites were not cooperative in making this proposal into a serious policy line of social welfare with sufficient financial backup.

His administration also pursued neoliberal labor reform for the sake of labor market flexibility, leaving many workers and managers laid off and labor unions indignant. But the Kim Young-Sam government remained too shy in the (neoliberal) reform of *chaebol*, so the collusive relationship between the government and *chaebol* remained unchanged and, in some cases, grew stronger. On the other hand, financial deregulation and liberalization were hastily pursued to the liking of both the Wall Street and *chaebol*. A national financial fiasco broke out due to excessive corporate borrowings and risky industrial investments. A degenerated version of the developmental state in economic policy combined with a neoliberal regime in social policy drove the country into an unprecedented economic-cum-social crisis against which no social protection mechanisms had been prepared. Kim Young-Sam's presidency ended leaving his country in a state of economic collapse without any meaningful social safety net.

4   THE CAUSE AS REMEDY? THE 1997 FINANCIAL CRISIS AND NEOLIBERAL RESPONSES

A decade of unconstrained corporate investment in heavy industries, lavish governmental spending on mega-size public projects, and even financial firms' incautious engagement in suddenly increased overseas transactions was followed by an instant financial collapse of the South Korean economy in late 1997. The more immediate cause was, of course, the irresponsible rush and flight of speculative global financial capital. The economic crisis came at a moment social conditions of a great many grassroots' livelihood were extremely unstable due to the outright neglect of social policy by the previous administrations commonly under developmental liberalism. Even without a national economic crisis, many numbers and sections of grassroots South Koreans may have experienced unbearable living conditions. There were no effective mechanisms for social buffering against the unprecedented national economic breakdown. Developmental liberalism as a regime of social governance would not function when development itself is brought to a halt. That was exactly what happened to South Koreans in the late 1990s. A *societal crisis* was in order as massive unemployment due to corporate bankruptcies and structural adjustments were added to the already long list of deleterious conditions of grassroots livelihood.

A blunter version of neoliberalism was adopted by the Kim Dae-Jung administration as a quick remedy for the economic crisis (Chang, K., 2019, Ch. 3). As discussed above, neoliberalism had influenced the preceding two administrations so that the establishment of a serious social policy regime had been inhibited. As the developmental liberal ideology had lost its appeal by the mid-1980s, developmental technocracy and business coalesced to insist that the national economy was supposedly in a serious crisis and that redistributive and welfarist policies should not be in the way of national economic stability (Chang, K., 2006). As neoliberals in the West preached that welfare expansion had supposedly led to the weakening of economic growth potential, the developmentalist coalition of technocracy and business in South Korea gladly turned to neoliberalism in the 1990s. An apt timing for redressing the national developmental strategy into a socially sustainable one was thereby lost. In less than a decade after the strategic, if not ideological, conversion to neoliberalism, a *real economic crisis* broke out and the intensification of neoliberalization ensued as the crisis management strategy practically coerced by the mastermind of the crisis itself—that is, global finance represented by the International Monetary Fund (IMF). Kim Dae-Jung— "the IMF's man in Seoul" (Cumings, 1998)—and the IMF concurred on what were the structural causes and basic solutions of the economic crisis. Severe austerity and unconstrained labor reshuffling were immediately forced on middle and poor classes whereas financial and organizational restructuring, albeit not as instantaneous as labor reform, was demanded of *chaebol*.

As they had revived from war ruins, grassroots South Koreans were accustomed to the austere mode of living. As far as someone in their family earned income, family members would engage in various strategies of collective survival. In a near absence of public assistance and social insurance programs for ordinary people, paid or self-employed work was the only universally available mechanism for physical survival. However, the abrupt and massive unemployment came to displace the precondition of such collective survival (Chang, K., 2019, Ch. 3). Families with no income at all increased dramatically, and a widespread social dissolution of families was inevitable (Chang, K., 2018). Even austere living was no option when material resources totally ran out. Kin network for emergency mutual assistance functioned to rescue some people, but generous kin members themselves came to lose their jobs and incomes. To many families and individuals, unemployment meant nothing other than a free fall to the ground. For most of laid-off workers and bankrupt entrepreneurs in small-scale businesses, state programs for unemployment relief were unheard of or ineffective at best. A public unemployment insurance was instituted in a hurry, but its meaningful effect had yet to be realized.

It was rather obvious that workers would fiercely resist the structural reforms that would sacrifice their jobs and threaten their sheer survival. In addition, labor activism was nothing new in this contentious society. Experienced and militant South Korean unions would not endure the neoliberal reforms targeted asymmetrically at their members. Without any effective material and institutional resources to pacify the anger of unfairly threatened workers, political persuasion and compromise were the last resort for the state leadership. Fortunately, Kim Dae-Jung was the best candidate to undertake the heavily demanding political task of eliciting cooperation from organized labor. The Labor-Employer-Government Committee (Nosajeongwiwonhoe) was thereby constituted to reach agreement on the terms of structural reforms concerning labor, business, and the public sector (Nosajeongwiwonhoe, 1998). Kim's core objective behind this seemingly corporatist political arrangement, of course, was to exhort labor to accept massive layoffs as the key condition for corporate survival and, ultimately, for national economic revival. Labor leaders accepted the pact expecting that the government and business would engage in sincere reforms on their parts. However, the government and business accepted the utility of the tripartite committee only when and where labor reforms were necessary. This sly tactic angered workers bitterly so that unions repeatedly pulled out of the tripartite committee (Chang, K., 2019, Ch. 3).

Nonetheless, the government came to realize the true cost of lacking a sound social security system. If an economic crisis of any sort immediately threatens the sheer survival of ordinary people, economic development is not socially sustainable anymore. Structural reforms cannot acquire legitimacy when they lead to the total alienation and impoverishment of weak social groups with no reliable public rescue programs. This was realized by conservative officials and politicians only after the national financial crisis had led to a total societal crisis. The business community also came to share this realization. In the opinions of international advisors (such as the IMF, the World Bank, and the OECD, and so forth) and Western lenders, the near absence of social security programs in South Korea was a serious obstacle to the neoliberal economic reforms they were encouraging to South Korean officials, industrialists, and workers. In this context, the notion of *social safety net* became a serious political catchword for public policy for the first time in history (Chang, K., 2019, Ch. 3).

However, the administrative effort has mainly been confined to the unemployment issue. Government officials refused to accept the need for a comprehensive social security system and instead focused on *unemployment as an economic issue* (Chang, K., 2019, Ch. 4). They had been dealing with laborers as an economic input, not citizens with social citizenship rights. They insisted that the public budget should be spent "productively" for those programs directly necessary in redeploying unemployed laborers, and thereby neglected the public protection of discharged workers' immediate livelihood. Widespread waste and virtual embezzlement of the emergency public funds in those *economic* programs set up for the unemployed were reported, whereas most of the laid-off and bankrupt people complained that they had not benefited from—and were not even aware of—public relief programs of any sort. At the same time, more general welfare concerns received rather diminished governmental commitment. At one point, the government even planned to reduce welfare expenditure while the structural adjustment of various social insurance programs required workers to pay substantially higher premiums.

Despite these problems, South Korea made a remarkable recovery economically. The national economy recorded an astonishing 10.7% growth of GDP in 1999 after a 6.7% decline in 1998. Even cautions against a possible "overheating" of the economy were pronounced. But it was also clear that "growth with equity" was not a South Korean attribute anymore. On the contrary, abrupt employment destabilization, wide income inequality, and rampant poverty were coerced as the primary conditions for corporate and national economic recovery (Chang, K., 2019, Ch. 4). The social pulverization under a sort of *rescue neoliberalism* transformed South Korea into a society distinctly different from even her immediate past. Its radical labor reshuffling stripped itself of the basic condition of developmental liberalism (and developmental citizenship) without replacing it with any other form of social governance.

In September 1999, according to the National Statistical Office, the proportion of non-regular workers (i.e., temporary workers and daily workers) surpassed that of regular workers for the first time in history by 53% vs. 47% (*Hankyoreh*, 16 November 1999). The Korean Labor Research Institute estimated that 92% of the newly employed workers in the first half of 1999 were either temporary or daily workers (*Hankyoreh*, 16 November 1999). Those who were excluded from unemployment statistics (because they had given up job search) may have numbered as many as two-thirds of the unemployed (*Hankyoreh*, 22 November 1999). Thus, the gradual decline in the overall unemployment rate since March 1999 was highly deceptive (cf. Kim, Y., 2003). However, the misery of these workers had an ironic effect of reforming the nation into neoliberalism's model student. In early 2003, *Forbes* (30 January 2003) indicated that South Korea ranked third (only after the United States and Canada) in labor market flexibility among all OECD member countries.

The lower strata of the proletariat were hit particularly hard. Even those earning less than the country's legal minimum wage—which itself has remained far below an internationally comparable level vis-à-vis per capita GDP—have constantly grown in number and proportion. Given its relatively low rate of unemployment in (both domestically and internationally controversial) official statistics, the economic hardship mostly concerns the working poor, a high majority of whom are the so-called *bijeonggyujik* (non-regular employees), including temporary, part-time, dispatched, on-call, and home-based workers.[12] As aptly analyzed by Yoon, et al. (2005), their earning on average amounts to a mere half of that of regular workers in a period of a supposed economic recovery period. Moreover, as the country's Continental European-style social security system used to be predicated on stable regular employment, the rapid and massive disappearance of regular jobs has only helped aggravate the hardships of the economically precarious citizens (Shin, K., 2013).[13] More specifically, the post-crisis structural adjustment lopsidedly focused upon "labor market flexibilization" has produced an additional impoverishment effect by nullifying, rather than strengthening, social security benefits to those workers who have been demoted or stuck to nonregular wage jobs and informal sector work. As shown in Fig. 1, a

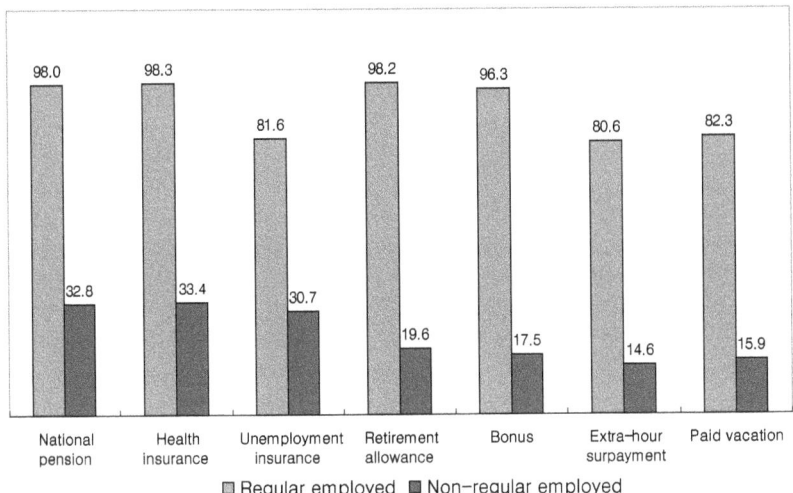

Fig. 1 Proportions benefitting from social insurances and fringe benefits by employment status after the national financial crisis (*Source* Created from data in Yoon, J., et al., 2005, Figure 4)

majority of non-regular employees have been omitted by work-based public social insurances (in pension, health, and unemployment) and excluded from company-level employee benefits (in retirement, bonus, extra-time surpayment, and paid vacation). Many of them may have been covered by residence-based social insurances in pension and health, but a huge disadvantage has to be accepted by residence-based pensioners. A similar fate has to be shared by most youth as only a tiny minority of them have been admitted to regular permanent jobs. A majority of non-regular employees, whose number has kept bloating ever since the 1997–1998 financial crisis, have not been arranged to fairly participate in the public social insurances.

Given the above problems, the widening of income disparities and even the increase of those citizens below the poverty line were pervasively pronounced. Before the economic crisis, according to official statistics (KOSIS; http://kosis.kr/statHtml/statHtml.do?orgId=101&tblId=DT_1L9I008), the richest 10% of the urban worker households used to earn six to seven times as much as the poorest 10%. Immediately after the economic crisis, however, this ratio surged to frequently surpass nine times. If statistics including non-worker households were examined as well, the income gap grew much bigger. The expansion of absolute poverty was alarming. The national economic crisis and instant recovery turned out to be a financial bonanza to the richest group as they garnered huge incomes from the IMF-forced high interest rates in 1998 and the overheating of the stock market in 1999. In a research report delivered to the United Nations Development Plan (UNDP), by contrast, Chamyeoyeondae (People's Solidarity for Participatory Democracy; PSPD) estimated the size of the population below the poverty line during the first quarter of 1999 as 10.3 million (*Hankyoreh*, 11 November 1999).[14] The corresponding figure was 9.2 million for the first quarter of 1998 and 7.6 million for the first quarter of 1996. Obviously, economic recovery failed to alleviate the destitution of the poor. In a more conservative appraisal, a study by the government-affiliated Korea Development Institute (KDI) estimated that the absolutely poor households increased from 8.8% in 1994 to 11.7% in 1998 and 12.0% in 2001 (*Yonhapnews*, 16 February 2003).

The changing structure of taxation also dampened economic inequality. The necessity of the expanded government spending for economic structural adjustment at a time of economic depression led to the sharp increase of indirect taxes vis-à-vis direct taxes. The alienation and impoverishment of future taxpayers—i.e., young people—were also a serious social problem. While confronted with the structurally jeopardized prospect for their stable long-term employment, they were practically being asked to underwrite rapidly increasing public debts with their (uncertain) future incomes. The year-end total state debt was predicted to be 109 trillion won (or 23.0% of GDP) in 1999 (*Hankyoreh*, 14 December 1999). The corresponding figure was only 49.7 trillion won (or 11.9% of GDP) in 1996, 65.6 trillion won (or 14.5% of GDP) in 1997, and 87.6 trillion won (or 19.5% of GDP) in 1998. If corporate debt repayments guaranteed by the government had also been included, the state debt would have doubled. Most of the expanded debts had been used to rescue defunct financial institutions which, in turn, had rescued financially troubled industries. Still more public spending was needed to complete the reform of financial industries. Such heavy indebtedness of the state was unprecedented in the South Korean context and would inevitably require future taxpayers' grave sacrifice.

The still developmentalist state's obsession with "rescuing the economy first" instantly reconfigured young people's citizenship with coerced duties of self-sacrifice in employment and taxation. Besides these social and economic concerns, neoliberal retreat and encroachment in the areas of environmental protection, public safety and health, high education, and cultural life were also condemned by intellectuals, civil activists as well as involved experts. Policy statements on these matters, if any, called for deregulation, commercialization, liberalization, globalization, and so forth (Chang, K., 2012b). All these neoliberalizing affairs would require additional sacrifices and dues by next generations.

5 South Korea's Post-Developmental Liberal Transition to the Welfare State?

Kim's successor from the basically same political faction, Roh Moo-Hyun, practically kept his eyes closed to such neoliberal socioeconomic pulverizations by professing, "Power has been transferred over to the market" and "The origin of the power that moves our society derives from the market" (*Hankyoreh*, 16 May 2005).[15] During his reign (2003–2008), the supposedly provisional conditions created under Kim's emergency neoliberal reform became congealed into a permanent structure in itself. If anything new, the impromptu liberalization of domestic consumer finance in all categories induced crisis-hit households and individuals to massively turn to borrowings for immediate livelihood. In the early 2000s, for instance, credit cards were issued almost randomly and credit card debts—about a half of them being cash withdrawals at usury-level rates—increased explosively (Chang, K., 2019, Ch. 6). Young citizens who had heavily voted for Roh turned particularly frustrated and angered, so they took a different political course of strongly supporting a conservative neo-developmentalist candidate, Lee Myung-Bak, in the next presidential election in 2008. Lee and his successor from the same party, Park Geun-Hye only intensified such neoliberal havocs on social citizenship while revealing to citizenry the cold reality that the developmental state and its developmental citizenship were not practical options anymore (Chang, K., 2019, Ch. 7).

Lee's apparent failure in the nation's developmental regeneration, for all his showy developmentalist propaganda, immediately induced progressive intellectuals, civil activists, and critical media to commonly explore alternative paradigms for national socioeconomic advances. The nation's transition to a welfare state was most prominently discussed, echoing the late 1980s and early 1990s (when South Koreans converged on social democracy as a Korean "third way" in envisioning the nation's future with the proudly achieved democracy and economic development).[16] In the early 2010s, however, their call for a welfare state was quite desperate under a societal realization that both democracy and advanced capitalism would not automatically bring about fairly and stably shared humane livelihood.[17]

In a highly interesting development, it was Park Geun-Hye, Park Chung-Hee's daughter, who most promptly accommodated civil society's yearning for a serious welfare state (Kang, B., 2016; Kim, T., 2012). Park had lost the main conservative party's candidacy for presidential election to Lee Myung-Bak in 2007, but somehow managed to drive her way back into the same party's presidential candidacy in the next election of 2012. In spite of her political capital as a daughter of the nation's developmental hero Park Chung-Hee, Park Geun-Hye could not replicate Lee's developmentalist campaign especially after his notorious political failure. She instead proposed, as a key election pledge, "the construction of a Korean-style welfare state" (Kim, T., 2012).[18] The main opposition party's would-be candidate, Moon Jae-In, could not but promptly trail Park's lead in welfare state pledges. To most of those who eagerly favored her, however, Park's main political appeal derived not from her progressive pledges for social welfare but from her political cultural status as a key signifier of the nation's developmental heyday under her father's leadership (Kim, S., 2013). Nonetheless, Park's practical political profit from her welfare state propaganda, by consequence, lay in preempting Moon's critical opportunity of establishing himself firstly as a potential national leader for social democratic transition. Park may not have to feel sorry for this political effect to Moon because he would not adopt the welfare state as a key political pledge anyway in the next presidential election in which he finally won (Chang, K., 2019, Ch. 7).

Park's actual presidency did not have much to do with the welfare state. In fact, she ended up being impeached by the Constitutional Court after shocking revelations about her corruption scandals involving secret cronies. To ordinary citizens' embarrassment, there was not much room for political reprimand or praise on her socioeconomic policy and administrative performance because she virtually idled on her job until her departure from the Blue House (the presidential office complex). If she did anything comparable to her father, it was the practical annulment of the welfare state promises politically pledged and administratively publicized.

Constitutionally speaking, South Korea had already been a welfare state during her father's lengthy rule. This legal feature of the Republic of Korea was not necessarily devised for the sake of political deception but reflected the particular mode of reflexive institutional modernization in which the so-called West had been syncretically copied for the best institutional makeup of the state (Chang, K., 2022, Ch. 3). Park Chung-Hee's neglect of citizens' social welfare rights—and, in fact, even his suppression of citizens' civil and political rights—did not entirely enrage them because his performance in national development was unprecedentedly strong to the eyes of most South Koreans. Park's actual regime of social policy, *developmental liberalism* as explained above, was effectively applied to South Koreans amid the nation's literally explosive industrialization and economic growth during most of his presidency. If his daughter had differed by actualizing meaningful welfare state programs, Park Chung-Hee's (developmental liberal) slogan, or strategy, of "growth first, distribution later" would have been upheld by South Koreans as a truly clever policy scheme. Unfortunately, his daughter did nothing much except reminding herself of being her great father's daughter.[19]

Park Geun-Hye, on her impeachment, ended up suddenly transferring presidency to Moon Jae-In virtually as a political gift and thereby helped usher in another period of socioeconomic instabilities. Curiously, in the presidential election of 2017, Moon somehow abandoned his previous election pledge on the welfare state and instead presented an ambiguous congery of selective social benefits and economic as well as political reforms.[20] His rather moderate yet vague policy line in socioeconomic affairs, called *poyongjeokbokji* (inclusive welfare; http://www.korea.kr/news/policyNewsView.do?newsId=148860605), appears characterizable more as selectively populist than as social democratic. His initial drives in "regularizing" (*jeonggyujikhwa*) non-regular employees in public sectors, raising the legal minimum wage substantially, and legally moderating weekly labor hours all reflected a serious effort at rectifying various labor market irregularities accumulated during the developmental and neoliberal eras (*Maeil Labor News*, 6 November 2017). But these measures have failed to address the most fundamental predicament of ordinary South Koreans' massive disenfranchisement from the mainstream industrial economy.[21] In all logical accounts and actual appearances, the Moon government is not likely to effectively lead South Korea's perplexed and troubled post-developmental citizenry into a new systemic terrain of socioeconomic governance in which either developmental or social citizenship is realized in a fully inclusionary way. This is particularly frustrating to young citizens who have to agonize about their current and prospective socioeconomic difficulties without any optimistic clue to a viable alternative system of economic order and social policy in so many remaining years of their life.[22]

6 Erosion of (What) Citizenship?

> The basic assumption behind Marshallian citizenship was that 'almost all adults would be steadily employed, earning wages and paying taxes, and the government would step in to help take care of the unemployable- the young, the old, the sick and disabled' (Colin and Palier 2015). Social insurance was designed to support income security for citizens with stable employment. In the USA and Britain (and in those societies that have adopted what we can call 'Chicago economic theories') in the last four decades, these 'basic assumptions' have been eroded. Privatization, tax cuts, the reduction or cancellation of pension rights, market-driven policies, the rolling back of the state, the casualization of the labor force, and individualism have subsequently eroded the public domain and diminished the social rights of citizenship. These neoliberal measures to enforce the free market have been further intensified by a variety of austerity packages that emerged after the economic crisis of 2008 and onwards. (Turner, 2016: 680–681)

> [M]arket criteria increasingly determine the relationship between the citizenry, the state, and the civil society in which the citizen is embedded. The actual economic worth of both citizens and migrants, and private provision for health care, education, and security are increasingly underpinned by what Margaret Somers (2008) has called 'market fundamentalism. (Turner, 2016: 681)

South Koreans' dramatic experiences in economic crisis, neoliberalization, and widespread loss of employment and welfare, only shortly after their nation's developmental miracle, imply that the erosion of citizenship is not a social phenomenon confined to neoliberalized Western societies only. It may not be a similar kind of social citizenship to those of the West that has been seriously eroded in South Korea. However, its citizens have been fiercely protesting their current and future livelihood that has been radically disenfranchised from whatever main (political) economic system exists or has evolved in the nation under the critical influence of externally coerced and domestically accommodated neoliberalism. It seems there are varieties in the erosion of citizenship in conjunction with varieties of capitalist political economies and their respective neoliberalizations.

Despite neoliberal political influences blanketing across Europe, most countries in Continental Western Europe and Scandinavia, with their welfare systems structurally embedded in the corresponding (political) economic systems, have remained fairly robust in the welfare state qualities and espoused social democratic citizenship (Abrahamson, 2012). In particular, Germany's corporatist inclusion of labor coupled with Bismarckian social insurances and Sweden's communalist entitlements to comprehensive social security have survived economic instabilities and uncertainties under neoliberal globalization. By contrast, the UK has been subjected to more aggressive neoliberal reforms to social services and insurances that used to be only loosely integrated with the national economic system, with its citizens' social citizenship thereby exposed to serious neoliberal erosion. Among the core social infrastructures for its putatively inclusionary liberalism, free health care has remained largely unchanged, but public education, in particular at high levels, has been subjected to rampant liberalization in cost and access, with all Tony Blair's loud promotion of the so-called social investment state under the slogan of "education, education, education" (see Chapter 6 in this book). In the US, its laissez-faire liberal state had not anyway offered much social citizenship except residual social security in poverty and health, but the nation's economic neoliberalization—in terms of off-shoring, automation, and digitalization in industrial production and financialization of both dominant economic interest and grassroots livelihood—has socioeconomically disenfranchised increasing numbers of citizens in various regions and classes. The subprime crisis in 2008 and Donald Trump's election into presidency were all crucial testaments to American citizens' subjection to the erosion of whatever social citizenship had existed (Peters, 2018).

In the South Korean context, as above analyzed in this chapter, neoliberalism was initially utilized by the state-business developmentalist coalition as a counter-democratic defense to the surging pressure of organized labor and civil society for progressive, mostly social democratic, reforms in socioeconomic affairs (Chang, K., 2012b). This strategy was effective at least in buying time before the rise of any seriously progressive state leadership. As far as social citizenship was concerned, while there was not much to be neoliberalized or eroded, neoliberalism helped to delay the formation of a meaningful social citizenship regime and thereby elongated the political lifespan of developmental liberalism in social policy. When the national financial crisis broke out, radical labor reshuffling as a neoliberal rescue remedy widely removed stable employment as the most essential condition of developmental liberalism and thereby liquidated developmental citizenship. Besides, it also came to nullify not only the current importance of the existing welfare system of regular employment-based social insurances to those suddenly deprived of regular employment, but also the future importance of the same system as an institutional guiding pole for ultimately enfranchising the entire working population in public welfare (Chang, K., 2007). In this context, young workers have been forced into a situation where neither developmental nor social citizenship can be envisioned as a reliable mode of socioeconomic participation in the nation. To the extent that labor reshuffling and flexible employment had been dictated by global finance as a key condition for its supposed rescue of South Korea from an impending national bankruptcy—and, though less explicitly, for its takeover of South Korean industries through capital market liberalization—its citizenry seems to have been *transnationally neoliberalized*. Having been forced into such a transnationally neoliberalized economic system, South Korean youth have confronted an inescapable prospect of their entire socioeconomic future's erosion.

In a great paradox, South Korea is a nation in which the construction of a welfare state has been called for by a possibly largest variety of social and political agencies in the world—including organized labor, progressive civil society, various religious groups, media of all political spectrums, nearly all sworn-in governments and their heads, and, not least importantly, political parties of all ideologies (Kim and Sung, 1993; Nam and Cho, 1995; Kim, B., 2011; Lee, C., 2016).[23] Such diverse advocates may have mutually different political motivations and backgrounds, but all of them consider the welfare state something like a "good society".[24] To those conservative political and social agencies, the (future) welfare state has been regarded as a developmental raincheck for persuading workers and poor people to be patient about immediate misery ("growth first, distribution later"), and/or as a political strategy of diverting labor interest and public attention about the immediate (in)justice in class relations and public affairs. To those progressive ones, it has been a sort of *reflexive* political goal envisioned after some model welfare states in Western Europe—Sweden in particular.[25] The common attribute of all these calls for the immediate or future welfare state is that they reflect *collectively* framed long-term political and/or institutional goals and largely lack fundamental and/or systematic references to *individual* citizens' inherent (social) citizenship as sovereign right. A critical question remains as to whether even this liberal ideological basis of citizenship can be reflexively learned or borrowed (from West Europe), or whether it should be found or generated indigenously in accordance with South Korean society's philosophical foundations and historical heritages.

CHAPTER 6

Education as Citizenship, or Citizenship by Education

1 Introduction: Education as Korean Distinction?

On January 13, 2014, Arne Duncan, the American education secretary of the Barack Obama administration, emphatically echoed his boss in stressing the national developmental importance of education by drawing public attention to South Korea as a supposed model case for his country. In a speech to a parents summit sponsored by the National Assessment Governing Board, he expressed his conviction as follows (*Washington Post*, 14 January 2014; https://www.washingtonpost.com/news/answer-sheet/wp/2014/01/18/arne-duncan-why-cant-we-be-more-like-south-korea/?utm_term=.810a73d7643f):

> In 2009, President Obama met with President Lee of South Korea, and asked him about his biggest challenge in education. President Lee answered without hesitation: parents in South Korea were "too demanding." Even his poorest parents demanded a world-class education for their children, ... President Lee was very serious. Korean parents were relentless and had the highest of expectations – insisting their children receive an excellent education. .....
> Because right now, South Korea – and quite a few other countries – are offering students more, and demanding more, than many American districts and schools do. And the results are showing, in our kids' learning

and in their opportunities to succeed, and in staggeringly large achievement gaps in this country. ....Just one generation ago, we were Number 1 in the world in college completion among young adults. Today, we have dropped to Number 12 in the world. Dropping from 1st to 12th – that's not something any of us can be proud of. ....That Number 1 spot is now occupied by – guess who? — South Korea. So, you may be asking: What are countries like South Korea doing for their kids that we aren't? The answer is, a lot.....

Let me be clear: I'm not saying we should be just like South Korea, where – as President Lee told President Obama – the pressure to study can get out of hand. ....In her book, Amanda Ripley talks about how Korean authorities have to enforce a 10 pm curfew on extra-tutoring schools, and students so exhausted that they wear napping pillows on their wrists in school.[1] We absolutely shouldn't aim to emulate all aspects of Korea's education system – there should be a sense of balance and common sense.

His president, Obama, was no less outspoken in emphasizing the critical significance of education in American social renewal with almost customary allusions to South Korea.

Education has been one of the most distinct aspects of South Korea's (compressed) modernity. South Koreans boast themselves as the world's best educated population in terms of their highest level of enrollment in colleges and universities. According to the latest data of OECD (2020), as shown in Table 1, the proportion of people aged 25–34 with tertiary education was the highest in South Korea (69.57%), distantly followed by Canada (61.75%), and far above the average of all OECD countries (44.48%). As these tertiary institutions of learning are quite hierarchically positioned, they require students at the lower levels of schooling to study excessively for acceptance into better colleges and universities. South Korean teenagers at the middle and high schools are known to be internationally unrivaled in their daily length of study, so sleep deficiency is rather a normalized feature of student life (*Yonhapnews*, 24 April 2019).[2] In fact, even most children at elementary schools and kindergartens are known to "study hard". The contents of their study are virtually the same to everyone because their ultimate purpose is to pass the commonly standardized entrance examinations of the most preferred colleges and universities. Such common contents of study do not imply that the range and diversity of school subjects are limited. To the contrary, South Korean schools at all levels teach larger numbers of different subjects

Table 1 OECD countries with higher proportions of population aged 25–34 with tertiary education (latest: 2018 or before)

Country	% population aged 25–34 with tertiary education
1. South Korea	69.57
2. Russia	62.66
3. Canada	61.75
4. Japan	60.73
5. Ireland	56.17
6. Lithuania	55.58
7. Luxembourg	54.78
8. Australia	51.39
9. Switzerland	51.21
10. United Kingdom	50.75
11. United States	49.37
12. Norway	48.21
13. Israel	48.03
14. Netherlands	47.60
15. Sweden	47.51
OECD average	44.48

Source Constructed from "OECD Data: Population with Tertiary Education" (https://data.oecd.org/eduatt/population-with-tertiary-education.htm)

than their counterparts in most other countries (KICE, 2002). Unsurprisingly, South Korean students have frequently been rated among the world's best in many internationally standardized tests on math, science, and so forth. Such achievements have chronically been accompanied by widespread fatigue and stress among most students, leading many of them to suffer mental disorder and, tragically, to commit suicide (Hwang, Y., 2013; Lee, et al., 2012).

Education-related competition is not necessarily confined to students themselves. At the huge expenses by their parents, most students at the primary and secondary levels of schooling take up additional learning by *sagyoyuk*, i.e., lessons at private institutions and/or with personal tutors that help facilitate and/or complement their study at regular schools (Kim, K., 2019). As of 2018, according to *Korean Social Trend 2019* (NSO: 127), 82.5% of primary school students, 69.6% of middle school students, and 58.5% of high school students took up such private lessons. Even when they manage to minimize or avoid the expenses for private learning as high school or lower level students, their parents will confront very high tuitions charged by colleges and universities, whether formally public or private, that operate on the basis of direct financial contribution from education recipients (or their parents). Until the early 2010s, the average tuition level of South Korea's public colleges/universities was second only to that of American counterparts (OECD, 2011, 2019).[3] Parents' financial burden reaches its extremist when their children are sent to overseas secondary schools (mostly in the United States and other Western societies) either because of their poor performance or dissatisfaction at a domestic school. Many middle-age fathers have ended up living a substantial part of their lives as *gireogiappa* (wild geese fathers) as their wives insistently stay with overseas studying children for intimate care (and supervision).[4]

With all such expenses added up, South Korean citizens' private share of the entire public education budget and the proportion of their educational spending in the nation's GDP are known to be respectively the world's highest.[5] The nation's elderly population are known to suffer from the industrialized world's highest level of relative poverty, to which their virtually universal spending, across all strata of income and asset, on children's education up to the college/university level has contributed most decisively.[6] Given the wide differential returns in income and status by educational credentials (Park, K., 2014), such parental commitment to children's education may appear as much pragmatic as moralistic in so far as their children remain thankful and pious to them permanently. Unfortunately, children's betrayal is pervasive, not to mention even many pious children's failure in occupationally establishing themselves at levels commensurate with their expensively won education.

At the societal level, education, especially at higher levels, has been crucially instrumental to the nation's all fundamental transformations since its liberation from Japan, including the condensed institutional modernization into a liberal system of sociopolitical governance and economic regulation, the expeditious and extensive capitalist industrialization buttressed by human capital, the potent democratization movement propelled by the allied forces of intellectuals, students, and workers, and the technological and cultural surge into global leadership.[7] Whether it is the quality, the intensity, or the universality of education that has been the most decisive for education's such contributions is debatable. Nonetheless, it is beyond dispute that South Koreans' educational fervor has both bolstered and been intensified by these societal transformations. In citizenship terms, education has critically enabled South Koreans to march into modern institutional, developmental, political, and scientific/cultural citizenship.

In a great paradox, however, South Koreans' access to education itself has remained quite dubious as a citizenship right. Public education has been constitutionally stipulated both as every citizen's right and duty ever since the nation's independence. The South Korean government has been consistently effective in promptly establishing public schools and mobilizing civilians to set up private schools that operate by the largely same curricula and financial rules, leaving virtually no children beyond reasonable access to universal public education. However, the same government used to keep balking, even until the beginning of the twenty-first century, on its legal duty to provide free public education up to the constitutionally designated level of middle school (7th to 9th grade).[8] In fact, even high school (10th to 12th grade) education has long been universalized at the parental expenses, leaving those very few youth with less education formally classified as unfit for ordinary military conscription.[9] Needless to say, the virtual universalization of tertiary education at colleges and universities came about under the private payment of tuitions and other school expenses. The government's budgetary support for most colleges and universities has remained negligible and civil society's charitable support for them has been rare, requiring them to survive by collecting quite expensive tuitions from most students. Most South Korea adolescents attain college/university diplomas not as a citizenship right but as a parental gift (Korea Higher Education Research Institute, 2017). Inevitably, a majority of their parents have felt extremely stressful about the heavy educational expenses—in particular, as indicate earlier, college/university tuitions that are more expensive than those in almost all other countries (except the US, the post-Thatcher UK, etc.).

Some conservative (!) politicians tried to strategically capitalize on such parental burdens through election pledges to substantially curb the tuition levels. One of them, Lee Myung-Bak, was elected into national presidency in part thanks to a radical proposal to halve the tuitions, which was practically impossible under the given budgetary structures of the state and colleges/universities.[10] Such political tactics nevertheless induced students and parents to judge that the tuitions are too expensive and that political efforts should be made to lower them. Halving the tuition levels thereby became a major social movement by activist citizens and students across the nation, which in turn drove nearly all political parties to converge on controlling the tuition levels.[11] Quite curiously, the commonly spoken political pressure for substantially cutting the tuitions has not been accompanied by political calls or administrative plans for enlarging the state's financial contribution to make up for the thereby reduced college/university budgets. The contradictory social demands and political pledges have been settled in terms of freezing the tuition levels during most of the 2010s and significantly expanding the public educational loans—a development not strictly characterizable as enhancing social citizenship but as regulating the educational market as to both suppliers and consumers.

An aspect of education in which South Koreans do make a strong citizenship claim is the governmental regulation and management of various components of college/university entrance examinations. In presidential and parliamentary elections, the reform of *daehakipsijedo* (the system of college/university entrance examinations) is quite frequently presented as a key election pledge, whereas the problem of nearly universal and excessive financial burdens for college/university education has curiously remained untouched until recently.[12] The popular apprehension about fair and transparent exams for college/university entrance sensitively reflects the above-mentioned instrumentality of higher education in all major components of modern citizenship. To the extent that such citizenship instrumentalities of education are conditioned upon meritocratic differentials and hierarchies, South Koreans' commonly shared anxiety about college/university exams falls short of constituting a clear sociopolitical basis of social citizenship.

This chapter analyzes the historico-social conditions and sociopolitical consequences of the so-called education zeal of South Koreans in a citizenship perspective. It reflects the theoretical and analytical necessity to examine the long-term historical context and multidimensional effects by which education takes on decisive significance for South Koreans' citizenship on all fronts. The immediately following section examines how decisively South Korea's essential modern transformations and its people's related citizenship rights have been framed and propelled by public education. The subsequent section appraises whether public education itself meaningful constitutes citizenship rights in its accessibility and substance and compares its sociopolitical nature as citizenship versus class property. The final section concludes the chapter by bringing in a broad international comparative perspective on the extraordinary significance of public education in South Korea's transformative citizenship.

2 SOUTH KOREAN TRANSFORMATIONS AND CITIZENSHIP BY EDUCATION

As South Korea's postcolonial achievement in economic development and political democratization has drawn wide global attention, a diverse range of explanations has been presented internationally as well as domestically. South Koreans' extraordinary education zeal and actual educational attainment have been among the most frequently discussed factors. However, the common explanatory logic in such attention to education has been a simplistic functionalist argument on educationally augmented human capital and civic consciousness. For this reason, education has remained a frequently discussed but not necessarily decisive factor for South Korean development and modernization. While not rejecting such conventional functionalist argument, this section offers an alternative account emphasizing the structural historical conditions and processes by which public education has decisively shaped the social institutional, economic developmental, political, and cultural transformations in postcolonial South Korea.

First, the South Korean economy has not simply developed with rapidity but traversed from the one end of the modern industrial-technological spectrum to the other end within a few decades. The human capital basis for such unprecedented and unparalleled industrial restructuring cannot be explained without noting South Koreans' no less extraordinary advancement in educational attainment at the world's very highest level (McGinn, et al., 1979). Second, on its cultural front, South Korea has been modernizing in an extremely pluralistic manner such that South Koreans often take a high pride in the notable plurality and diversity of their cultural experiences.[13] To a critical extent, such pluralist cultural citizenship has been systematically nurtured and shaped by public education at all levels, which in turn is characterized by excessive diversities and pluralities in formal school subjects (KICE, 2002). Third, South Korean democracy was *reflexively* adopted as a postcolonial polity of the nation, but, after two decades of its stoppage under military dictatorship, it had to be *reflectively* rehabilitated through an allied struggle of civilian politicians, activist intellectuals (including academics and students), and educated workers.[14] The dramatic expansion of tertiary education had a critical side effect of politically enlightening and activating ever increasing numbers of South Koreans. Fourth and finally, while often neglected or simply taken for granted, South Korea's nearly overnight social institutional transformation from a structurally tattered postcolonial social entity into an organized modern system of public governance and social order, however incomplete and unstable, has been a tremendous historical task, in which public education has functioned as the core enfranchising mechanism for both elites and grassroots citizens (Seth, 2002; Sorensen, 1994). In particular, as the US-transplanted/emulated liberal institutions in political, economic, and social affairs have had to be adopted and utilized without any corresponding historical and social conditions as embedded in civil society, public education has served as a surrogate environment for technocratically appropriating such advanced foreign institutions of polity, economy, and society (Son, I., 1992). The above aspects of public education's decisive significance in South Korea's modern transformations reveal that its people's developmental, political, and even basic civil citizenships have been acquired through their broad and active participation in public education. Thus, without being properly educated, a South Korean citizen may well end up becoming or feeling like a nobody in nearly all aspects of the nation's proud civilizational transformations.

2.1 Educationalization of Institutional(ist) Liberal Modernization

From the nineteenth century, Koreans began to debate the basic direction of their nation's post-traditional civilizational and political transformation. Much like in China, their early judgment was to reluctantly emulate the apparently powerful Western nations, but they would soon be subjugated by Japan, a much earlier and more aggressive emulator of the West. This situation began to drive the Koreans into a gradually defiant position about the international capitalist order as mainly mediated by Japan (Shin, Y., 2001). As a social subject controlled and exploited by imperial capitalist Japan, the Koreans began to develop a sort of *dialectical consciousness* as (ethno)nationalist civil society and collective proletariat against it.[15] Such dialectical national consciousness was systematically embodied by the Provisional Government of the Koreans (Imsijeongbu)—an independence movement organization in exile broadly representative of both domestic and overseas forces for anti-Japanese national struggle. Japan's defeat to the United States in the Pacific War, however, would not politically enthrone a progressive nationalist polity. To the contrary, the United States did everything to violently eradicate the widespread socialist influences across South Korea (Cumings, 1981). The new colonial authority would fundamentally circumscribe the basic direction of South Korea's systemic and civilizational transition along its own model of liberal politics and economy. The Korean War fought over the intense ideological rivalry between South and North Korea critically helped reinforce the supremacy of "free democracy" (*jayuminjujuui*) and capitalism in South Korea.

The liberal order of democracy and capitalism thereby arrived in South Korea as an outcome of international political circumstances, rather than through an indigenous sociopolitical revolution or evolution propelled by civil society. Such political superimposition of the liberal order would not automatically effectuate the broad social conditions necessitated for the firm and stable rooting of liberal institutions in political, economic, and social affairs. *Liberal institutional modernization without liberal historico-social backgrounds would find a sort of surrogate enforcement mechanism in public education.* Thus the curricula of public education from primary to tertiary education have been systematically coordinated in accordance with the new political, economic, and social orders internationally sanctioned and domestically absolutized.[16] School grades and academic diplomas have thereby become the formalized certificate of citizens' conception and absorption of the liberal public order. In addition, the ubiquitous exam systems for school entrance at all levels, appointment in state offices, and even corporate private employment have reinforced the unconditional effect of public educational curricula because the respective examinees have been required to prove their mechanical mastery of school-processed knowledges on liberal social institutions and related civilizational and technological matters.[17] In a sense, it has been a process of *educationalizing* the grand historical project of liberal sociopolitical modernization.[18]

The broad educationalization of South Korea's liberal modernization rendered public school curricula to incorporate a vast range of subjects compressively reflecting the institutional, civilizational, as well as technological conditions of those advanced nations emulated enthusiastically. Up to the secondary education (i.e., middle and high schools), every student has had to cram an extensive variety of standardized subjects under the threat of authoritarian disciplinary measures for ensuring their mechanical absorption of knowledges therein (KICE, 2002). However, from the tertiary education (i.e., colleges, universities, and graduate schools), a radically sudden transition in the education system takes place under a very minute and rigid disciplinary division of knowledge mechanically accommodated in the formal academic departments and schools at colleges and universities. A modernization regime of *compartmentalized institutional simulation* governs each academic discipline's West-benchmarking strategy of supposedly scientific advancement (Chang, K., 2022, Ch. 3). Once a student gets accepted into a certain academic department, he/she would often expect to lead a whole life rigidly subordinated to the societal division of labor institutionally incorporating the academic disciplinary partitions that in turn reflect the Western knowledge system.

This academic system assumes the practical utility or indispensability of a sort of *civilizational/scientific reverse engineering*. As no individual or group can master the entire construct of the Western civilization, it is minutely divided into pedagogically manageable segments that, in turn, are incorporated in the formal academic departments. Fortunately (?), the US-led twentieth century system of scientific research and learning has also facilitated a similarly minute division of knowledge labor, so that South Korean colleges and universities have comfortably adopted or copied, above all, the academic institutional structures of the United States (Kim, J., 2015). On top of such academic institutional transplantation, South Korean colleges and universities have further partitioned the advanced knowledge system according to immediate practical needs for urgently securing the basic manpower in the economically and/or administratively necessitated tasks. Under this strategy, many of the hierarchically sequenced subjects in the applied knowledge fields (usually accommodated in the specialized graduate schools of the West) have ended up being horizontally placed side to side with various subjects in the basic knowledge fields. This has led major South Korean universities to top the world in the number and variety of academic disciplinary departments.[19]

The assumption of civilizational/scientific reserve engineering entitles each of these minutely partitioned disciplines to the status of supposed societal requirement or necessity. Their existential ground has often been assumed to be automatically established from the correspondent institutional existence of each of them in the context of advanced Western nations where their assembled whole supposedly defines the civilizational/scientific structure of these model societies (Chang, K., 2022, Ch. 3). Consequently, academic disciplines have been rigidly segmented from each other, leaving colleges and universities in an institutional state of total mutual dislocation among their constituent units of teaching and research. Such academic institutional order has been structurally extrapolated into society since many of the academic disciplines have helped construct independently institutionalized colonies as the authoritative (or authoritarian?) kernel of South Korea's modern system of socioeconomic life and public governance.[20] In fact, the very first stage in South Korea's postcolonial reflexive institutional modernization was to formalistically (re)organize society according to the socioeconomic sectors, occupational divisions and professional boundaries, and administrative dissections that in turn were defined, substantiated, and certified by the mutually segmented academic disciplines. The educationalization of South Korea's liberal modernization has incurred a historico-structural cost of compartmental monopolization of society by the academic discipline-based sectoral, occupational/professional, and administrative divisions. Within such divisions, alumni and graduates of certain elite colleges/universities prevail as dominant cliques.[21] Without entering a recognizable college or university, one cannot be incorporated into this kind of social system. Ironically, the consequent increase of college/university students at a literally explosive pace has inevitably liquidated the likelihood of an averagely performing student of an averagely reputed college/university to actually enter and meaningfully benefit from such educationalized monopolies in society.

2.2 *Developmental Workfare, Education, and Citizenship*

South Korean development has often been appraised as an achievement based primarily upon human resources. As of the early 1960s, South Korea was beset with extremely low income, scarce natural resources, rare industrial technologies, and unrecognizable industrial entrepreneurship. On the other hand, its human resources in the form of economically underutilized labor force arrested in farming had increased quite rapidly due to the postwar baby boom among mostly village-based South Korean families. The Park Chung-Hee government set off a typical process of Lewisian industrialization "with unlimited supplies of labour" (Lewis, 1954) in which "surplus" labor from rural subsistence farming was transferred to urban capitalist industries at such low wages as to enable them to rapidly accumulate corporate capital (and to constantly augment international competitiveness in the export market). It is important to recognize that the rural-to-urban transfer of mostly young members of farm families was not confined to industrial work at sweatshop factories but involved a critical social process in which most rural parents made strategic investment in children's public education designed to facilitate human capital formation for industrial capitalism. As elsewhere, higher-level schools have been located in urban areas and even rurally located schools have taught students under the formal curricula that are fundamentally "urban-biased" by idealizing and assisting the nation's developmental transformation into urban industrial capitalism (cf. Lipton, 1977). South Korea's capitalist industrialization at a miracle pace was to a critical extent an educationalized process in which peasant families earnestly collaborated with the industrialist developmental state in terms of aggressively investing (or, in a sense, diverting) their human and financial resources in urban-biased public education.[22] Schooling at all levels has practically functioned as a systematic mechanism for rural-to-urban migration. Until very recently, virtually no rural parents wanted their children to succeed their farming after schooling, whereas a very few children thought about farming as their lifetime occupation (Chang, K., 2010, Ch. 6).

By the early twenty-first century, South Korea's industrial success has far surpassed the earlier level of labor-intensive industrialization. Some of South Korean—in fact, substantially global—industries and firms are now leading the global economy technologically and socioculturally. This implies that the country has economically traversed the very full distance from traditional family farming to state-of-the art advanced industries within several decades. Needless to say, such unprecedented economic restructuring has been critically facilitated and sustained by the nation's human capital endowment blessed with the world's highest rate of tertiary school enrollment. South Korea remained a predominantly agrarian society until the 1960s, turned into a labor-intensive industrial economy by the mid-1970s, was restructured into a heavy industrial economy by the late 1980s, and became a global ICT pacesetter by the early 2000s. Now, the South Korean government, business, media, and public intellectuals nosily debate the nation's irresistible fate in the so-called fourth industrial revolution.[23] All along this process, universities and academics have been publicly urged, scolded, and supported for their critical role in driving the nation's ceaseless economic structural upscaling. Students accepted into the strategically designated fields of science and technology have been given all sorts of priorities and privileges, including generous scholarship, exemption of military service, job guarantee, and so forth. Where strategically necessitated, private industries and firms have set up their own education/training institutions for employees and/or have sent talented workers and researchers to reputable overseas schools.

The South Korean government has continued to take on the nature of a *developmental workfare state* in conjunction with public education's strategic industrial instrumentality. As systematically analyzed in my other work (Chang, K., 2019; also see Chapter 5 in this book), the developmental state has been *developmentally liberal* in its social policy, keeping social welfare and other elements of social citizenship at a margin. It has instead tried to maximize market-based economic opportunities for its citizens, including wage jobs and own businesses, on the basis of maximized national economic growth. South Korea's rapid and sustained economic growth, in turn, has been propelled by a strategic developmental regime of continual industrial restructuring into sequentially advanced sectors. Accordingly, the Ministry of Education reserves a legal authority to determine the national composition, regional distribution, and even department sizes of academic disciplines in tertiary education. An ordinary citizen could not join and benefit from this developmental process without his/her educational attainment in the circumstantially relevant fields of study in each stage of industrial upgrading. In a fundamental dilemma arising out of this developmental opportunity structure, virtually no one's educational attainment at any level would remain industrially useful throughout his/her economic lifespan, which may amount to the period of the nation's industrial restructuring across a few technological ages.

2.3 Liberal Pluralist Cultural Modernization, Education, and Citizenship

The global prominence of South Korea's contemporary pop culture, dubbed "the Korean wave" (*hallyu*), has added another chapter to the nation's civilizational and developmental achievement story (Kim, Y., 2013; Chua and Iwabuchi, 2008). While this ancient nation's traditional culture and history have certainly drawn due international attention, the Korean wave is not mainly about its indigenous thoughts and arts. Nor is it a simple copycat pop culture extended from the West. The stories, feelings, and technologies conveyed in South Korean cinemas, dramas, and K-pops may be best summarized as inventive hybridities from all possible sociocultural sources in the modernized regions of the world, including South Korea and its immediate neighbors (Ryoo, W., 2008). Such hybridities are not necessarily a studio outcome of arbitrarily arranged combinations of diverse cultural contents and forms.

An ordinary South Korean's daily life is full of sociocultural hybridities whether at work, at home, or on streets. On its cultural front, South Korea has been modernizing in an extremely pluralistic manner such that South Koreans often take high pride in the plurality or diversity of their cultural experiences itself.[24] Pluralist cultural citizenship has long characterized South Korean society before the recent surge of a sort of *officialized multiculturalism* amid the sudden expansion of transnational marriages (see Chapter 8 in this book). Consciously and unconsciously, South Koreans are ordinarily engaged in generating endless sociocultural hybridities besides separately managing diverse sociocultural experiences. For most people, such sociocultural practices systematically begin through public education.[25]

The basic educational premise of reflexive institutional, cultural, and technological modernization has governed schools and their curricula at all levels (Chang, K., 2010, Ch. 3). Reflexivity herein has focused upon all major advanced nations and their institutional, cultural, and technological traits. While such *pluralist reflexivity* is mainly justified by its pragmatic and instrumental utilities in catching up with the advanced West in all envious aspects, it has ended up becoming a popular social value itself, as explained in terms of "complex culturalism" in my other work (Chang, K., 2022, Ch. 5). Ironically, but not surprisingly, pluralist reflexive modernization has been espoused by a concurrent neotraditionalist modernization, particularly in terms of socially generalized (or equalized) Confucian ethics, relations, and rituals at the family level (see Chapter 8). Public education curricula at all levels have accommodated all such diverse lines of sociocultural references and traditions and have thereby required students to study intensively in understanding all of them (KICE, 2002). In tertiary education, colleges and universities have established quite minutely divided units of education in history, literature, philosophy, music, fine arts, performing arts, and so forth and have separately taught these subjects according to national and world regional divisions.[26] Thus, it is possible for a South Korean student to major in the language, literature, philosophy, history, music, fine arts, or performing arts of any influential nation or world region at a domestic college or university. As inundated by certain numbers of annual graduates from these globally exhaustive and finely divided units of civilizational and artistic education, South Korea has become a sort of *expo society* in its cultural configuration. In this *expo society*, every culture has a civilizational citizenship, and the pursuer of every culture has a (nominal) social citizenship (in terms of his/her entitlement to public encouragement and support).

The simultaneous exposure of a South Korean citizen as well as South Korean society as a whole to all such diverse sources of culture indispensably leads to inventive hybridities in individual life and social arena. Their food, housing, clothing, hobby, leisure, travel, courtship, friendship, and spiritual pursuit are all about cultural pluralities and hybridities, which define the basic nature of cultural citizenship in this society. To a critical extent, such pluralist cultural citizenship has been systematically nurtured and shaped by public education at all levels. This educationalization of cultural citizenship used to have a particular significance for women from middle- and upper-class families. Well into the 1990s, women's economic participation was concentrated in poor class people, whereas women's attainment of tertiary education surprisingly lowered the possibility of their economic participation. Women with four-year university education evaded the least employed status only in the mid-2000s as men and women with high school education or less turned less employed than them (Chang, K., 2010: 34–35). Curiously, despite such paradox, women's tertiary education has kept expanding no less rapidly than men's. In terms of majoring fields of study at colleges/universities, music, fine arts, and performing arts used to be dominated by women, whereas most humanities—literature and languages in particular—have also been greatly outnumbered by women. As so many of them would pursue even higher degrees in prestigious Western institutions, they sometimes outnumbered native students in such institutions.[27] While South Korea's patriarchal developmental capitalism used to systematically discriminate women, its pluralist cultural modernization has been critically buttressed by women's educational pursuit. As another manifestation of the nation's patriarchal order, women's attainment of tertiary education used to serve a decisive qualification for marriage with better-educated and higher-earning men (Park, M., 1991). In this respect, the dim economic prospect for a woman majoring in various genres of arts and culture has not necessarily discouraged or penalized her tertiary education—at least not until the "IMF economic crisis" in the late 1990s (Chang, K., 2019).

2.4 Democratization from Below, Education, and Citizenship: Political Citizenship Through Education

South Korea's democracy began basically as a reflexive conceptual construct in its postcolonial pursuit of US-dictated liberal modernization. With its left-bent civil society violently suppressed in the US-controlled political space of the late 1940s, its formally declared democracy would soon be subjected to the manipulation and monopolization by those opportunistic political elites with suspicious careers and interests during the Japanese rule and with strategic collusive connections with the American military occupation authority (Cumings, 1981; Park, T., 2008). In the 1960s, Park Chung-Hee's military junta outright suspended democratic institutions and procedures until they were ready to cling to state power by manipulatively normalized political elections. The Park regime excused itself of suppressing and distorting democracy under the supposed national exigencies of economic development and military security (Kim, D., 2006). Its actual developmental success helped to intensify political authoritarianism (see Chapter 4). Park's unexpected assassination in 1979 briefly nourished a public hope for democratic restoration, but another period of brutal military rule ensued until the anti-military popular uprising in 1987. In this year, South Korean democracy took another launching, now as a realistic political purpose.

Throughout such political turbulences, activist students and critical academics and intellectuals played the role of key agencies of democratic debate and struggle, and college/university campuses became the very central arena of democratic resistance (Kim, S., 2000; Choi, H., 1991). West-originated academic social sciences, despite their protracted limitation in properly theorizing and analyzing local sociopolitical realities, did play a critical function of enlightening students about the nature and utility of liberal democracy as a philosophical-cum-institutional possibility of South Koreans' political liberation. In a sense, they functioned as an institutional handbook of West-derived democracy in the South Korean context. Many other variants of political ideas and systems were also introduced and discussed both within and without classrooms. In the 1970s and 1980s, activist students organized innumerable underground study groups on campus, called *hakhoe* (academic association), in order to disseminate—and, arguably, indoctrinate—critical theories and progressive thoughts that were not formally taught in class and sometimes legally censored (according to the National Security Law) (Lee, C.,

2012). This may be considered as a sort of *bottom-up educationalization* of the democratization process.

The West-derived notion of colleges and universities being an institutionalized safe haven for intellectual freedom enabled students and academics to courageously activate their learned knowledge into critical political voices and actions.[28] In fact, almost every crucial juncture of South Korea's political transformation has been marked by the decisive role of activist students and academic and civil intellectuals—above all, the April 19 Student Revolution (in 1961) and the June Uprising (in 1987), in each of which dictatorial state power surrendered to the civil demand of democratization. South Korea's political history cannot be properly read without paying serious attention to sociopolitical activism on campus that used to be shaped both by formally and informally learned knowledge. This was another aspect of the educationalization of South Korea's liberal modernization. To the extent that college/university attendance remained a sort of middle-class experience until recently, many poorer and older South Koreans had to remain content about a spillover effect of educationally promoted and fortified political citizenship.[29]

3 Education as Citizenship? The Limits of Education as Social Citizenship

In South Korea's social institutional, developmental, cultural, and political transformations, public education has functioned as an essential crucible for a contentiously reflexive modernization in which all confrontational social forces and interests have exercised their maximum influences and efforts at driving the nation's historical transformations into own preferred directions. That is, South Koreans' citizenship in the nation's social institutional order, economic development, cultural life, and democratic politics has been decisively facilitated and shaped by their participation, competition, and struggle in public education. Their "education zeal" (*gyoyukyeol*) should be understood in this broad historical context of postcolonial modernization and development (Seth, 2002). It should be pointed out that South Koreans' globally unrivalled educational attainment has not necessarily been driven by the state's aggressive investment in public education and/or its generous guarantee of ordinary citizens' free or affordable access to higher learning. In fact, the state kept balking on its constitutionally stipulated duty to offer free public education up to the middle school, whereas nearly all parents as private citizens have not abstained from paying for their children's education up to the tertiary level. In a great paradox, public education beyond the primary level has hardly constituted a meaningful social citizenship itself.

South Korea has kept showing the world's highest proportion of private citizens' share in the national public education expenses. (This figure excludes the notoriously costly expenses of after-school cram institutions and private tutors that afflict nearly all parents.) In particular, an overwhelming majority of colleges and universities in South Korea are private establishments, whose financial dependence on highly expensive student tuitions has been decisive. Even the tuition levels of public colleges and universities are not much lower. South Korean colleges and universities have allegedly charged the world's arguably second most expensive tuitions for the universalized tertiary public education, which, in turn, is fulfilled by the world's highest proportion of high school graduates at their parents' expenses. In this respect, South Korea may boast a sort of *social investment family* as opposed to "the social investment state"proposed by Tony Blair in his "third way" policy vision under the advice of Anthony Giddens as below[30]:

> Education and training have become the new mantra for social democratic politicians. Tony Blair famously describes his three main priorities in government as 'education, education, education'. The need for improved education skills and skills training is apparent in most industrial countries, particularly as far as poorer groups are concerned. Who could gainsay that a well-educated population is desirable for any society? Investment in education is an imperative of government today, a key basis of the 'redistribution of possibilities'. (Giddens, 1998: 109)

> The guideline is investment in *human capital* wherever possible, rather than the direct provision of economic maintenance. In place of the welfare state we should put the *social investment state*, operating in the context of a positive welfare society. (Giddens, 1998: 117)

Despite public education's decisive significance for South Korea's all societal transformations and concomitant citizenship rights, most of its expenses beyond the primary school level have been borne by universally enthusiastic parents in the hope of enabling their children to participate in and benefit from the nation's modern progresses. South Korea's actual successes in social institutional modernization, economic development, cultural advances, and political democratization seem to have meaningfully rewarded such pragmatically devoted parents as far as their children have cooperated by "studying hard". The state has rarely been criticized for dumping over public educational expenses to private citizens—to a potential retrospective envy of Tony Blair (and Barrack Obama)?[31] (The British emphasis on the social investment state was accompanied by the drastic inflation of college/university tuitions as its colleges and universities were sternly asked to financially stand on their own feet.)

If the allocation of public education is contingent upon private citizens' great sharing of its expenses, there should be a danger of estranging poor youth from fair educational opportunities. However, this danger has been manifested not in poor youth's foregone access to public education but in their parents' financial hardship after exhausting all earnings and savings for children's education up to the college/university level. In particular, the industrialized world's highest rate of old-age poverty among South Koreans has been most seriously caused by their nearly universalized investment in children's tertiary education.[32] Actually, the disadvantages of poor youth have been revealed in terms of their increasingly lowered likelihood of entering more competitive colleges and universities (see Table 2). For instance, academic and sociopolitical controversies abound about the strategic efficacy of rich people's excessive spending in their children's private tutorials for college/university entrance examinations. Popular enthusiasm, envy, and jealousy about private tutorial-aided admission to reputed colleges/universities abound so much so some of the most successful dramas and movies have dealt with this issue as a key expression of the nation's class inequalities— including *Gisaengchung* (*Parasite*), a black comedy thriller which was celebrated as the Best Picture and the Best International Feature Film at the Academy Awards in January 2020 (https://www.youtube.com/watch?v=LUf3-LvMrBg).[33] Major cities have popularly envied particular residential-cum-commercial districts in which proactive middle-class locals live and educate their children with the possibly best infrastructures of both public education and private tutorials.[34] At the opposite end of this social spectrum, most of rural young parents have opted to send their children to cities for better chances for college/university acceptance, or move altogether to cities for the same purpose.

Table 2 SKY university students by familial income strata in the first semester of 2018 (SKY: Seoul National University, Korea University, Yonsei University)

University/ Income decile	SNU		Korea Univ		Yonsei Univ		SKY		Nation	
	Stud's	Share	Stud's	Share	Stud's	Share	Stud's	Share	Stud's	Share
1st	517	7%	771	8%	766	9%	2,054	8%	154,513	11%
2nd	400	5%	568	6%	528	6%	1,496	6%	117,171	8%
3rd	390	5%	529	5%	476	6%	1,395	6%	114,837	8%
4th	329	4%	484	5%	456	6%	1,269	5%	108,165	8%
5th	157	2%	249	2%	185	2%	591	2%	51,097	4%
6th	341	5%	491	5%	391	5%	123	1%	95,821	7%
7th	488	7%	730	7%	592	7%	1,810	7%	126,929	9%
8th	795	11%	1,243	12%	1,028	13%	3,066	13%	170,195	12%
9th	1,180	16%	1,600	16%	1,207	15%	3,987	16%	178,791	13%
10th	2,357	32%	2,884	29%	2,002	24%	7,243	30%	163,520	12%
Total	7,405		9,971		8,179		24,455		1,391,546	

Source Tabulated by *Ohmynews*, 19 June 2019, with data from Korea Student Aid Foundation, acquired by Congressman Kam Hae-Young.

The basic nature of the state's formal engagement in public education can be summarized in terms of its regulatory roles and infrastructural functions. While the South Korean government has been quite effective in mobilizing both public and civilian resources into a nationwide network of reliable schools from very early on, its regulatory roles have frequently been subjected to intense public debates, controversies, and criticisms.[35] Its education ministry has widely been rebuked for behaving like a grand national principal with its interventions in educational institutions at all levels virtually unconfined.[36] However, there is an area in which the ministry's authoritative determination has never been compromised or downplayed—namely, the governmental management of the college/university entrance examination system and the high school student recruitment system.[37] In this context, if the national aptitude test for college/university entrance in a certain year turns out too difficult or has erroneous questions, it can sometimes be considered as the ministry of education's worst possible mistake, letting media demand the education minister's grave public apology.[38]

The strictly meritocratic principle of college/university admissions is arguably the most sacred institutional basis for South Korea's modern social order that has been constructed under public education's extraordinary functions and impacts (Chang, K., 2010, Ch. 3).

The above-mentioned historical educationalization of social institutional order, economic development, cultural life, and democratic politics has inevitably generated uneven statuses, opportunities, benefits, and praises in accordance with each citizen's diverse educational endowments such as the level of his/her educational attainment, the prestige or competitiveness of his/her final-level school (which is, in most cases, a college or university), the popularity or profitability of his/her majoring discipline, and so forth. Such educationally contingent differentials in various citizenship rights can be accepted if and only if each citizen's access to public education is legitimately decided. In the South Korean context, perhaps in part thanks to the nation's aged historical tradition of appointing public officials by formal written exams, veritably objective meritocratic exams have been upheld as the only practically legitimized method of distributing access to public education in preferred institutions of learning. On the mind of South Korean citizens, the meritocratic order in the distribution of public educational access seems to constitute a citizenship right in itself.

4 In Comparative Perspective

In every major aspect of South Korea's swift liberal modernization, public education has spawned decisive impacts. Its social institutional, developmental, cultural, and political transformations have reflected not only the ordinarily expected effects of public education such as human capital formation and civic culture, but also, more crucially, various complex structural effects generated from the unique contexts, conditions, purposes, strategies, and manners by which public education has been incorporated into postcolonial modernization and development. Public education has functioned as a civilizational-cum-political economic crucible for South Korea's contentiously reflexive modernization in which all confrontational social forces and interests have exercised their maximum influences and efforts in driving the nation's historical transformations in preferred directions.

South Koreans' citizenship on all fronts has decisively been facilitated and shaped by their participation, competition, and struggle in public education. Their globally renowned "education zeal" is not just a modern manifestation of the Confucian ancestors' literary tradition but a strategic and even desperate expression of their will to postcolonial survival and prosperity whether collectivist or individualist. While the national transformative significance of education has been underscored by every each government, Park Chung-Hee, as the nation's foremost architect for development and modernization, was particularly keen to upholding it in an authoritarian nationalist perspective. This was aptly illustrated in the National Chart of Education, which was declared on 5 December 1968 through Park's own speech as follows:

> We were born into this Land charged with the historic mission to revitalize our nation. ..... With sincerity in our minds and strength in our bodies, we shall engage in scholarship and the arts, develop the innate faculties in each of us, and, using the current challenges as stepping stones for speedy progress, cultivate our creative power and pioneering spirit. .... Realizing that a nation grows through creativity and cooperation and that individual growth is grounded in the prosperity of the nation, we shall do our best to fulfill the responsibility and duty attendant upon our freedom and rights and to raise the national consciousness to participate and serve in building our nation. The love of country and fellow countrymen, together with the spirit of democracy that resists communism, paves the way for our survival and lays the ground for realizing the ideals of the free world. Looking forward to the glory of a unified homeland for our posterity and as an industrious people with confidence and pride, let us pledge to make new history with ceaseless effort and the collective wisdom of the whole nation. (*Source* Translated from Korean by the President Parkchunghee Memorial Foundation; https://www.youtube.com/watch?v=3Syifru8BR8)

Park's propagandic exhortation of his citizens for making "new history" through education was taken as a grand political endorsement of their universal education zeal. If South Koreans' such education zeal is not easily replicable in other societies, it is much more due to the nation's particular historical and sociopolitical conditions for *educationalized modernization and development* than its literarily focused historical heritage.

In fact, many of those Western nations in which public education is frequently touted as a key platform for socioeconomic regeneration tend to show somewhat comparable historical and sociopolitical conditions. In particular, those liberal political economies with the historical backgrounds as European settler colonies in the "new continents"— the United States, Canada, and Australia, among others—are known to have quite respectable systems of public education, including world-class universities, and show relatively high levels of citizens' tertiary education attainment (as shown in Table 1). For these nations, both postcolonial nation-building and rationalistic social management seem to have critically necessitated an active meritocratic enfranchisement of its citizens in conjunction with social institutional modernization and techno-scientific progress. It is quite suggestive that they are among the most popular destinations to South Korean and other East Asian students seeking overseas tertiary education.[39] When political leaders from these New World liberal nations emphatically remark that they should learn from East Asia's education zeal, it may attest to the very fact that they have also taken public education as a critical foundation for national progress in all aspects.[40]

CHAPTER 7

Reproductive Contributory Rights: From Patriarchal to Patriotic Fertility?

1 Introduction: Reproductive Citizenship Under Compressed Industrial Modernity

The seminal analysis by W. Arthur Lewis (1954) on "economic development with unlimited supplies of labour" fundamentally turned around the once prevalent perception about most developing countries' "surplus population" as a chronic economic liability. These countries, according to Lewis, could enjoy a sustained process of capitalist industrialization by systematically transferring their huge labor forces redundantly engaged in subsistence family farming to labor-intensive urban industrial sectors at costs that would enable industrial enterprises to reap sustained high profit without damaging the subsistence needs of newly employed workers. South Korea's "miracle" industrialization in its early phase took place exactly in this manner. As a result, its otherwise "surplus population" became the key basis for a national economic development primarily based upon "human resources".

The devoted mothers of such human resources, however, have not been duly acknowledged by the developmentalist state for their services in procreation and childrearing (even though they may have been thanked by their pious children, if not by their own authoritarian parents). To the contrary, they were subjected to the same developmentalist state's aggressive campaigns and authoritarian measures for "family planning" under an explicit subscription to Americans' Malthusianism-based theory of economic development in which population, as equated with gross consumption, supposedly inhibits economic development by reducing gross industrial investment (Oh, Y., 2019; Kim, H., 2002). At best, their motherly contribution should have been reframed from quantity to quality under such governmental slogans as "Let us have two children only and raise them well without differentiating son and daughter" and "Even one child from each family will make the three thousand *li* fully stuffed" (the three thousand *li* meaning the national territory). Such public pressure, and virtual insult, seems to have effectively functioned to reduce fertility although there were no less important social factors for the so-called (classic) fertility transition in the 1960s to 1980s.

In a great historical paradox, it has been in the latest period of "deindustrialization" (and industrial globalization) that South Korean mothers and potential mothers are finally acknowledged for their critical contribution to sustaining the national economy and society. The so-called jobless economic growth, especially since the national financial crisis in the late 1990s, has become a structurally normalized feature of this increasingly post-developmental nation, to which young women and men have strategically responded by a sort of long-term measures of self-austerity in life—namely, delay or avoidance of marriage, minimal or no fertility, and so forth. These sociodemographic trends do constitute the act of self-sacrifice because even a majority of young South Koreans are still *familialist* in terms of normally accepting marriage and procreation if under favorable conditions. Their timid hiatus from the so-called social reproduction through familial relationships has been so drastic that South Korea's fertility has reached the world's lowest level—e.g., a TRF of 0.84 in 2020, which renewed the historical lowest of 0.98 in 2018 and 0.92 in 2019 (KSO, 2021). Other demographic indicators such as marriage, divorce, and even suicide rates have shown similarly abrupt changes, pointing to the same phenomenon of a social reproduction crisis. In public policy discussions, South Korea has become a nation supposedly or statistically confronted with the risk of demographic extinction, which would be prevented only by young people's—in particular, young women's—courage to enter marriage and parenthood.

Having a family has become a crucial patriotic act, as implicitly insinuated in floods of policy statements, public slogans, media campaigns, and so forth. In a sense, the collectivist conception of transformative citizenship has been desperately applied to young people's marriage and fertility. It is true that these trends of demographic hiatus are sometimes reanalyzed as an outcome of defective social citizenship, but the primary thrust of the public policy is placed on the long-term political and economic predicaments of a national demographic meltdown. In another fundamental paradox, the thereby insinuated patriotism in young citizens' supposedly private sphere of life seems to have been rather counterproductive because of their widely shared feeling that their fundamental individual(ist) rights to marriage and parenthood, as well as their possible children's future, are arbitrarily subjugated to the only suspiciously sympathetic state's imminent technocratic necessities.

2 DEMOGRAPHIC RESTRUCTURING UNDER COMPRESSED AND GENDERED INDUSTRIALIZATION AND ITS CITIZENSHIP IMPLICATIONS

South Korea experienced one of the most drastic fertility transitions, along with one of the most rapid urbanizations, in human history. In 1960, the total fertility rate (TFR) was as high as 6.0. But, by 1987, it had dropped to 1.6, accounting for an impressive 73% decline (Kim, et al., 1993). Since then, fertility briefly stabilized at that level, but TFR began another phase of decline into the 2010s.[1] In other words, South Korea became a "below-replacement" society in the demographic sense merely after two decades of rapid capitalist industrialization. Soon after, it joined the "lowest-low fertility" group of nations in the 2010s and even became the group's lowest by the late 2010s (KSO, 2020; see Table 1). As a result of this precipitous fertility transition along with a sustained mortality decline, the age structure (age pyramid) of the population changed into a "bell shape" and then is becoming a "jar shape" rapidly. That is, the South Korean population is aging rapidly.[2]

At the same time, South Korea became one of the most urbanized countries in the non-Western world, at least in the demographic sense. According to the 1990 Census statistics (EPB and NSO, 1990), 74.43% of the 43.41 million national population lived in cities (*shi*), 8.30% in towns (*eup*), and 17.27% in townships (*myeon*). Since the towns would be classified as "urban" by the usual international standard, South Korea's actual urbanization rate in 1990 was 82.73%. Even this already high rate of urbanization would keep bloating into the twenty-first century—for instance, the population proportion of cities and towns was 90.6% in 2015

Table 1 Countries with the world's highest and lowest levels of total fertility rate in 2018

Rank	Country	TFR
Highest 1	Niger	6.9
2	Somalia	6.1
3	Congo, Dem Rep	5.9
3	Mali	5.9
5	Chad	5.7
6	Angloa	5.5
Lowest 1	South Korea	1.0
1	Puerto Rico	1.0
3	Hong Kong	1.1
3	Singapore	1.1
5	Macau	1.2
5	Malta	1.2
World		2.4
OECD		1.7

Source Constructed based upon World Bank (2020) data on "Fertility Rate, Total (births per woman): All Countries and Economies" (https://data.worldbank.org/indicator/SP.DYN.TFRT.IN)

and rose to 91.0% in 2018 (*e-Narajipyo*, 2020). The generational (or age-related) selectivity in rural-to-urban migration has been responsible for a disproportionate aging of the rural population. Also, the gender selectivity in rural-to-urban migration further complicated the rural population structure by leaving numerous rural men unable to find brides locally (Chang, K., 2018, Ch. 6; also see Chapter 8 in this book).

For the early phase of this fertility trend, the governmental program of family planning was initially a forceful factor, but the most decisive determinant was young parents' adaptive attitude in the context of rapid urbanization and industrialization (Kim, D., 2005). In most of the urban proletarian families, in accordance with Caldwell's (1982) intergenerational wealth flows theory, children became a social liability, not a helping hand as in the traditional peasant family. Also, the new culture of "childhood" made that liability even more costly (Chang, K., 2001). Quite interestingly, the same situation developed even among most peasant families because they hoped that their children would become successful not as a peasant but as an urban citizen with a professional, entrepreneurial, or skilled worker career (Chang, K., 2010, Ch. 6). Both in cities and villages, young parents came to realize that the good care of one or two children, rather than a desperate struggle in raising too many children, would not only relieve their own burdens but also benefit their children. The pragmatic attitude of young parents, as virtually universalized across the nation, radically changed the demographic magnitude and structure of the national population as well as those of their own families.

This pragmatism, however, had a highly controversial aspect, which in turn led to a very problematic side-effect. A severe distortion of the demographic balance between boys and girls developed as young parents tried desperately to have "at least one son" (Park and Cho, 1995). When they intended to have only one or two children, the possibility of failing to get at least one son was quite substantial. In order to avoid this possibility, many young parents asked doctors to release the result of an ultrasonic detection of their conceived child (fetus) and, if it turned out to be a female, they asked for an abortion operation.[3] The rationale for this aggressive—and formally illegal—behavior in part reflected their subjection to the (neo)traditional sociocultural system of patrilineal and patrilocal kinship, but its critically decisive factor was women's widespread discrimination under the patriarchal structure of the "modern" industrial capitalism and of the political and social order as its infrastructural conditions (Chang, K., 2010, 2018).[4] Rather than criticizing and resisting the conservative system's gender bias, many young parents opted to sacrifice their unborn daughters and thereby colluded in socially reproducing the patriarchal socioeconomic establishments.[5]

The demographic consequence of this misled pragmatism was a serious distortion of the sex ratio at birth and thereafter. For instance, as of 1990, the sex ratio (female = 100) was as high as 112.0 among the 0–4 age group, 107.1 among the 5–9 age group, and 106.5 among the 10–14 age group (Kim, et al., 1993). The 50–54 age group showed a sex ratio of 100.3, a level which should have been reached by the age group of around 15 in a normal population. The sex ratio of the 0–4 age group had been over 107 for a few decades, but the rise from 107.8 in 1985 to 112.0 in 1990 was a startling phenomenon. Even a brief stabilization of fertility between the mid-1980s and the mid-1990s did not eradicate but intensified this scandalous procreative behavior. The sex ratio at birth remained above 110 until 1996, except in 1987 (www.kosis.kr). In 1990, 1993, and 1994, it was even above 115. Living in the heyday of popularly based industrial developmentalism, South Koreans seem to have been quite confident about a men-centered future for their national economy and family structure. However, primary school teachers began to find it quite hectic and even embarrassing to listen to the complaints of those unlucky boys and their mothers on not being seated next to a girl in classroom (*KBS News*, 1996). Before long, this sex ratio distortion would be translated into a marriage market distortion, an even worse social problem with notable regional differences reflecting socioeconomic disparities (Sung, et al., 2012).

This social trend reflected a sort of *triple violations of women's citizenship*—namely, the suppression of women's social rights in the public sphere of economic and social activities, the violation of pregnant women's right to health, maternity, and motherhood, and, most seriously, the denial of female fetuses' most fundamental right to life. The first problem is about the broad societal conditions of gender discrimination, so it may not need additional elaboration here. What needs an emphasis is the fact that such societal discrimination of women was internalized into mother women's procreative behavior, usually under the severe pressure of their patriarchal stem families in marriage (Chang, K., 2018, Ch. 4). The second and third problems reflect not only the prevailing social order of gender discrimination and/or hierarchy but also, more critically, the fundamental ethos or moral about women's existential dignity and right as human being. To the extent that those pregnant women undergoing abortion of female fetuses were dictated by (extended) familial pressure for having at least one son as well as by their own similar desire, the latter two problems may have been considered as citizens' private responsibilities. However, the medical technological possibility and availability in abortion and the legal tolerance—or the administrative pretense of unawareness—of basically illegal abortions were all direct consequences of the Malthusian developmentalist state's antinatal posture and its aggressive policy measures for restraining women's procreation (Park and Cho, 1995). In a sense, pregnant women's subjection to abortion and their unborn daughters' subjection to extinction constituted, though anachronistically, developmentalist citizenship duties.

3 Economic Meltdown, Demographic Meltdown: An Instantaneous Transition to "Lowest Low" Fertility

South Korea's unprecedented national financial crisis in the late 1990s and the accompanying radical industrial restructuring required a majority of its citizens to abruptly confront a post-developmental or even post-industrial era without meaningful public and private preparations (Chang,

K., 2019, Chs. 3 and 4). The impressive recovery and renewed growth of the now substantially globalized industrial conglomerates (*chaebol*) have ironically necessitated and caused a pervasive economic disenfranchisement of current and prospective laborers, with immediate damages concentrated on male economic prerogatives.[6] Such historically unfamiliar economic distress foisted on contemporary South Koreans came to trigger a South Korean version of "second fertility transition". South Korea's fertility became "lowest-low", now competing against Taiwan, Hong Kong, and Singapore whose fertility has been additionally subjected to exceptional political and socioecological pressures.[7] As noted above, the latest figure of its TFR, 0.84 in 2020, placed South Korea as the world's least reproduced demographic entity (KSO, 2020).

In a paradoxical and unexpected development, the latest fertility cutback in South Korea has produced a corrective effect on its citizens' gender-biased procreative behavior. That is, the average sex ratio at birth has all of a sudden recovered its "natural" level (of about 105). As the hitherto advantageous economic prospect for sons has fundamentally crumbled amid the nation's jobless economic growth, South Koreans have rapidly veered to the "romantic" value of having daughters (Chang, K., 2011). It is quite interesting to note that South Koreans, nonetheless, have maintained exceptionally high levels of gender-specific preference—as opposed to gender neutrality or indifference—in childbirth (Eun, K., 2013). Their propensity to find a strategic fertility reason in respect to their children's gender has notabated in spite of an apparent demise of the aged patriarchal sociodemographic culture. Their familialism may be changing in content, but not disappearing.

More broadly, there arose since the late 1990s a conspicuous social trend among the young generation to indefinitely postpone or give up marriage, to have no or a minimum number of children in marriage, and to choose separation or divorce without hesitation. The nation's current fertility at one of the world's lowest levels has been systematically linked to its extremely high divorce rate and rapidly rising age of first marriage (Byun, et al., 2010). Behind this trend lies a rapid growth in young individuals who feel extremely burdened about the formation and maintenance of familial relationships for social reproduction and even feel doubtful about the practicality of social reproduction itself. This development, nevertheless, does not necessarily attest to their abandonment of familialism or a sociocultural change toward more individualistic life.

Instead, it should be understood as *individualization without individualism* (Chang and Song, 2010) because even young people's familialism still remains strong as evidenced by their general willingness to get married and to have children in marriage.

Since the national economic crisis of the late 1990s, however, the devastating impacts of economic turbulences and social instabilities on the material conditions of family-centered social reproduction have made most young women and men extremely cautious about marriage and procreation from the perspective of *risk aversion* (Chin, M., 2013; Chang, K., 2018). As familial relationships are increasingly prone to function as the transmitter of social risks rather than that of social resources, the motivation for securing a partner (spouse) and successors (children) for family-based social reproduction has been critically undermined.[8] At the same time, due to the "social democratization" in familial order and gender relations and the expanding job opportunities for women in tertiary sectors, more and more young women now pursue active social participation and individually resist the social pressure for marriage and procreation (Chang and Song, 2010).

Whereas South Koreans' recent familialism often serves only to deter (materially unprepared) marriage and fertility, this normative dilemma has not been relieved by any meaningful compensatory ideational development. For instance, the remarkable improvement in women's sociopolitical and cultural status has not been accompanied by a more individualistic or autonomous culture of procreation and motherhood as would be comparable to that found widely in Western societies. The (neo)traditional era of *familialist procreation* has apparently subsided, but a new era of *individualist procreation* is not yet in clear sight.[9] The aggregate consequences of such motivational crisis in social reproduction—namely, marriage reduction, fertility decline, and aged demographic structure—inevitably cause serious destabilizing effects on the maintenance of the macro social and economic systems. Thereby arose an active, and loud, pronatal policy regime in South Korea in an instantaneous succession, or replacement, of the antinatal policy regime, of which various remnants remained well into the 1990s.[10] Communicated in a similarly authoritarian technocratic tone to the (not so much) earlier birth control campaign, the pronatal policy discourses, by highlighting the prospect for related social and economic crises incautiously, are suspected to have aggravated the familial risk concerns of young women and men.[11]

4 DEMOGRAPHIC PATRIOTISM, REPRODUCTIVE CITIZENSHIP, AND POST-FAMILIALIST FERTILITY

The more low fertility is emphasized as a crisis, the more reluctant I become about procreation because I am made to think that it is a really difficult world for childbirth. (Participant A; https://www.yna.co.kr/view/AKR20180901018400017)

Noting the state's warning and move on the recent low fertility crisis, fertility seems to be coerced in order to preserve the nation. (Participant B; https://www.yna.co.kr/view/AKR20180901018400017)

Through these events, [we] have confirmed the resistance and burden of young people about the beneficialist approach that the state will come out to help such individual choices as courtship, marriage, and fertility. .... [We] will endeavor to realize, through concrete policies, a paradigm shift for recognizing marriage and fertility as individual choice. (Presidential Committee on Ageing Society and Population Policy, 2018b)

The above passages are, respectively, two opinions expressed by participating citizens and the official conclusion at a series of special forums ("Youth Talk") on courtship, marriage, and fertility, organized by the Presidential Committee on Ageing Society and Population Policy (PCASPP) in August 16–30, 2018 (https://www.yna.co.kr/view/AKR20180901018400017). Quite interestingly, the low fertility "crisis" has induced South Korean youth and their government to concretely and systematically think about basic principles of citizenship in their mutual relations.

In the twenty-first century, South Koreans have been warned about a prospective demographic shock that even the unprecedentedly radical sociodemographic transformations of the previous century cannot match. As South Koreans' "lowest-low" fertility shows no sign of immediate recovery, their national population is predicted to be halved by the mid-twenty-first century.[12] Furthermore, such demographic shrinkage will be marred by an abruptly bloated proportion of aged people as the country is undergoing population aging with an internationally unparalleled velocity (see Chang, K., 2022, Ch. 8). South Korea—for that matter, North Korea as well—is a society founded and sustained by historically fortified (ethno)nationalism (Shin, G., 2006). Even its modern capitalist economy is a product of state-driven (ethno)nationalist development and, despite various tendencies of economic globalization, may well remain a (ethno)nationalist entity in the coming decades in terms of Korean control of regulatory coordination, corporate governance, and core human capital. Besides, its continuing confrontation and hoped reunification with North Korea are fundamentally framed through (ethno)nationalist competition for historical, political, and socioeconomic legitimacy. Under these circumstances, the South Korean state and society have perceived the projected demographic meltdown as a potential national pandemonium that should be counteracted with all possible efforts. Thus, all of the recent administrations, whether conservative or progressive, have dealt with population issues as a policy of presidential priority. Familial procreation of children—who shall sustain the nation's future as productive laborers, dependable consumers, willing taxpayers, as well as regenerative sociocultural subjects—has all of a sudden become an issue of nation-saving, so a patriotic atmosphere abounds, if implicitly, in policy debates, public appeals, and media coverage (PCASPP, 2018a).

Paradoxically, as noted above, such patriotic suggestions have insinuated a fundamentally contradictory message to current and prospective parents that their born and unborn children could confront various structural future risks associated with national demographic imbalances and shortages—namely, a hyperaged population requiring unbearable welfare expenses, national economic contraction due to shrinking labor force and consumption basis, and so forth. While South Koreans are encouraged to procreate despite (and because of) such risks, no one would voluntarily base actual childbearing on a patriotic ground.[13] There have arisen a series of ideological and programmatic changes that now constitute an explicit regime of *reproductive citizenship*—that is, childbearing and childrearing as citizens' rights (and implicit duties) that should be duly respected and supported as (national) public good.[14]

The generous and sometime aggressive programs of both the national and local governments for encouraging fertility as a supposed national exigency have critically complemented South Koreans' rather weak *social citizenship* that has even worried the United Nations in respect to its Economic, Social and Cultural Rights Covenant (see Chapters 4 and 5 in this book). In particular, child allowance—that has long been called for by welfare activists and experts as the last remaining requirement for completing the full institutional configuration of the South Korean "welfare state"—has been rather abruptly promoted by multiple public agencies largely as a pronatal incentive.[15]

Another (arguably) progressive aspect of the pronatal policy has consisted in its strong emphasis on the easing of working women's childbearing and childrearing through provision of more and better childcare services, protective encouragement of childcare leaves for both parents, and so forth (Park, B., 2006). The combined political emphasis on women's economic and reproductive citizenship, however, is sometimes subjected to opposing voices that criticize the hidden (neo)liberal thrust for overexploiting women (Kim, G., 2011). Most policy practices are openly geared toward work-family combination, rather than work-family balance, and thereby help reinforce the "second shift" (Hochschild, 1990) as South Korean women's generalized life situation.

Nonetheless, the overall direction of the pronatal policy does not seem to be mistaken, particularly in the post-IMF crisis context where the so-called socioeconomic bipolarization has caused a fundamental destabilization of most citizens' general material conditions for social reproduction.[16] However, it remains doubtful if the recent consolidation of reproductive citizenship alone can effectively motivate young South Koreans to marry and procreate in numbers that would make significant demographic upturns. South Korean women used to bear children mainly as a patriarchal familial subject, but such patriarchal force—whether from stem family or nuclear family—has critically waned in both material and cultural terms (Chang, K., 2011a, 2018). The apparent demise of the patriarchal familial regime of fertility has yet to be counterbalanced by a new socioculturally consolidated regime of fertility that is compatible with women's liberal individuality and democratic inter-gender and intergenerational relations. Motherhood now has to be socially reconstructed from below, rather than culturally inherited or reinvented from the past or politically superimposed from above.

5 Conclusion

South Korea's demographic restructuring in many aspects has been no less radical than its socioeconomic transformations under compressed modernity. This is no coincidence in that individual behaviors and familial choices determining demographic parameters such as marriage, fertility, and migration have closely reflected South Koreans' intense desires and active efforts to participate in their nation's literally explosive development and modernization on all fronts. In a sense, the full realization of their citizenship rights in national socioeconomic progresses has been conditioned upon their active demographic behaviors attuned to the qualifications for and opportunities from such progresses. Likewise, the unprecedented and unparalleled drastic transitions in marriage/divorce, migration, and fertility rates all have mirrored the notable fulfillment, enhancement, and, most recently, erosion of various citizenship rights.

Until recently, in a fundamental paradox, such demographic behaviors themselves have not been subjected to strong social demands and active political proposals in terms of citizenship rights. They have mostly been perceived as private choices and responsibilities both by the state and citizens themselves. This does not imply that the state has not intervened in such supposedly private choices and responsibilities. Its family planning program was one of the most draconian instances of governmental intervention in demographic behaviors. Its industrialization strategy was accompanied by a comprehensive range of urban-centered infrastructural, educational, and housing policies for accommodating the urban migration of a majority of villagers. But these policies were rarely classified or publicized in citizenship terms.

In the long run, South Korea's industrialized capitalist economy and social security system have socioeconomically frustrated rapidly increasing segments and proportions of its population. Much like during the earlier period of socioeconomic progresses, the latest era of South Koreans' massive socioeconomic disenfranchisement has been accompanied by drastic changes in demographic indicators with which the country now appears almost scandalous—the world's lowest fertility rate, the world's third highest suicide rate (and, among aged persons, the world's highest suicide rate), a divorce rate rivaling those of the liberal West (such as the United States and the UK), and so forth. While these trends are sometimes reanalyzed as an outcome of defective social citizenship, the primary thrust of the public policy is placed on the long-term political and economic predicaments of a national demographic meltdown. The collectivist conception of transformative citizenship has been desperately applied to young people's marriage and fertility. Such insinuated patriotism in young citizens' supposedly private sphere of life may have been rather counterproductive in that they tend to develop a feeling that their fundamental individual(ist) rights to marriage and parenthood, along with their possible children's future, are bluntly subordinated to the conservative state's technocratic necessities.

CHAPTER 8

Ad Hoc Cultural Citizenship: Neotraditional to Multicultural (Non)transition

1 Introduction

South Korea's breathtaking social and economic transformations have predominantly been concentrated in urban areas. Accordingly, the country has experienced an internationally incomparable pace of rural-to-urban movement of people and socioeconomic resources. Many of South Korean villages and townships are now predicted to disappear before too long because of their unstoppable demographic thinning (KREI, 2004). In a great paradox, it is this crisis of rural people and society that has suddenly ushered South Korea into a supposedly cosmopolitan era in which multiculturalism is hailed as a "new-normal" attribute of the nation. The mass arrival of foreign brides from various poorer Asian countries to marry South Korea's rural bachelors, many being in their forties and fifties, has been both intellectually and administratively characterized, and epistemologically improvised, as multiculturalization.

South Koreans' long cherished pride in supposedly being a nation of millennia-sustained ethnic homogeneity, as if its use-by date had expired, has all of a sudden been replaced by a fervent public campaign of national multiculturalization. The rural origin of the nation's cosmopolitan cultural self-reinvention is not logically deducible from its modern history of externally dependent urban-based social modernization and capitalist industrialization that have recently been extremized under neoliberal globalization. "Global Korea" is touted as a new national identity for culturally lubricating South Korea's unbridled economic and social globalism as a core member of neoliberal global capitalism (Watson, 2010, 2011). It is a stark irony that rural families and villages, the worst victim of both the earlier and latest phases of South Korea's externally oriented development and modernization, have been arbitrarily staged to serve as pioneering subjects in multiculturalization as a core trend of sociocultural globalism.

The government policies and social campaigns for multiculturalism are no empty words. Foreign brides and their Korean family members have been offered a wide range of public and communal social services, including language lesson, job training, family counseling, health support, parenting assistance, and cultural experiences (*Danuri*, 2020; *Bokjiro*, 2020; Kang, B., 2012). These benefits may be considered in part as a sort of (multi)cultural transformative contributory rights because both the state and society have aspired to promote multiculturalization, at least nominally, by taking advantage of transnationalized rural marriages. It is not only foreign brides and their Korean family members but also local Korean citizens, activists, corporations, and communities engaged in multicultural advocacy that are acknowledged as subjects of such transformative contribution in culture.

Curiously, South Korea's multiculturalism as a culturally framed regime of cosmopolitan citizenship has officially excluded foreign guest workers—another significant group of foreign population that has no less crucially facilitated the country's neoliberal globalization.[1] Such differentiation, or discrimination, of foreign guest workers reflects, on the one hand, the neoliberal labor regime governing foreign workers through transitory terms of work and, on the other hand, the sociocultural non-necessity of their permanent status in South Korea for mostly sweatshop industrial labor (Seol, D., 2002, 2014). By contrast, foreign brides arrive in South Korea basically as subjects of social reproduction labor (such as homemaking, childbirth, and family care) that necessitates their permanent sociocultural membership in the nation as legally mediated by marriage relations with local Koreans. Seen in this angle, governmental and social multiculturalism does not necessarily points to the very core dimension of foreign brides' citizenship. It is their reproductive contributory rights in the context of rural depopulation by which their permanent citizenship status is established.

In an unprecedented cultural paradox, foreign brides from across Asia have been mobilized as substitutive labor for Korean rural families' social reproduction that is still very (neo)traditional in terms of familial role divisions, gender/generation hierarchies, behavioral normativities, and so forth. In a sense, modern Korean families, particularly in rural areas, may be more traditional (or Confucian) on average than their ancestral counterparts in Chosun (the last dynastic state in Korea) because postcolonial modernization rendered them to universally appropriate the traditionally aristocratic sociocultural system of Confucianism despite, or in conjunction with, their universalized socioeconomic status as smallholding peasant after land reform (Chang, K., 2018, Ch. 3). Such neotraditionalized attributes of rural families, besides the chronic economic depression and infrastructural backwardness of rural areas, have widely been rejected by local Korean women in their long-term preferences and decisions in life. Unable to find willing Korean women, "forced bachelors" in rural areas, frequently in their middle ages, have desperately sought for foreign spouses who would help mend the badly destabilized conditions of social reproduction in neotraditional rural families. The loudly publicized notion of multicultural citizenship, as touted in South Korea's latest all-front globalization, more hides than reveals most foreign brides' everyday conditions of life and work.

2 Neotraditional Cultural Citizenship in Postcolonial Modernization and Developmentalist Social Governance

During the colonial era, Japan formally reaffirmed the nominal abolition, by the short-lived Daehanjeguk, of the feudal status system of Chosun (comprised by *yangban*, *jungin*, *sangmin*, and *cheonmin*; or by gentry, middlemen, commoners, and slaves). But its position as to Confucian culture remained syncretic and flexible in accordance with pragmatic considerations for cost-effective control and exploitation of Koreans (Rhyu, M., 2005, 2007). Japan dealt with *yangban*, the landed aristocratic class of Chosun, as local socioeconomic elite, whose material interest and customary social status would be tolerated in exchange for their cooperation in colonial rule and exploitation.[2] In this context, Confucianism changed from the feudal status culture of a hegemonic caste to the class culture of local socioeconomic elite. In fact, many members of *yangban* endeavored to make up for their loss of national and social hegemony by practicing Confucian rituals earnestly, whereas many newly enriched Koreans from non-*yangban* backgrounds tried to culturally cement their material success by emulating Confucianism (Park, S., 2019). Japan found Koreans' effort to reproduce the conservative social order (pivoting around loyalty, filial piety, and chastity) useful to its colonial rule, but attempted to moderate the ideological rigidity and financial cost of the formerly aristocratic rituals by enacting "The Standard Rules of Rituals" in the 1930s (Lee, H., 2011).

Japan's colonial family policy and law impacted complicated changes in gender relations, both legalizing men's status as "household head" (*hoju*) in the socio-administrative control of Korean population (Yang, H., 2006, 2011) and instituting women's formal legal status in the increasing nuclear families (Lim, S., 2019). During Japan's colonial rule, its familial custom of primogeniture for family enterprise (*ie*) was replicated onto Koreans' primogeniture custom for the Confucian religious status, establishing the *hoju* (household head) system. This arbitrarily *reinvented* tradition has thereafter been upheld by Koreans as a historical fact, leading to the eldest son's (and his wife's) extraordinary rights and duties in the material livelihood as well as sociocultural representation of each family. (Many eldest sons in rural families, even during the recent period of rapid economic development, would become particularly unpopular as marriage partner to South Korean women, with many of them, as explained below in detail, searching instead for foreign brides from poor Asian countries.[3]) On the other hand, Korean women's status norms had also been influenced by the Japanese ideology of *ryosai kenbo* (wise mother, good wife) (Choi, H., 2009). This influence was not incompatible with Confucian family norms but would normatively reinforce them, with a complicated impact of nurturing a womanly status betrayed by their everyday realties of agricultural and other production labor besides home management. It was not institutionally articulated through the patrilineal kinship system but, in fact, accompanied by the colonial legalization of women's formal status in the increasing nuclear families (Lim, S., 2019). However, as discussed below, postcolonial neotraditionalization in family culture would help to substantially liquidate the practical effect of women's such legal status in everyday life.

Korea's liberation from Japan was immediately accompanied by various dispersed efforts by members of some previously influential Confucian families and schools at reinstating Confucian principles in public life and sociopolitical order (Yi, H., 2014). Although such elite efforts turned out mostly ineffective, ordinary South Koreans, nevertheless, widely and fervently began to consummate Confucian culture in their private spheres. This phenomenon was contextually combined with the new political order of universal democratic citizenship, the new socioeconomic order stabilized under land reform, and the new system of universal (elementary) public education (Chang, K., 2018, Ch. 3). As full members of the Republic of Korea, a new nation-state of equally sovereign commoners, virtually all South Koreans endeavored to assert a dignifying cultural status in tandem with their new citizenship rights in politics, farming, and education.[4] Almost instantaneously, culturally self-serving aristocratization (*yangbanhwa*), mainly in family relations and rituals, took place throughout the country, rendering modern South Korea more Confucian on average than its ancestral society of Chosun.[5] This trend enraged descendants of many traditional aristocratic families who claimed a supposedly exclusive status of being or remaining Confucian more properly.[6] Family-based Confucianism, regarded as a socially superior cultural asset, thereby came to form the core sociocultural foundation of postcolonial liberal modernity (in the South Korean version), allowing every citizen to feel equally superior through responsible participation in traditionally revered forms of family life. This constituted a sort of cultural self-citizenship by which grassroots South Koreans endeavored to dignify themselves after decades of political, socioeconomic, and civilizational alienation as colonial subjects. It may also be seen as an aristocratic cultural citizenship from below—an individually and socially costly practice that, as discussed below, would worry Park Chung-Hee in his urgent pursuit of national economic development.

Conceptually, this phenomenon was *neotraditionalization*, rather than *retraditionalization*, in that Confucianism based upon such cultural egalitarianism fundamentally deviated from Confucianism as the core status asset of an aristocratic class (*yangban*) as in Chosun. As explained authoritatively by Eli Zaretsky (1973), the aristocratic nature of modern (nuclear) family life, as a neotraditionalist modernity, has also been found in the Western historical context where the Victorian-age family culture has sequentially been appropriated by bourgeoisie and proletariat along the historical transformations of the capitalist production system and its labor regimes. In comparison, the Western case is more a long-term political economic phenomenon attendant upon industrial capitalism's evolution and expansion, whereas the South Korean case is more a circumstantially driven sociopolitical phenomenon derived instantly from a suddenly attained national liberation.[7]

Materially, such cultural aristocratization of the populace was complemented by the socioeconomic conditions stabilized through land reform. As Japan's colonial capitalist industrialization fell short of industrially and occupationally transforming Koreans in any significant proportion, postcolonial land reform in South Korea implied a nearly universal (re)enfranchisement of its predominantly agrarian population in traditional family farming. Despite the common smallholding nature of their farming, most South Koreans' quickly stabilized livelihood began to be culturally celebrated by their universal adoption and practice of Confucian family norms and rituals and demographically accompanied by rising fertility and increasing lifespan (Kim, J., 1994). There arose historically unprecedented communities of socioecologically standardized, organizationally enlarged, and culturally aristocratized peasant families, with all macroeconomic uncertainties and political instabilities haunting this postcolonial society.[8] Despite commonly experienced poverty and seasonal hunger, South Korean rural citizens managed to lead a self-contained regime of livelihood that compared far more favorably to their earlier livelihoods under the civil war, Japanese colonialism, and the decayed feudal order. To the eyes of the resource-poor state, grassroots South Koreans' Confucian norms for familial support and protection at least helped to familialize the otherwise burdensome political duty of materially looking after its citizenry (Chang, K., 1997).[9]

The seemingly oxymoronic social entity of aristocratized smallholder peasantry, however, necessitated women's multifaceted alienation and exploitation (Kim, J., 1994; Yang and Kong, 2016). The critical material defect of poor peasant families in practicing those aristocratic familial rituals and services that, in ancient times, even required substantial slave labor, not to mention various in-kind private resources, was coped with by improvised measures for mobilizing and abusing women as a socioculturally inferior gender. In particular, the subservient labor of daughters-in-law was maximally utilized in sustaining poor peasant families' aristocratic virtues as well as managing primitive agricultural work. In a sense, all married women ended up becoming a sort of *double-outsider* in that marriage did not enable them to become full members (or familial citizens) of their families-in-law in economic and cultural terms, while they were normatively regarded as *chulgaoein* (outside person after on-marriage departure from own family) by their parental families.[10] The only way to escape this stressful status was by becoming the mother of a male family member, so their procreative son-preference was as much a strategic desire as a cultural norm.[11]

By the time Park Chung-Hee took over state leadership by a military coup in the early 1960s, however, the post-war baby boom had led to rapidly worsening conditions in farming and livelihood as the rural economy was rigidly constrained by increasingly adverse man-land ratios. The urban economy, without a noticeable industrialization yet, was no exception to this social ecological hardship. Such material difficulties, however, did not immediately discourage ordinary South Koreans from (over)expending familial efforts and resources for Confucian rituals and services.[12] In an era of Malthusian liberal developmentalism when even human lives began to be perceived as a redundant liability to the nation, the lavish (neo)traditional cultural rituals of poor peasants and urbanites seriously worried the Park government, especially in the early stage of aggressive state-led industrialization and rapid economic growth. Thus, it prepared and declared, in 1969, the Standard Rules on Familial Rituals (*Gajeonguiryejunchik*) in order to formally regulate and moderate citizens' excess practice and consumption in ancestor worship, funeral, wedding, sixtieth birthday, and so forth (Chang, K., 2018, Ch. 3).[13]

Such governmental intervention in civilians' cultural life was not to deny or rebuke the contemporarily universalized neotraditional norms and values. To the contrary, it effected a formal ratification of South Koreans' neotraditional cultural identity, including the patrilineal/patrilocal family system and its patriarchal order of family relations. This policy stance was, on the one hand, to avoid a potential social enragement of grassroots citizens by politically negating their precious cultural (self-)citizenship, and, on other hand, to maintain the convenient social effect of citizens' material self-protection under Confucian norms for familial support and care (Koh, W., 2006). Not unrelatedly, the state's mobilization of women in this campaign of cultural rationalization did not attempt to structurally reconfigure the patriarchal gender order in familial and social relations. South Koreans' self-asserted neotraditionality thereby became certified into a formalized form of cultural citizenship, which in turn obliged them to cooperate with the developmentalist state for frugal management of Confucian familial rituals and services.

3 THE SOCIODEMOGRAPHIC MELTDOWN OF RURAL FAMILIES AND COMMUNITIES AND TRANSNATIONAL ADAPTATIONS: THE ARRIVAL OF FOREIGN BRIDES

Despite its chronic economic strains and cultural contradictions, South Korea's peasantry did manage to stably contain a severely accumulating population pressure until the onset of what would later be considered as one of the world's most explosive instances of capitalist industrialization. The country's socioeconomic conditions in the early 1960s almost perfectly approximated the immediate preindustrialization stage of W. Arthur Lewis's (1954) "dual sector model" of economic development. Under various opportune circumstances (that are not addressed here in detail but have been explained in many other studies), the South Korean state was able to help trigger an extremely rapid and sustained industrialization along with no less speedy social modernization and urbanization (Amsden, 1989). As elsewhere, labor-intensive manufacturing sectors enticed both men and women, particularly in young ages, into various levels and types of urban places (Koo, H., 2001). Even as the national economy swiftly matured into capital/technology-intensive sectors that would disproportionately employ men, women's rural exodus did not attenuate but, in fact, exceeded that of men (Kim, J., 1994). Their home villages and towns could not be favorably compared to cities in the aspects of attractive jobs, alluring sociocultural atmosphere and infrastructure, and, not least importantly, marriageable men's availability.

As a sincere subscriber to the so-called unbalanced growth strategy (cf. Hirschman, 1958), the developmentalist government did everything to maximally concentrate public and private socioeconomic resources into the sequentially selected industrial sectors (excluding agriculture permanently). Throughout this process of late but swift capitalist industrialization, farming has been socioeconomically regulated with the constitutional stipulations on equitable family-based production (dubbed *gyeongjayujeon*, meaning "tillers own land" equally). South Korea was no exception to the macroeconomic rationality of family farming under the condition of "economic overpopulation" that is defined by worsening declines in marginal labor productivity below its average rate—if not below the level of meager subsistence consumption (Georgescu-Roegen, 1960, 1970). Thus, as has been the case throughout its history and as is evidenced in a majority of other (over)populous nations, the legally stipulated family farming has served as a production regime that maximizes the total agricultural output on the basis of all physically able individuals' universal participation in familially organized farm work. The developmental state's expectation of the rural society and economy kept remaining precisely at that level or stage, exempting itself of any major new duties except basic infrastructural improvements and enhanced supplies of "modern" inputs (such as chemical fertilizers, insecticides, and so forth) (Chang, K., 2010, Ch. 6).

Paradoxically, or quite rationally, most rural families did not complain about the state's lopsided development strategy of urban industrialization but instead *internalized such developmental dualism* into themselves. South Korea's swift capitalist industrialization in various levels and types of urban places did not require such arbitrary social measures like the British enclosure because virtually all individual families opted to promptly diversify their economic activities (and organizations) by allowing and encouraging the urban migration of able-bodied children and siblings for immediate industrial work or education for higher-level urban jobs. The velocity of this nearly universal rural-to-urban migration was accelerated in proportion to the country's miracle-pace urban industrialization, generating the world's most extreme instance of urbanization during the latter half of the twentieth century—that is, South Korea's urbanization rate reached the 90% level merely a few decades after its industrial kick-off in the early 1960s from a predominantly agrarian society (*e-Narajipyo*, 2020).

While this kind of radical population movement cannot but be accompanied by all sorts of side-effects to both places of origin and places of destination, what mattered most crucially was the aggressive developmental judgment and execution of peasant families in systematically transferring rural socioeconomic resources to urban areas through *moral-cum-strategic investment* in the city-based work and education of children and siblings.[14] To begin with, the selective urban migration of young individuals, leaving parents behind, was itself a systematic act of resource transfer. Under this circumstance, farming soon became an occupation that no rural parents—not to mention urban parents—would recommend to their children and very few rural youth would hope as their future.[15] Marriage to a farmer also became the least preferred future to young rural—not to mention, urban—women (Kim, J., 1994). Farming and village life all of a sudden became a signifier of a developmental outlier, if not a loser, whose fate has been taken much more as a subject of private remorse than as an issue of sociopolitical grievance.[16]

As a key sociodemographic outcome of a sort of "Don't look back" industrialization, most of South Korean villages and townships have been confronted with rapid declines in their overall population size, proportion of young people, and, not least importantly, and women-to-men ratio among never married adults (Kim, T., 1996, 2001). These trends have been structurally reflected in the highly skewed distribution of rural families among various stages of family life cycle—that is, those families which are in the organizationally shrinking or dissolving stages account for preponderantly large proportions across the country. (Table 1 shows the distribution of rural families by the family life cycle stages in the 1990s, that is, on the eve of the sudden transnationalization of rural marriages.) In many regions, the rural economy and community are literally in an existential crisis due to the pervasive interruption or even cessation in the normal social reproduction of peasant families as the basic organizational unit of rural production and livelihood. Except in the suburban regions of major cities, elderly-only-villages are not exceptional but commonplace. Despite such organizational destabilization or even meltdown of peasant families, the basic institutional framework

Table 1 Family life cycle distribution of rural households on the eve of the sudden increase in international marriages

1992	Farm only	Farm plus	Non-farm	All
Formative	1.5	1.9	3.3	1.9
Expanding	2.5	5.3	8.6	4.2
Expansion completed	36.4	48.3	47.4	41.1
Shrinking	46.4	35.4	19.7	39.3
Shrinkage completed	9.3	8.1	8.6	8.9
Dissolved	4.0	1.0	12.5	4.7

2000				Farming and fishing[a]
Formative				0.43
Expanding				1.70
Expansion completed				35.32
Shrinking				37.73
Shrinkage completed				13.33
Dissolved				11.49

[a]Households of employed women
Source Abridged from Chang, K. (2010a), Table 6.3

for rural socioeconomic management has remained virtually unchanged, whether as rural people's own practice or as the state's rural policy. As Sorensen (1988) observed, most rural families managed to maintain their (neo)traditional organizational structure and culture even under rapid industrialization and urbanization. In fact, their strategic support of urban-headed/based children as a new basis of (extended) familial economic progress and status advancement enabled themselves to feel relaxed about not changing their comfortably accustomed way of rural livelihood (Chang, K., 2010, Ch. 6).

With South Korea's neoliberal globalization accelerated in the new century, all such social displacements and contradictions in rural areas have been even more intensified, particularly due to the developmental state's aggressive pursuit of free trade with major agricultural exporter countries such as the United States, China, Australia, Canada, and Chile, on top of its proactive participation in the global free trade regime of the World Trade Organization (WTO) (Jin, H., 2015). Agriculture has been systematically sacrificed practically as a lure to those countries whose consumer markets can be significantly enlarged to South Korean industrial goods. However, South Korea's globalization has not been confined to the nominally economic front, but has also encompassed a virtually unlimited range of social and cultural affairs. Perhaps the most abruptly staged affair among them has been the explosive growth of international marriages largely between South Korean men in urban peripheries and rural areas and women from various poor Asian countries (see Fig. 1).

The notable increase in peripheral urban men's international marriage, mostly with Korean Chinese (Chaoxianzu) and Han Chinese women, began in the early 2000s as an individually based side-effect of a selective liberalization of the nation's labor market.[17] That is, many of the originally economic sojourners from China have ended up helping to fill the shortage of brides in South Korea's urban marriage market (Kim, et al., 2010). By contract, the sudden upsurge in rural men's international marriage, particularly with Vietnamese women, started in the mid-2000s virtually as a strategic social project involving not only rural bachelors and their parents but also rural communities, local governments, and advocacy campaign organizations.[18] Within a few years, this social project got officially recognized under the rubric of *multiculturalism* (namely, "the multicultural family support policy") (Kim, H., 2012, 2014). Henceforth, the nation of South Korea as a whole has been reinventing itself as a supposedly cosmopolitan entity, socioculturally comparable with its global economic prominence.[19]

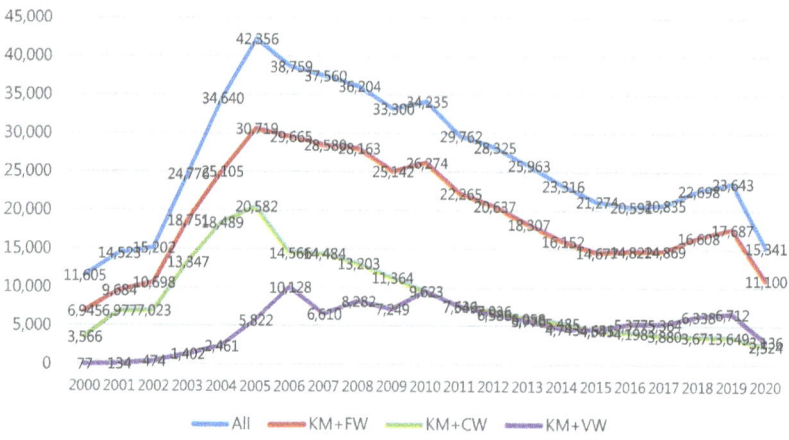

Fig. 1 Growth and composition in international marriages in South Korea (KM, FW, CW and VW stand for Korean men, Foreign women, Chinese women and Vietnamese women respectively) (*Source* Created from data in National Statistical Office, 2020, *The Statistical Yearbook on Population Dynamics 2019* [http://www.index.go.kr/potal/stts/idxMain/selectPoSttsIdx Search.do?idx_cd=2430])

4 Neotraditional to Multicultural (Non)transition: Dual Cultural Citizenship as Antinomy

Massive numbers of foreign brides recently arriving in South Korean villages and townships have served as a *dual functionary for the nation's globalization*—that is, as substitute social reproduction laborers for those rural bachelors (and their parents) rejected by domestic women amid the country's accelerated economic globalization and as a convenient signifier of a sociocultural cosmopolitanization deemed necessary to match its prominent global economic status. Foreign brides, particularly in rural areas, are thereby confronted with an existential antinomy in which they have to simultaneously deal with culturally framed expectations for both neotraditional Korean family life and publicly staged "multicultural" ethnicity (Kim, H., 2012, 2014). They have been greeted by most local communities and governments, various voluntary associations, and innumerable business enterprises with all eagerly paternalistic gestures and services offered to help ease their adaptation to South Korean society while celebratively welcoming their cultural differences (see, for instance, in Photo 1, a video reunion between foreign brides and their home families organized by a government ministry). However, many of them have increasingly felt uncomfortable and even alienated about the multiculturalism campaigns and slogans (Chu, B., 2011; Kim and Choi, 2016). Usually dressed in home-country costumes and expected to exhibit home-country culture (in cooking, singing, etc.), they are staged, paraded, and photographed in frequently repeated multiculturalism events and frequently feel weary and estranged (*Wando Times*, 9 January 2013).[20]

Most crucially, multiculturalism policies and services rarely help exempt foreign brides from neotraditional Korean norms and duties in their everyday lives and relationships in respective Korean families. In essence, neither the social project of multiculturalism nor the familial system of neotraditional social reproduction has been intended to serve foreign brides as main subjects. At best, they are instrumentally utilized for both

Photo 1 "Korea-Vietnam/Philippines Family Video Reunion" organized by Ministry of Public Administration and Safety (MOPAS) (*Source* Ministry of Public Administration and Safety, 14 April 2011)

purposes (Yoon, I., 2008). As most foreign brides from other Asian countries have married rural bachelors, they are much more likely to live in the social setting of (neo)traditional family relations and rituals than their native Korean counterparts (most of whom live in urban places). To them, local cultural experience is not just a special "multicultural" event, but constitutes their everyday reality. Consequently, as a great paradox, foreign brides live far more Korean (neo)traditional types of family life than their Korean native counterparts by whom rural families have been deserted (Chang, K., 2018: 158–169; KWDI, 2016; MOGEF, 2019).

This has been clearly documented time and again in comprehensive public surveys (triennially carried out since 2009) as well as by numerous individual research investigations.[21] In these observations, rural foreign brides are much more likely to coreside with parents-in-law and/or siblings-in-law than both foreign and Korean brides in urban areas. Even when they live only with their spouses (and children), their parents-in-law frequently and closely interact with them and their spouses for care, assistance, and/or intervention in daily life. Not unrelatedly, what has drawn the biggest attention from media is the in-law women's intergenerational-cum-intercultural relationship, called *damunhwagobugwangye* in Korean (meaning multicultural relationship between a mother-in-law and a daughter-in-law). The conflictual intergenerational relationship between the in-law women (*gobugaldeung*) used to popularly typify the authoritarian sociocultural order of neotraditional Korean families. Now, local scholarly attention has moved on to *damunwhagobugaldeng* (e.g., Kong, E., 2009; Seong, et al., 2012). Furthermore, much curious native Koreans are watching television shows and documentaries about the country's late modern version of *gobugwangye* between foreign brides and their Korean mothers-in-law.[22] With all such relational complexities and cultural antinomies, most of foreign brides and their spouses and children are not necessarily unhappier than their counterparts of between-native marriage (Chang, K., 2018; KWDI, 2016). It is yet to be clarified if such positive sentiment reflects decent objective realities or their modest life view based upon earlier experienced destitute and hardship.

The above-explained role transfer between native Korean women and foreign brides in the social reproduction of (neo)traditional rural families is directly contradicted by the already routinized usage of the term "multicultural". In South Korea as a supposed multicultural society, there exist the respective binary categories of "multicultural family" versus ordinary (Korean) family; of "multicultural bride" versus ordinary (Korean) bride; of "multicultural child and youth" versus ordinary (Korean) child and youth, and so forth. Not infrequently, all these multicultural categories of persons are derogatorily simplified as "multiculturals", making South Korea a society composed of ordinary (reads native) Koreans and multiculturals.[23] As the notion of "multicultural" has frequently been abused to segregatively denote marriage migrants and their mixed-blood children, there is an increasing antipathy among these "multicultural" subjects and their sympathizers against the arbitrary linguistic order of discriminatory multiculturalism. (see Photo 2, showing children protesting the linguistic abuse of "multicultural" at a staged event.) Such linguistic practice allows native South Koreans to remain socioculturally unchanged in entering their nation's enthusiastically declared multicultural or cosmopolitan era. The physical presence of foreign brides as human embodiment of permanently frozen and repeatedly staged ethnocultural differences is considered as a sufficient condition for such new era.[24] This social ethos has frequently been capitalized on

Photo 2 Children shouting, "Let us do away with the word, "multicultural"!" (Source *Free Mouth Paper*)

by international matchmaking agencies that cunningly attempt to project racist images and perceptions about foreign brides as useful commodities (Kim, H., 2014; see Photo 3).

Another, no less crucial, contradiction consists in the formalized exclusion of foreign guest workers, most of them being men, from the government programs and public campaigns of multiculturalization. Under the official term of "the multicultural family support policy" (*damunhwagajokjiwonjeongchaek*), foreign guest workers are not categorized as related policy subjects and remain ineligible for related social benefits and services. Not unrelatedly, they have been disallowed from inviting their family members to live together in South Korea. In fact, this group of late modern members of South Korean society has a longer history of wide presence, particularly under the country's aggressive drive of economic globalization since the late 1990s in the wake of the Asian

Photo 3 Vietnam students in South Korea protesting against international marriage brokers' racist and sex-selling practices and South Korean society's neglect (Source *Yonhapnews*, 17 February 2012)

financial crisis (Seol, D., 2014). Their exclusion from being recognized as "multicultural" subjects is in no sense a cultural affair. It reflects a flatly instrumental consideration that their industrial labor mostly at sweatshop factories does not require a permanent stay (Seol, D., 2002). By contrast, "multicultural" brides' labor in the social reproduction of neotraditional Korean families—spousal union, childbirth and childrearing, and even filial services for aged parents-in-law—cannot but require them to become permanent members of South Korean society. A sort of *particularistic neoliberalism* has governed the country's changing immigration policy in mobilizing foreign human resources for industrial production and familial social reproduction.

5 Discussion: The Neoliberal Hospice State, Disguised Cultural Citizenship, and Peasant Social Citizenship

South Koreans' postcolonial neotraditionalization was an epochal incident of popular cultural self-reinvention. Through this incident, grassroots South Koreans came to translate their newly won democratic citizenship into a collective historical nexus to the precolonial Confucian system of sociocultural self-governance. None of the post-independence governments, whether conservative or progressive, or whether authoritarian or liberal, have dared to deny or liquidate the ad hoc cultural self-citizenship of all South Koreans. However, the Park Chung-Hee government paid a special attention to the mixed instrumentalities of grassroots familial neotraditionalism—namely, sociocultural stability, familial material self-protection, wastefulness of Confucian rituals, misuse of women's labor, and so forth. The developmentalist government under Park ended up formally ratifying its citizens' neotraditional cultural (self-)citizenship while carefully moderating Confucian familial rituals into reasonably frugal forms and sustaining the universal familialization of its citizens' material support and care with Confucian norms. In a sense, grassroots South Koreans traded their social citizenship for an ad hoc cultural self-citizenship. This arrangement, particularly in rural areas, was widely resented by women because of their asymmetrical sacrifices and contributions for the neotraditional social reproduction of families, most of which were even rapidly growing in size and complexity. In a widespread *liberal* reaction to their current and/or prospective hardship in rural life, most of young women have opted to head to urban places, leaving villages devoid of women in marriageable ages. Of course, even a majority of young men have also moved to cities for work and/or education, except those few who have reluctantly or willingly succeeded their parents' farms, while thereby risking their marriage prospect.

As many of them have ended up marrying foreign brides since the mid-2000s, the South Korean state and society have coalesced to invent another ad hoc cultural citizenship of "multiculturalism". This late modern citizenship has seemingly been conferred on foreign brides in terms of various paternalistic assistances and benefits under the loud welcoming of their home-country cultural traits. However, the hidden desire of South Korean society consists in its strategic cultural self-reinvention into a supposedly multicultural or cosmopolitan entity— multicultural in terms of South Koreans' physical coexistence with foreign bodies with permanently frozen and repeatedly staged ethnocultural diversities. By inventing various new binary categories of "multicultural" subjects versus ordinary (native) Koreans, South Korean society has very conveniently characterized itself as "multicultural" without asking its native citizens to socioculturally transform themselves.

More fundamentally, the loudly publicized notion of *multicultural citizenship* more hides than reveals most foreign brides' everyday conditions of life and work, particularly in rural families. In a great paradox, foreign brides usually live far more Korean (neo)traditional types of family life than their native Korean counterparts by whom rural families have been deserted. This situation has been clearly shown time and again in a series of comprehensive public surveys and many individual studies. The simple fact is that what has been mobilized from poor Asian countries is not so much the cultural attributes of foreign brides as the *material instrumentalities of their gender as women* in coping with the wide meltdown of rural families' (neotraditional) social reproduction. In a sense, the neoliberalized developmental state's latest policy stance of dumping domestic agriculture in exchange for augmented overseas markets for industrial products has been accompanied by a hidden *hospice* regime of rural policy under which foreign brides have functioned to significantly slow down and ease the organizational dissolution of rural families. At the societal level, foreign brides' sudden and massive arrival in South Korea could be characterized as a sort of socioeconomic hospice migration.

CHAPTER 9

Risk Citizenship in Complex Risk Society

1 Introduction: Transformative Risk Citizenship in Perspective

Numerous South Koreans have angrily told their society that they would leave away forever because of the unbearable traumas from personally experienced yet socially endemic complex accidents and disasters. Many have actually left, with their preferred destinations being such immigrant-welcoming and seemingly safe societies as New Zealand, Canada, and so forth. Most of those who remain behind in a complex risk society like South Korea tend to lead their everyday lives with extreme cautions about probable risks and threats in various aspects—namely, preferring to live in crime-secure high-rise apartments, purchase foodstuff from brand franchise stores, use large passenger cars, take medicine and visit physicians as often as possible, and so on. On the other hand, many South Koreans frequently offer cynical glances and opinions about social, environmental, and other risky conditions in their supergiant neighbor country, the People's Republic of China. Sometimes South Korean media proudly carry reports on Chinese people's love of South Korean-brand consumer goods—not to mention South Korean music and drama—in a great part due to their supposed safety and trustability.

© The Author(s), under exclusive license to Springer Nature Switzerland AG 2022
Chang K-S, *Transformative Citizenship in South Korea*, International Political Economy Series, https://doi.org/10.1007/978-3-030-87690-6_9

These contradictory feelings between the two complexly risk-prone societies are not unrelated with their common, globally envied fast development and wide prosperity. They are a sort of developmental risk societies, albeit with much proud outcomes. South Koreans' personal and public anger generated from widespread physical dangers, accidents, and disasters reflect not so much some probable technoscientific, industrial, and/or institutional backwardness in risk management as the repeatedly revealed reality of intentionally, strategically, and/or cunningly opting to neglect, ignore, or even utilize risky conditions in social, industrial, and administrative activities. The nation as a whole may develop more rapidly and diversely in that way, but the profits (or prizes) and costs (or sacrifices) from such risks are very unevenly distributed, adding to vast social inequalities embedded in the already disequalizing system of a state capitalist political economy. In other words, while South Korean citizens may feel that endemically risk-ridden conditions of public and personal life are socially unavoidable and even developmentally instrumental or contributory, their apparently uneven and unfair subjection to such worrisome conditions frequently infuriate them as a fundamental breaching of their (social and other) citizenship rights.

It is necessary to adopt the notion of *risk citizenship* and elaborate on its practical (and possibly theoretical) characteristics in sociopolitical and other domains if we are to understand the unique (but perhaps not unprecedented) nature of such risk-accommodative political economies as South Korea, China, etc.[1] Broadly speaking, risk citizenship in such complex risk societies should encompass: first of all, simultaneously as social citizenship, effective protection of all citizens from almost normally generated multifarious and ubiquitous risks, dangers, and hazards; second, reasonable remuneration or reward for any identifiable transformative contributory risks and concomitant hazards, accidents, and disasters; and third, acceptable or fair allocation of access to transformative contributory risks with presumably satisfactory compensation. Where risks are perceived, diagnosed, commanded, praised, and rewarded in terms of their probable or supposed transformative contributory quality, they cannot simply be prevented, avoided, minimized, or hedged in personal, familial, communal, industrial, and governmental activities. Where whatever transformative contributory risks are detected or promoted, we should explore their citizenship implications.

2 SOUTH KOREA AS COMPLEX RISK SOCIETY

From the early 1990s, South Koreans were celebrating their historical achievements in rapid economic development and robust political democratization amid the praise and envy of other late developing or modernizing nations. This was symbolized by the country's acceptance to the OECD in 1996. Paradoxically, a host of unprecedented physical disasters and accidents began to break out then, including the collapse of a huge bridge over Han River and a mammoth department store in Seoul, the subway station fires in Seoul and Daegu, and so forth (see Photo 1). Each of these incidents claimed tens or hundreds of innocent lives. In media coverage and social commentaries, these shocking accidents were instantly juxtaposed with the country's shameful records of industrial and traffic accidents at some of the world's highest levels as well as recurrent man-caused ecological disasters.

As citizen safety was subjected to nearly indiscriminate threats, the Western discussions on "risk society" as led by German sociologist Ulrich

Photo 1 The collapse of Sampoong Department Store, 29 June 1995 (*Source Yonhapnews*, 29 June 1996)

Beck attracted an immediate attention of South Korean academics and experts. Behind the material affluence accompanying sustained rapid industrialization and economic growth—namely, "compressed development" that enabled the country to catch up with the West in economic terms—the unwelcome phenomenon of the routinization of widespread accidents and disasters came along. Western societies have also faced enormous costs of risk as a result of their development, for instance, from nuclear power-related accidents to the hazards of GM foods. In Ulrich Beck's (1992) observation, extending his theory of "reflexive modernization," these accidents and disasters are not accidental events but rather routinized aspects of daily life under advanced industrial capitalism.

South Korea's economic development has also subjected the country to such symptoms of an advanced risk society, in particular, including high-intensity industrial disasters at the supposedly advanced production lines of global leader enterprises. However, most of the aforementioned incidents of disasters and accidents were not necessarily classifiable as symptoms of an advanced risk society. For instance, lack of rudimentary safety management has led to continuous instances of a sort of backward society-type disasters and accidents. During the monsoon season, due to obvious neglect or failure in basic preventive measures, many towns have been submerged underwater and many villages buried in dirt from landslides. Across the country, what are cynically called "death roads"—poorly built roads left unmonitored or undermanaged—keep claiming human lives incessantly. In addition, South Koreans have been inflicted by a wide range of slapdash, or faultily rushed, society-type catastrophes, including the collapse of shoddily constructed buildings and infrastructures whose workmanship reveals commonplace irregularities and deviations. Furthermore, the country is also a compressive risk society in that the compressed paces and scopes in production, construction, consumption, and movement are inevitably accompanied by no less compressed extents of physical risks in safety.

The particular manners and intensities of South Korea's compressed economic development and social change have made the country become a risk society with correspondingly particular characteristics. South Korea can be defined as a *complex risk society* in which various risk factors and symptoms of developed, un(der)developed, slapdash, and compressive societies are present simultaneously and interactively. In the following, various qualities and tendencies in South Korea as advanced, backward, compressive, and slapdash risk society are briefly explained.

Advanced vs. Backward Risk Society Ranging from nuclear energy to bio-engineering, South Koreans have shown a sort of *high-tech fetishism*. News media so frequently carry, with loud headlines for urging the public to celebrate nationally, stories of South Korean companies and researchers making significant new technologies and scientific discoveries. Besides, South Korean industrialists and technocrats are quite liberal in spending money to learn and borrow new foreign technologies. Their economy and society seem to be operating under the extensive use of high-efficiency— and, for that matter, high-risk—technologies. South Koreans' success in compressively achieving many aspects of an advanced industrial civilization warrants that risk concerns presented by Ulrich Beck (1992), Charles Perrow (1984), and other scholars are also meaningfully applicable to the South Korean situation. Ceaseless incidents of high-tech disasters such as nuclear leakage, chemical and metal poisoning, biomedical mistreatment, and electronic and digital hazards remind that South Koreans cannot avoid the costs of the high-efficiency, high-risk industrial civilization while only enjoying its benefits. This is particularly so because many of the utilized theories and technologies are borrowed from the West without sufficient knowledge and information concerning their internal scientific reliability and contextual relevance.

On the other hand, unbalanced development is not only an economic theory (Hirschman, 1958) but also has been a core mandate in South Korean development. Significant imbalances have been pronounced between industrial and agricultural sectors, between material and cultural development, between economic growth and welfare provision, between physical development and environmental conservation, and, not least importantly, between production/consumption expansion and safety promotion. Such imbalances imply that South Korean society remains much un(der)developed in various noneconomic aspects. A brief survey of frequent physical accidents in South Korea immediately reveals that this society suffers from many symptoms of an un(der)developed risk society— namely, chaotic cross-sections without proper norms, regulations, and facilities for guiding traffic; supergiantic buildings of all purposes lacking proper facilities, regulations, and/or daily cautions for fire prevention, dangerous construction and public work sites exposed to passers-by without due cautions or barricades; home and industrial energies (in particular, various types of gas) supplied and used with lax observance of safety regulations; rivers and shores unprotected from organic wastes, chemicals, plastics, and so on.[2] Due to these (and other) factors, South

Korea still remains one of quite risky societies in terms of physical accidents and accident-caused casualties.

Compressive Risk Society To contemporary South Koreans, their society is particularly problematic as a slapdash and compressive risk society. Compressive society-type risks stem from the enormous economic and social changes South Korea has undergone in a remarkably short period of time. As indicated by Krugman (1994), rapid economic growth in Asia has been achieved in large part by intensifying the mobilization (or exploitation) of labor and natural resources instead of improving the efficiency and safety of the production processes, ushering in a rapid increase in disasters and pollution. South Korea's rapid development has been manifested in terms of explosive growth in human activities of production, construction, consumption, and movement which in turn has been accompanied by no less explosive growth in risk factors and experiences. The costs of compressive risk society do not end here. There are dangers attending upon the rapid and ceaseless changes in industrial structures and technologies and public lifestyles. These changes are usually considered as upgrading or progress, but the particular nature and pace of such changes, if undermanaged or mismanaged, can bring about various problematic consequences. The growth of South Korea's national economy and businesses has been a result of continuous diversification and upgrading of its industrial structure, and the change to citizens' lives has been characterized by compulsively ceaseless exposure to unfamiliar lifestyles. This has placed South Koreans in the perpetual status of "novice" or "learner" during which accidents tend to concentrate. Moreover, while new production technologies and goods may outshine the old in terms of efficiency and utility, they are often much riskier if handled improperly. The dilemma of remaining a perpetual novice or learner is shared by both the general public and the respective expert groups.

Slapdash Risk Society South Korea's publicly promoted processes of rapid economic growth and social modernization have helped formed a unique culture of *speed efficiency*—measuring the effectiveness of economic and social activities in terms of time taken. This culture has spawned rampant practices of corporate, governmental, and civil irresponsibility as to public safety, thereby making South Korea a slapdash risk society. On the national political level, whenever the ruling government sets forth a major policy goal—be it economic growth, infrastructure construction, crime control, or else—there is a keen interest in accomplishing it in a shortest time possible and presenting such speedy accomplishment as evidence of a superior government.[3] On the corporate level, in response to the explosive economic growth and industrial restructuring, a corporate growth strategy of completing each business project as early as possible and moving into the next, more profitable projects has prevailed. Such governmental and corporate obsession with speed efficiency has resulted in the collusive aggravation of safety in production lines, construction sites, public spaces, and infrastructures, as well as consumer lives. It has repeatedly been revealed that the government, far from enforcing strict rules, has tried to accomplish its national developmental goals by tacitly encouraging private enterprises and public agencies to run at "full" operational speed even if it would mean breaking safety regulations. The business community has had no qualms in complying because it would imply quicker profits. In a sense, the developmental state's obstinate policy line of "growth first, distribution later" has had a corresponding, albeit tacit, policy line of *growth first, safety later*, intensifying symptoms of a slapdash risk society.

3 Transformative Contributory Risks and Social Inequalities

South Koreans' subjection to multifarious risks, dangers, and threats are reasonably expectable from their country's multi-front, expeditious transformations and their personal, communal, and organizational lives situated in such transformations. Unless South Korea had pursued an exceptionally risk-averse line of developmental, institutional, and civilizational progresses, its citizens would not have been exempted from normally contingent risks from all modern activities. However, a systematic probing into the structural nature of South Korea as complex risk society leads to a revelation that virtually all categories of risks have practically reflected the pragmatic, strategic, and/or urgent efforts to expedite and aggrandize developmental, institutional, and/or civilizational purposes and utilities in the nation's particular historical and international contexts.

Those risks normally associated with a Beckian advanced society have been heavily amplified amid South Korea's brave endeavor for technoscientifically and industrially catching up with the West, often by arbitrarily compromising risk-assessment/management principles. Many of those backward society risks have not necessarily been attributable to South Korea's possible technoscientific, organizational, and/or other backwardness, but pragmatically (?) neglected or even extended in order to developmentally (and sometime politically) concentrate in certain strategic sectors and areas under the premise (if not a pretext) of "unbalanced growth," or by the above-noted tactic of *growth first, safety later* (corresponding to the Park Chung-Hee government's open developmentalist policy of "growth first, distribution later"). Most of those compressive society risks are simply taken for granted and accustomed to as South Korea's phenomenal success in temporal abridgement and growth maximization in development and modernization has resulted from a sort of national existential paradigm in the extremely turbulent postcolonial and post-Korean War era. Those slapdash society risks have practically been manufactured under the specific developmental, institutional, and civilizational purposes and utilities that are narrowly, exclusionarily, and/or shortly decided, defined, or improvised by the often opportunistic yet dominant political, corporate, and/or personal interests.

As these diverse risks are seen and accommodated in terms of various transformative functions, those citizens, communities, and organizations otherwise liable for or knowingly scarified by them are often praised and rewarded in risk-reflective citizenship. To begin with, a sort of national fetishism prevails in glorifying those experts with some supposed scientific, technological, and/or industrial achievements (particularly in catching up with the West), at whatever risks would be revealed later on.[4] Many of those managers, workers, farmers, researchers, and local residents who have bravely overcome or sacrificially endure dangerous outmoded conditions in carrying out either prioritized or neglected yet essential functions have been offered to be praised as indispensable national, industrial, or organizational heroes under their tacit acceptance (or forced excuse) of such otherwise problematic dangers. Those hard-working South Koreans—with the world's longest hours and/or incomparable intensity in work, study, human care, and so forth (see Chapters 4 and 6 in this book)—have been portrayed domestically and internationally as model citizens of South Korea's miraculously compressive economic and other marches. Those South Koreans who have cooperated or contributed in executing overambitiously targeted and often irregular or illegal activities and operations (without regulatorily or legally challenging them) have been preferentially given stable employment, positional promotion, extra wage or revenue, and so forth, on top of inner-circle honors and influences. In these diverse recognitions of transformative contributory risks, both formal arenas and personal spheres have been inundated by political, organizational, and private discourses on transformative risk citizenship.[5]

As South Korea as complex risk society is still driven forward under the premise of multifarious risk citizenship, its citizens are intensely sensitive to risk-based social inequalities. First, as consumer citizens, they have, one the one hand, manifested conspicuously risk-averse patterns of consumption, indulging in high-rise apartment homes, large passenger cars, high-intensity drugs, habitual hospital visits, etc., and, on the other hand, expressed particularly strong social anger when unable to fulfill such patterns of consumption.[6] South Korea's worsening social bipolarity critically intensifies such anger. Second, those individuals with weaknesses in educational credential, occupational knowledge, industrial skill, and/or even legal residential status have had to accept risk exposure as a compensatory leverage in economic participation—as exemplified by the so-called 3D (dirty, difficulty, dangerous) jobs predominantly occupied by undereducated, less trained/skilled, less experienced, and/or non-Korean workers, who are already under disproportionate alienation and destitute.[7] Third, the frequent (or even usual) inconsistencies between risk-generators/profiteers and risk-receivers/victims tend to constitute crucial and even increasing parts of South Korea's social inequalities, often under the strategic, yet unfair or irregular, intervention of the developmental and/or plutocratic state, as exemplified in labor disputes, environmental damages, product hazards, and so forth.[8] (This line of inequality in risk citizenship then also breaches the very basic liberal principle in legal citizenship, namely, all citizens' equality before the law.) Fourth, the developmental state has been asymmetrically protective of corporate risks (vis-à-vis workers', farmers', consumers', and local residents' risks) practically as a sort of *industrial policy*.[9] This practice is in direct contrast to the welfare state's protection of the latter groups' livelihood risks through various social security programs. Apparently, these risk-based inequalities assume a much more problematic sociopolitical nature than sheer material inequalities of an ordinary capitalist system.[10]

4 Risk Citizenship, Risk Democracy

4.1 The State-Business-Expert Developmentalist Collusion in Risk Management

In Middle East and South East Asia, South Korean construction companies have built so many buildings and infrastructure facilities with the world's largest sizes and most complicated technologies.[11] The durability and safety of these physical structures are fully satisfactory by any rigorous international standards. One big irony in this regard is that the same South Korean companies have been responsible for so many defective and fraudulent construction projects within South Korea which sometimes claim tens or hundreds of people's lives as well as enormous property losses. It is more often moral, ideological, and/or political failure than technological backwardness that once created and kept an "accident republic" in the southern part of the Korean peninsular.

In order to achieve economic growth at highest rates imaginable, South Koreans have suppressed, neglected, and ignored various requirements which are necessary for socially, ecologically, physically, as well as economically sustainable development. For instance, under the ideology of "growth first, distribution later," the South Korean government used to intentionally neglect social security measures and instead poured most of the public financial resources in economic development projects and for corporate industrial subsidies. The potential risk of such welfare-suppressive development strategy was not difficult to comprehend, but the successive administrations adamantly maintained it (Chang, K., 2019; also see Chapter 5 in this book). Only after the "IMF economic crisis" in 1997 broke out to create massive unemployment and poverty, technocrats, politicians, and even business leaders began to discuss the urgent need to establish a comprehensive "social safety net" (Chang, K., 2019). It was of course all too late. The same developmentalist doctrine has also been responsible for a hidden or implicit policy of *growth first, safety later* among public officials in carrying out administrative activities and supervising private economic activities. In order to help produce larger volumes of product, fulfill economic growth and construction targets within shorter periods, and sometimes receive bribes, public officials have neglected, ignored, and negotiated risk regulations. The potential cost of such risk-neglective development strategy was even easier to comprehend, but it did not constitute even a serious topic for public discourse until the time of "big collapses" in the mid-1990s.

Perhaps by minimizing governmental and corporate expenses on safety matters, more resources could have been mobilized to maximize inputs for production and thereby achieve maximum economic growth. This may have comprised a significant part of what Paul Krugman (1994) calls "input-driven" economic growth. It is also an important, though hidden, dimension of the state-business alliance for the South Korean developmental drive. When severe accidents and disasters broke out due to obvious violations of risk regulations, killing and injuring so many people, neither corporate personnel nor administrative supervisors received fully accountable punishments. This outraged injured and bereaved individuals inevitably, but their protest rarely changed the seemingly deplorable situation. Safety-breaching has been considered as what everyone is guilty of and what makes the economic growth system functioning. In fact, strict safety-keeping (risk prevention)—under the slogan of "*junbeoptujaeng*" (law-abiding struggle)—has become one of the most powerful forms of labor protest in many industries where workers are ordinarily forced to break safety principles and regulations supposedly for the sake of higher organizational efficiency or industrial productivity.[12] In this context, many risk elements of preindustrial years have remained uncorrected, new high-risk technologies and industries have been brought in without due attention and preparation concerning safety matters, and explosive increases in risk-prone activities have been left unchecked. More recently, democratic social pressure for reforms in risk assessment and management has been resisted or bypassed by business under the neoliberally driven "deregulation" (*gyujegaehyeok*) in the state's supervision over corporate activities.

What have those professionals and experts specialized in risk assessment and safety enforcement done? To one's dismay, these specialist groups have rarely challenged the safety-suppressive government-business developmental alliance. On the one hand, they have lacked sufficient organized political or social power to resist the hegemonic state-business coalition. More crucially, however, they have seldom showed such intellectual will or devotion as to lead South Korea into a meaningfully risk-free society. Instead, they have often cunningly adapted to the given politico-legal culture and industrial market structures and thereby reaped bountiful rents in terms of bribe for willful connivance, generous compensation for lax work, and profits from monopoly expert service. In this respect, the social success of the supposed risk specialists has often required not only technoscientific capacity in practicing the concerned expertise but also political economic knack in adapting to the dominant developmentalist order.[13] In this respect, broadly in line with his analysis of Western societies, Ulrich Beck could have called South Korea a *developmental risk society* (vis-à-vis "risk society" in his pioneering work).

The list of publicly known foul instances is endless (Lim, et al., eds., 1998): The collapse of Sampoong Department Store was crucially associated with the irresponsible and incapable architectural professionals whose duties in building design, construction supervision, and safety control were negotiated for profit and bribe; the breakdown of the Seongsu Grand Bridge was predestined under the collusive neglect of safety regulations by technocratic regulators, corporate construction managers, and professional safety supervisors; numerous private contractors of the environmental impact evaluation of various public construction projects were disclosed to have copied each other, practically presented replica (after reordering the same contents), and even borrowed other people's licenses; the safety certification of gas containers has been habitually fabricated by private inspection contractors whose leniency toward container manufacturers leads to higher numbers of inspected containers and thus to larger amounts of service profit; many fatal side-effects of chemical drugs have often been concealed intentionally amid the dispute over legal responsibility between physicians and drug manufactures; and subway workers and bus drivers would not mind routinely ignoring a series of obligatory safety measures with all their aggressive confrontations with employers for wage negotiation under *junbeoptujaeng* (law-abiding struggle).[14]

One area in which they do show some social and political efficacy is the lobbying and protest against governmental attempts and civil social pressure to reform the rigid monopolistic markets of risk-expertise. The increased issuing of licenses, the increase of expert training institutions, the opening of markets to other specialists performing comparable functions, and the establishment of alternative expert systems have always been met by staunch resistance of such specialist groups. For some reason, even the authoritarian political regimes were quite lenient in dealing with these skirmishes for immediate material interest—what are popularly called *bapgeureut ssaum* (rice bowl fight). Perhaps such leniency has been the core condition for incorporating these specialist groups into the developmental alliance, in which licensed experts and professionals trade their conscience and knowledge for comfortable and affluent life.

South Korea's dramatic (re)democratization in the late 1980s not only allowed its citizens to recover their formal political citizenship but also enabled them to courageously and often successfully fight for their asymmetrically sacrificed socioeconomic rights. In this context, the procedurally democratized state began to assume sociopolitical neutrality in regulating social, industrial, infrastructural, environmental, and other risks, thereby removing developmentalist (and sometimes plutocratic) privileges and excuses from corporate and specialist activities in risk affairs. Before long, however, neoliberalism entered South Korea as a sort of counter-democratic paradigm of the sociopolitically threatened developmentalist alliance in coping with subaltern or progressive pressures for socioeconomic reform (Chang, K., 2012b, 2019). The threatened yet still hegemonic bloc managed to reinvent neoliberalism into a business-led neodevelopmental approach in which all-front deregulation became a supposed panacea for whatever economic obstacles and impediments existed in the nation.[15] In risk affairs, the political economic utility of technoscientific experts and licensed specialists has been significantly yet ironically reinforced in actualizing deregulation in corporate and other private activities.[16] For this and other reasons, South Korea's structural nature as a complex risk society has remained or even become more complicated in the twenty-first century.

4.2 Grassroots Citizenship in Risk Democracy

When the failure in technocratic, corporate, and specialist capacity and accountability in risk assessment and management is made obvious simply by so many accidents, disasters, and hazards, grassroots citizens' effort at self-protection is indispensable. Their missions must include not only doing what technocrats, industrialists, and technoscientific specialists have failed to do but also undoing what these elite groups have harmfully caused. The latter mission requires grassroots citizens' thorough understanding and close supervision of the technocratic-corporate-specialist complex of risk construction and deconstruction, on the one hand, and their presentation of alternative modes of risk assessment and safety enforcement. Both missions require grassroots citizens' effectively and knowleably organized collective actions as well as their ideological and moral commitment to democratic risk management. South Korea's (revived) democracy since the late 1980s, despite its remaining institutional defects and political circumstantial tribulations, has helped to strengthen such civil efforts and attitudes by rapidly increasing citizens and social organizations.

To be a dignified citizen in this complex risk society is an overwhelming challenge. However, can grassroots South Koreans' pain and anger from so many horrifying incidents of physical collapse, collision, explosion, pollution, contamination, and poisoning generate a significant impetus for civil social contestation against the rulers and profiteers of the "accident republic"? As South Koreans themselves acknowledge, they have been so forgetful that all such accidents, disasters, and hazards have rarely been brought back into serious social debate and responsible political discussion. Even at the times of shocking accidents—not to mention in daily experiences of hazardous physical, environmental, and other conditions—chaos and confusion often drive them into extremely egoist, and ultimately self-abusive, responses.[17] Mutually hostile competition and opportunism in risk aversion, instead of collective social and political pressure on risk generators, tend to prevail among grassroots citizens. Moreover, the repeated economic depressions—in particular, the "IMF economic crisis" in 1997—has kept most South Koreans preoccupied with immediate economic concerns such as unemployment, income reduction, and poverty, whose alleviation supposedly requires immediate macroeconomic recovery (Chang, K., 2019). Perhaps it is not a small possibility that the pressure for sheer material survival, particularly under the increasing bipolarity in income and asset, may once again induce South Koreans to sacrifice physical safety and other social concerns for the sake of immediate pecuniary gains.

Nonetheless, under the interestingly combined conditions of the nation's (re)democratization and all citizens' common trauma from chronically experienced accidents, disasters, and hazards, South Koreans' risk citizenship has taken a meaningful turn in the new century. Grassroots South Korean citizens, with useful help from expert intellectuals and social movement organizations, have strived, not altogether unsuccessfully, to establish three lines of efficacious reflexivity in democratic risk citizenship.[18] First, they have realized that they are pitted against each other for physical survival while the rulers and profiteers of this complex risk society are effectively shielded from them by complicated technocratic, corporate, and technoscientific apparatuses, as dramatically and tragically evinced in the Sewol Ferry incident (Suh and Kim, eds., 2017) as well as so many other mostly man-made disasters. Unfortunately, their moral decay is not yet fully overcome—for instance, on streets where traffic rules are poorly kept and accidents so often lead to lies and fights. A sort of *moral self-reflexivity* concerning their misguided understanding of and responses to various risk factors is indispensable and has actually been ameliorating so that a right target for civil social struggle is to be set for the sake of justice in risk management. Second, they have acknowledged the need to organize themselves systematically for various lines of collective action against the risk tyrannies of the state-business-specialist coalition. Grassroots citizens' sociopolitical consciousness, or *democratic reflexivity*, is prerequisite for effective self-protection, as has been duly acknowledged in various organized civilian efforts for public safety promotion.[19] Finally, as Beck (1992) also emphasizes, they have tried to establish the capacity to monitor the failure and conspiracy in technocratic, corporate, and specialist practices and present alternative (and, of course, better) modes of risk assessment and safety enforcement. Applying Beck's terminology, it may be called (social) *reflexivity of* (technocratic, corporate, and specialist) *reflexivity*, or *double reflexivity*. Perhaps this cause demands the initiative from socially based (i.e., detached from technocratic, corporate, and specialist interests) intellectuals, but the wisdom and insight embedded in grassroots citizens' everyday life should be, and have often been, tapped actively.

5 Discussion: Risk Citizenship in the Pandemic Era—From Finance to Coronavirus

By March 2020, South Korea had become the second most devastated country (after China) by what would later be termed COVID-19.[20] In fact, China's political dictatorship enabled itself to contain the epidemic's nationwide spread through the forceful interregional blockade and the virtual home-arrest of Wuhan citizens, whereas democratic South Korea (under the self-proudly democratic government of Moon Jae-In) could not blockade Daegu, the epicenter of the epidemic with the Sincheonji (New World) cult functioning as the breeding ground of the Coronavirus. The Moon government was neither able nor willing to shut down the national border with China, with the peninsula nation so extensively depending on its economic relationships and social interactions with China for sustained national development. (Moon's political foes in the parliament and media loudly attributed South Korea's initial failure in blocking the China-originated virus to his alleged misjudgment and affinity about the socialist Republic.)

Such dilemma was seemingly reminiscent of South Koreans' painful collective experience in late 1997 when the Southeast Asia-originated financial crisis almost instantly engulfed South Korea in spite of all its "sound economic fundamentals" and the state's healthy budgetary conditions. It later turned out that many South Korean banks and firms had been partly responsible for causing the scandalous financial bubbles in Southeast Asia even though they had recklessly welcomed Western financial capital for their own domestic operations and expansions. Both the new Coronavirus and global hot money ended up blanketing the entire world, suffocating humanity in the respective socioecological and financial pandemics. From both pandemics, nevertheless, South Korea arose or recovered brilliantly, drawing praises from foreign state leaders, experts, and media across the world. The IMF's immediate endorsement of the then incumbent President Kim Dae-Jung's performance in managing the national financial and industrial recovery in the late 1990s led him to be (derogatorily) called "the IMF's man in Seoul" (Cumings, 1998), whereas in the latest G7+ meeting in the UK, South Korean president, Moon Jae-In was honorably congratulated by Western leaders for most successfully controlling the Coronavirus and thereby minimizing socioeconomic damages.

As emphatically argued by Ulrich Beck (1999, 2009), overcoming or surviving such (globalized) pandemics in finance, virus, air/water pollution, global warming, digital anarchy, and countless yet-to-come existential risks will be all humanity's everyday key concern. South Korea, of course, shares responsibilities, burdens, and damages regarding all such pandemic risks whether or not it would outshine other nations in coping with and even benefitting from them. However, South Korea has entered this omni-pandemic era without clearly or effectively overcoming its earlier burdens as an incomparably complex risk society. Thus, new-era pandemic risks are being stacked up upon the earlier-explained diverse risks accumulated through its successful, though unstable, economic, and social progresses. Relatedly, socioeconomic inequalities and instabilities engendered by both complex national risks themselves and political, corporate, and social manners in risk management are now coalesced with and aggravated by the globally shared threats and dangers of omni-pandemics.

In fact, South Korea's seemingly effective control of both the national financial crisis in the late 1990s and the recent Coronavirus crisis have not fundamentally differed from its earlier experiences and manners in which risk citizenship was sociopolitically constructed and popularly instrumentalized and even abused. Above all, beneath South Korea's globally admired success in controlling COVID-19, those groups who have most critically devastated in the earlier national financial crisis and concomitant neoliberal restructuring—namely, precarious workers, self-employed persons, un(der)employed youth, and so forth—are now struggling even more badly than during the financial crisis (Cho, M., 2020), whereas *chaebol* firms in main export industries and increasingly monopolistic commerce have rather enlarged their market shares and sheer revenues and profits, making Moon Jae-In proudly declare—quoting abundant official statistics from the IMF, the OECD, etc.—that the South Korean economy has been most successfully protected. At least in many recent domestic social surveys, however, ordinary citizens in increasing numbers do not seem to share Moon's such self-congratulatory appraisal in socioeconomic affairs and gradually veer toward opposition politicians for possible rescue measures.[21]

PART III

Whither Post-Transformative Citizenship

CHAPTER 10

Transformative Citizenship, Transformative Victimhood

1   Transformative Citizenship vis-à-vis Transformative Victimhood

> Making of 'a society that can be sustained even without economic growth' is a must. The present has become an era that cannot endure the lack of growth or change, but it is necessary to create a society that remains fine without development. (Karatani Kojin, in a New Year interview with *Kyunghyang Daily*, 7 January 2013)

Although the above advice by Karatani Kojin, a globally distinguished progressive liberal intellectual of Japan, is not necessarily confined to South Korea, its appeal may be particularly strong among those South Koreans who have opposed and criticized their country's extremely hasty, obsessive, and often unphilosophic pursuit of continual national and societal transformations and various problematic costs and consequences accompanying such transformations. However, a societal change into post-transformative society constitutes still another transformation that must be much more challenging than any of the previous ones because of the structurally established transformative order of contemporary South Korean society.

Since the mid-twentieth century, postcolonial war-devastated South Korea has kept impressing the world and even themselves by aggressively and precipitously carrying out institutional and technoscientific modernization, economic development, political democratization, economic and sociocultural globalization, and, mostly recently, ethnonational reformation. While each of these transformations is rather a generic experience in postcolonial societies, South Korea's impulsively proactive pursuit of them has induced the country to become a fixatedly transformative social entity. From this transformative modernity have arisen the transformation-oriented state, society, and population for which each transformation becomes an ultimate purpose in itself, the processes and means of the transformations constitute the main sociopolitical order, and the transformation-embedded interests form the core social identity. Reflecting these historical conditions, a distinct mode of citizenship has arisen in terms of *transformative contributory rights*—namely, effective and/or legitimate claims to national and social resources, opportunities, and/or respects that accrue to each citizen's contributions to the nation's or society's transformative purposes.

By the early twenty-first century, however, it has painfully turned out that the citizenship regime of transformative contributory rights, despite its apparent effectiveness in generating and accelerating successive societal and national transformations, has a fatal problem of structurally and precipitously engendering *transformative victims*, in numbers and extents that are no less conspicuous than those for transformative beneficiaries. There have been structural victims not only inherent in the substantive nature of each transformation (e.g., traditionalists and nativists in West-dependent modernization, peasants in urban-centered capitalist industrialization, local interests and communal agents in neoliberal globalization, and so forth) but also embedded in the impulsive, excessive, and violent manners of pursuing the transformations (i.e., students in cramming educational institutions, workers controlled and abused by the authoritarian developmental state, women abused at home and work under patriarchalized capitalism, foreign workers and brides maltreated respectively by opportunistic employers and in-laws, and so forth).[1] In fact, given the unevenly developmental and selectively democratic nature of South Korea's postcolonial capitalist modernization, virtually every category of transformative citizenship has been accompanied by the transformative victimhood of certain social groups.

In what follows, let us examine what transformative victims have been generated under the transformative citizenship regime in each socioeconomic domain, covered, respectively, in Chapters 4–8 of this book.

Developmental citizenship and its transformative victims As already indicated in Chapter 4, developmental citizenship has an inherent problem of disenfranchising those citizens without productive assets and capabilities—i.e., elderly, children, youth, handicapped, and so forth. Under an economic development-focused polity, these dependent social groups cannot be meaningfully incorporated into the national community, not to mention the national economy. The developmental(ist) state tends to organize even the minimal public measures for social security in tight conjunction with the developmental contribution of each would-be beneficiary group—an extremist application of the Bismarckian social security system. Therefore, many supposedly social democratic institutions in South Korea have rather exaggerated the existing market-linked inequalities. The concentration of poverty among the current elderly and handicapped has been particularly serious because too many of them have been left out of both developmental and social citizenship. Furthermore, in the post-IMF crisis era, the social security-based exaggeration of inequalities encompasses an increasing number of people *with* laboring capacities. Unemployed and underemployed workers in massively increasing numbers have been doubly disadvantaged due to their frequent exclusion from social insurances and services that are mostly attached to regular employment. If developmental citizenship is very narrowly defined in terms of access to a stable job and its concomitant social security benefits, it has become a rare aristocratic privilege enjoyed by a constantly dwindling number of regularly employed workers in public sectors, top-tier industries, and so forth.

Social citizenship and politically expired redistribution South Koreans' stratified and deferred social citizenship, as reflected in the nation's developmental liberalism and its neoliberal degeneration, could not but necessitate two critical conditions if it was to materialize into a universal system of socioeconomic benefits in the long run—namely, sustained long-term economic development and the ultimate realization of redistribution pledges (by the later governments). Unfortunately, neither of these conditions has been realized. The South Korean economy kept literally overheating into the mid-1990s, however, only to stumble into a national financial meltdown and the concomitant radical neoliberal restructuring of industries and labor markets. Politically, for whatever reasons, none of the one-term only governments since the 1980s have identified themselves as an underwriter of Park Chung-Hee's slogan of "growth first, distribution later"—including the one led by his daughter, Park Geun-Hye. This implies that those politically coerced sacrificial terms of industrial and other labor by a majority of the nation's laboring population have never been compensated. What they have held in their hands is a politically expired, if not economically nullified, raincheck of temporally sequenced redistribution. In particular, their retirement from work, mostly without meaningful pensions, has almost automatically placed them in poverty, making the country hugely discomfited at its status of the OECD's worst case of old-age poverty. (Many of them even lost their private savings during the 1997 financial crisis.) No need to mention that most of next-generation workers, as indicated above, could be worse off because of the chronic job market crisis as a routine feature of the radically neoliberalized and globalized economic system.

Educationalized citizenship and its transformative victims South Korea's relative sociopolitical stability is to a critical extent due to the universal legitimacy of the broadly meritocratic education system. In proportion to the extraordinary significance of public education, its rapid developmental, social institutional, political, and cultural transformations have been accompanied by wide inequalities based upon educational credentials. In so far as the national collective utilities of public education have remained unquestioned and all citizens' access to public education has appeared to be *fairly* distributed according to meritocratic competitions (i.e., formal exams), the nation has continued to be a very conveniently governable society. However, at the early stages of postcolonial modernization and development, privately financed tertiary education was not accessible to innumerable citizens simply due to their poverty. Even after most families became able to afford children's tertiary education, the mechanical meritocratic system of educational competition itself has kept devastating a predetermined proportion of youth every year by excluding them from preferred tertiary educational institutions in spite of their commonly excessive preparation of entrance examinations. Most recently, a virtual universalization of tertiary education in tandem with the joblessness of the nation's post-industrial capitalism has aggravated such regularized despair of youth by imposing a frightening prospect of un(der)employment on increasing numbers of them. All these torturous worries and experiences of youth have been shared by their parents as their educational commanders and financiers.

Mobilizational reproductive citizenship and its transformative victims In no doubt, the worst victim of South Korea's incomparably abrupt demographic transition was the innumerable female fetuses illegally aborted under the procreative son preference—or daughter hiatus—of their otherwise would-be parents and/or grandparents. In one of the world's most radical declines in fertility since the mid-1960s, South Koreans' tenacious desire to secure at least one son led to an arbitrary attempt to prevent their would-be daughter(s) from being born. It was not only their patriarchal cultural orientation but, more crucially, also the men-dominant political economic order of South Korean capitalism that rendered so many families to strategically approach their procreative decisions. Even in most of the early 2000s, the nation's sex ratio at birth remained even above 110, a literally extreme level unobservable in other industrialized nations. Paradoxically, it was the nation's total economic crisis and concomitant neoliberal restructuring that came to critically sap South Koreans' son preference in procreation. Under young people's generalized employment crisis, a son is not necessarily more advantageous to a daughter, and rapidly increasing numbers of young married couples now take it for granted to maintain their dual income earning. Young women's suddenly generalized economic participation has made their marriage and fertility much more costly, driving the nation's fertility further downward.

Ad hoc cultural citizenship and its transformative victims Virtually all South Koreans' postcolonial neotraditionalization in family life was certainly a culturally dignifying experience and even got practically certified by the state as a common cultural citizenship. However, in most young women's long-term preference and choice in life, neotraditionally aristocratized but materially meager rural families could not be favorably compared to their possibilities of urban-based work, livelihood, and marriage. Most rural young men have shared many of such reasons and considerations for urban migration. The disproportionate exodus of rural young women has kept driving increasing numbers of rural men into "forced bachelorhood" and their parents into lonely old age. As the neoliberalized developmental state's dumping of agriculture has been intensified in terms of its aggressive free trade deals with the world's major agricultural exporter economies, such despair of rural bachelors and aged parents has been even more aggravated. The sudden yet massive arrival of foreign brides from Vietnam and other poor Asian countries to their rescue has certainly helped to ease various problems and difficulties in the (neotraditional) social reproduction of rural families. But such international marriages do not necessarily help to improve the basic material destitute of rural families. Simply speaking, foreign brides—for all their material aspirations behind a marriage with a supposedly rich country's citizen—land in South Korea to become part of a destitute rural family. The showy yet genuinely paternalistic public campaign of "multiculturalism" falls short of meaningfully changing neither this cold material reality nor the tenacious neotraditional culture in the social reproduction of South Korea's rural families.

Transformative risk citizenship and its victims The particular manners and intensities of South Korea's compressed economic development and social change have engendered a risk society with correspondingly particular risk characteristics. South Koreans' subjection to multifarious risks, dangers, and threats are reasonably expectable from their country's multifront, expeditious transformations and their personal, communal, and organizational lives situated in such transformations. However, a systematic probing into the structural nature of South Korea as complex risk society leads to a revelation that virtually all categories of risks have practically reflected the pragmatic, strategic, and/or urgent efforts to expedite and aggrandize developmental, institutional, and/or civilizational purposes and utilities in the nation's particular historical and international contexts. South Koreans' personal and public anger generated from widespread physical dangers, accidents, and disasters reflect not so much some probable technoscientific, industrial, and/or institutional backwardness in risk management as the repeatedly revealed reality of intentionally, strategically, and/or cunningly opting to neglect, ignore, or even utilize risky conditions in social, industrial, and administrative activities. The nation as a whole may develop more rapidly and diversely in that way, but the profits (or prizes) and costs (or sacrifices) from such risks are very unevenly distributed, adding to vast social inequalities embedded in the already disequalizing system of a state capitalist political economy. Furthermore, South Korea has entered the latest omnipandemic era (involving global financial volatility, borderless pollution of air and water, global warming, Coronavirus, and so forth) without clearly or effectively overcoming its earlier burdens as an incomparably complex risk society. Relatedly, socioeconomic inequalities and instabilities engendered by both complex national risks themselves and political, corporate, and social manners in risk management are now coalesced with and aggravated by the globally shared threats and dangers of omni-pandemics.

The sacrifices and injuries made by these transformative victims have often been euphemistically considered as part of their transformative citizenship that should be accepted in conjunction with the supposed rainchecks of future benefits—as exemplified by the slogan of "growth first, distribution later," "save the economy first," and so forth. Since such rainchecks have been delayed unduly and sometimes indefinitely, many of these victims have tried to autonomously reconstitute their citizenship by reducing or avoiding duties (e.g., avoiding or minimizing procreation, refusing (underpaid) employment, resisting taxes, etc.), by transnationalizing their practical and/or legal belonging (e.g., pursuing overseas education and work, seeking (hidden) dual citizenship, etc.), and sometimes removing their sheer physical presence (i.e., committing suicide at one of the world's highest rates) (Chang, 2010a, Ch. 8). Do these, often desperate, reactions of innumerable transformative victims clearly and coherently indicate that they will sociopolitically support and practically contribute to a possible national transformation into a post-transformative society? Or do they still wish that the current societal and national transformations should continue until the moment that they can participate from more prepared or favorable positions or that the delayed rainchecks for their earlier transformative contributions finally arrive?

2 Beyond South Korea

Diverse and widespread transformative victimhood is far from confined to contemporary South Korea. In fact, it seems to decisively characterize social situations across the world in the twenty-first century, including not only most postcolonial developing nations but also numerous (post)industrial and virtually all post-socialist nations. In a sense, globally generalized transformative victimhood conversely testifies that various types and forms of transformative citizenship has shaped the sociopolitical order in most nations under modernization and development. It is not necessarily the failure of transformative citizenship but even its success (as well as failure) that has rendered late modern politics structurally and chronically destabilized by various unforeseen sociopolitical manifestations of such transformative victimhood as embedded in or necessitated by transformative citizenship. Crucial examples of such citizenship paradox include, above all, the Donald Trump phenomenon in the world's most powerful American political economy, followed by the widespread resurrection of despotic political regimes in post-socialist nations and, of course, the continuing or renewed dominance of populist developmental autocrats in so many (usually neoliberalized) un(der)developed capitalist nations. Ironically, but not surprisingly, the frequently self-serving rule of these conservative political figures and forces feeds on the social desperation and political nostalgia of severely alienated and deprived groups of people.

Donald Trump's dramatic election into American presidency was most crucially determined by the fervent support by massive precarious industrial workers and reluctant retirees in the nation's industrial "rust belt" (McQuarrie, 2017). While having once constituted the kernel of American economic citizenship, they have ended up becoming a sort of transformative victims in the American economy's radical post-industrial transformation, in particular, into ICT and financial sectors (geographically concentrated in the coastal superstates such as California and New York) and unconstrained offshoring of industrial production. In a great historical paradox, their initial rise in American economic citizenship had rendered citizens in many Southern and mid-Western rural regions to become another group of transformative victims. In these sequential transformations, citizens under transformative victimhood not just experienced material despair but, more essentially, felt their sociopolitical disenfranchisement, leading to unexpected drastic challenges to the mainstream political parties' platform for popular support. Similar sociopolitical trends have also been observed in numerous European countries in terms of the sudden prominence of ultra-rightwing populist figures and parties across the continent regardless of diverse economic structures and social policy regimes (e.g., including Italy, France, and even Nordic countries at different times).

Virtually all of the so-called transition economies both in Eastern Europe/Russia and East Asia have necessitated innumerable citizens in diverse sectors, regions, and occupations to confront drastic instabilities and losses in their socioeconomic life and political status, whereas whatever outcomes of system transitions or reforms have frequently been appropriated or even monopolized by politically collusive business elites (many of whom used to be Communist party-state officials themselves) (Windolf, 1998). It is ironically in the formerly underindustrialized economies in East Asia (China and Vietnam in particular) that system reforms have enabled large parts of the respective populations to be incorporated in the new process of (mostly labor-intensive) market-based industrialization, thereby attaining some meaningful post-socialist transformative citizenship (instead of just losing socialist entitlements in work and livelihood) and allowing the respective ruling Communist parties to hold on to power under a sort of developmentalist dictatorship (Chang, K., 2020a, 2020b).

In sum, transformative citizenship and transformative victimhood (or negative transformative citizenship) as the two sides of the same coin have fundamentally and universally characterized all the grand historical processes of modernization, industrialization, deindustrialization, globalization, and post-socialist transition, respectively, in diverse regions of the world at different times. South Koreans' experiences in transformative citizenship and victimhood may have been particularly distinct, but such experiences have constituted more of their commonness with other national citizenries in the sociopolitical, cultural, and developmental status since the mid-twentieth century. In every respect, the twenty-first century, as the previous century's institutional and developmental impetus is rapidly enervated across the world, tends to further reinforce such commonness more widely and intensely. This is the case even if virtually all states and societies remain fundamentally perplexed about what transformations are necessitated.[2]

NOTES

CHAPTER 1

1. This slogan, which reads "*Mungchimyeon salgo, heuteojimyeon jukneunda*" in Korean, was publicly uttered in late 1945 by South Korea's would-be first present Syngman Rhee at the welcoming ceremony for Korean returnees from across the world. It has the same meaning as "United we stand, divided we fall", a proverb which first appeared in Aesop's Fables. Rhee, a returnee from the United States himself, may well have had this Western proverb on mind.
2. See Park Myoung-Kyu (2014), *National, People, Citizen* (in Korean), for a useful conceptual analysis of the main categories of individuals' national sociopolitical status.
3. In Chosun, the middle-age dynastic state that lasted half a millennium since 1392, city was primarily an administrative space for enforcing governmental orders and demands, with suburban-residing local gentry serving as sociopolitical intermediary between the dynastic authority and local populace (Jeon, J., 2015).
4. It should be noted that, in this word, *guk* is the nation, and *min* is people (i.e., multitude of humans), not an individual or person.

5. *Guk*, derived from Chinese, denotes both the nation and the state, so such statist framing of citizenhood is even linguistically facilitated.
6. There were a series of Koreans' own political and social efforts, before and during the Japanese colonial rule, at establishing and promoting modern democratic principles for popular sovereignty, basic civil rights, the balance of state power, and so forth (Suh, H., 2006; Shin, W., 2008). While these efforts were not directly effective or successful in transforming the nation's sociopolitical order, they would be seriously reflected and incorporated in the first constitution of the Republic of Korea enacted in 1948.
7. For an interpretation of "reflexive" in the postcolonial context as extended from the work of Beck, Giddens, and Lash (1994), see Chang, K. (2022), *The Logic of Compressed Modernity*. Also, see Chang, K. (2017b), "reflexive modernization" in *The Wiley Blackwell Encyclopedia of Social Theory* for a formal synopsis on reflexive modernization, focusing on Ulrich Beck's position.
8. The most prominent and influential figure in this regard was Park Won-soon, the mayor of Seoul since 2011, whose lengthy experience as human rights lawyer and social rights activist was quite actively incorporated in the city's "citizen-centered" governance. His utterance of *simin* (citizen) as to Seoulites (and all South Koreans) connotes their status beyond the simple geo-administrative denotation of "city people" (as literally meant) and reflects serious political, social, and even philosophical/ideological concerns he had confronted before his mayor status. The latest national president, Moon Jae-In, has kept addressing South Koreans as *gukmin*, perhaps in the sense of national citizen, but there is no clear formal explanation or guideline for differentiating these terms.
9. Daehanminguk is the Korean expression of the Republic of Korea, literally meaning the great Korean people's country.
10. See Whittaker, et al. (2020), *Compressed Development*, for a broad comparative account of East Asia in this regard.

CHAPTER 2

1. East Asia here refers to Northeast Asia, excluding Southeast Asian countries.
2. I elsewhere analyzed North Korean civil society as a latent possibility (Chang, K., 1994).
3. In his classic observation of American society in the nineteenth century, Alexis de Tocqueville (1988) expressed his admiration about the freely associative nature of American people and communities.
4. See Wiarda (2003), *Civil Society: The American Model and Third World Development*.
5. This civic culture reflected both ethnonationalism (against the racist colonial state of Japan; *minjokjuui*) and nationalism (as a political aspiration for collectivist national survival and prosperity; *gukgajuui*).
6. See Park, T. (2008) on the American military occupation authority's peripatetic engagement with entrenched rightwing factions of South Koreans on its arrival in the Korean peninsula, which would set a course for a violent allied suppression of civil society under strong progressive and neutralist influences.
7. In my other work, *Developmental Liberalism in South Korea* (Chang, K., 2019), this "developmental cooptation of social policy constituencies" is explained as a key component of the state's *developmental liberal* governance until the mid-1990s.
8. In fact, even the outspokenly liberal president, Roh Moo-Hyun tried to co-opt the Samsung clan, for instance, by appointing Hong Seok-hyun, the publisher of Samsung-affiliated Joong-Ang Daily (who is in fact Samsung President Lee Gun-Hee's brother-in-law) as the South Korean ambassador to the United States and supporting him in the prospective candidacy for his lifetime dream, the UN Secretary General position. However, Hong was revealed to have delivered illegal cash donations of Samsung during an earlier presidential election campaign to the formerly pro-military party and had to resign from ambassadorship and face persecution.
9. This position was formally declared as Jiang Zemin's "important thought of Three Represents" in the 16th Congress of the Chinese Communist Party in 2002 (Dickson, 2003). This thought, or theory, which was first introduced in 2000 during an inspection

tour in Guangdong Province, underlined "the requirements for developing China's advanced productive forces, the orientation of China's advanced culture and the fundamental interests of the overwhelming majority of the Chinese people"—that is, economic development, cultural and scientific progress, and popular interests. For the first time, China's newly emerging business elite was politico-theoretically enfranchised in the formal rule of the party-state as a key contributor to national economic development.
10. Foreign observers call such entities "GONGOs" (government-organized NGOs). Their counterparts in South Korea are called *gwanbyeondanche* (para-government associations) by media and critical scholars and citizens.
11. In the era of high socialism, production was always conceived as politics in the everyday operation of collective farms and state factories. See Franz Schurmann (1966), *Ideology and Organization in Communist China*.
12. This is referred to as *xiaogang* in the so-called Xi Jinping theory.
13. In this respect, the Chinese order or practice of *guanxi* should not be easily derogated as an irrational cultural remnant despite all involved discriminations against unconnected others. On the other hand, such referential information has been officially filed, maintained, and utilized by the *dangan* system.
14. This is more a relationship principle (culture) than a relationship basis. If the term, "nepotism", is used for such relationships and interactions without due attention to concrete contexts, it can sometimes be an Orientalist or unjustly derogatory appraisal.
15. Some historians rediscovered how actively grassroots industrial workers utilized such referential associations in constructing their own civil society even in Anglo-American industrial revolutions (Thompson, 1963; Hareven, 1982). This means that social uprooting was not necessarily a precondition for free association. In many revolutionary instances, indigenous communities in their entirety reinvented themselves as proactive voluntary networks (for a Chinese example, see Thaxton, 1983). In the long run, this civil rebirth of established communities—ranging from villages to nations—is a key question concerning the possibility of liberal East Asia. This may be considered as an instance of what neo-Weberian Clifford Geertz (1973) calls "internal conversion" in the area of civil society. With all these progressive possibilities, it is also

true that the same referential communities or relations have often served as the basis for subversive or divisive sociopolitical actions such as military coup, regionalist politics, and so forth.
16. Paradoxically, Confucianism (in compromised versions) has become a mass culture in the modern era, encompassing each entire national population, whereas pre-modern East Asia used to uphold it as a statist and/or aristocratic social and political philosophy (Chang, K, 2010a, 2018). Then, the historically embedded prestige of (aristocratic) Confucian norms has been translated into contemporary East Asians' heatedly competitive consumption of supposedly Confucian lifestyles—e.g., extravagant wedding, showy burial, and so forth. This seems to constitute a sort of self-defined cultural (and material) citizenship on the mind of contemporary East Asians, regardless of the limited or non-existing practical support by their states (see Chapter 8 in this book).
17. In principle, Confucianism is not a societal religion but a familialized ritual system, so this diversity did not cause serious moral difficulties. When combined with politics, however, different interpretations of Confucian classics and practices oftentimes resulted in factional struggles of various sorts.
18. Japan's wartime emperor, China's Mao Zedong, South Korea's Park Chung-Hee, and North Korea's Kim Il-Sung were all perched in such positions.
19. See Chang, K. (2018), *The End of Tomorrow? Familial Liberalism and Social Reproduction Crisis* (in Korean), and also Chapter 7 in this book.
20. Singapore's self-conscious position as a flamboyantly Asian-way modernizer may not be entirely groundless. Highly suggestive in this regard is the debate between Singapore's state-paternalist leader, Lee Kuan-Yew and South Korea's liberal leader, Kim Dae-Jung about 'democracy with Asian characteristics'. See Zakaria and Lee (1994), and Kim, D. (1994).
21. An interesting yet tragic episode is the creation of KCIA (Korean Central Intelligence Agency) in 1961 after the model of the American CIA. The abuse of human and civil rights as well as the distortion of political rights by KCIA, mostly in the anticommunist framework, left indelible scar on political order and public mind.
22. See Giddens (1990), *The Consequences of Modernity*. Also, see Badie (2000), *The Imported State: The Westernization of the*

Political Order. Of course, this historical disembedding could not be thorough, so the contradictions between institutional rules and social realities would centrally characterize the turbulent political histories of South Korea and other postcolonial societies (Chang, K., 1999).
23. This phrase is *tongchuangyimeng* in Chinese; *dongsangimong* in Korean; *doushilyouimu* in Japanese.

CHAPTER 3

1. While sincerely serving *seomin* may be considered as a political virtue, addressing a specific person as such can be offensive. This is particularly the case if the concern person's socioeconomic status is actually humble because it could point to his/her failure in work and/or livelihood. The politico-moral utility of this notion consists in the commonly humble socioeconomic background of most South Koreans as children of poor peasants or as poor peasants themselves. This makes national economic development and citizens' participation in it a moral economy issue that overrides class divisions.
2. Democracy without serious labor politics has also been debated by South Korean scholars as to Japan (Choi, J., 2006) and West Europe (Ko, S., 1999).
3. I elsewhere address this aspect of colonial social change as *colonial dialectical modernity* Chang, K., 2022, Chapter 4).
4. See Kim, D. (2000), *War and Society: What Was the Korean War to Us?* (in Korean) for a pathbreaking analysis in this regard.
5. Estimates of the number of deaths and civilian casualties during the war vary by different researchers, but it is thought to be about two million among South Koreans (Kim, D., 2000). The number of refugees leaving their home regions during the war is thought to be about ten million (Seo, J., 2000). Even after the war, many regions suffered massive popular exodus due to chronic unemployment and destructed conditions of livelihood.
6. See Mobrand (2019), *Top-Down Democracy in South Korea*, as an excellent latest work in this respect.
7. This sort of "institutional parasitism" is not limited to party politics, but pervasive among various professions. If their entrenched

interests are threatened by state policies and social demands for restructuring or rationalizing their functions and/or jurisdictions, they will launch war-like resistance, however, without clear historico-social rationale. This was evidenced, for instance, during the government-led process of separating between prescribing (medicine) and dispensing (pharmacy), during the reform of law education and bar examination, and so forth. These incidents seriously damaged the public legitimacy and respect of the concerned professions.

8. Cho, H. (2000) denotes the chronic displacement between formal politics and civil society as a "political lag." He suggests to distinguish between "absolute political lag" and "relative political lag". According to him, "'Absolute political lag' inhibits political transformation and innovation due to various structural factors, whereas 'relative political lag' refers to a situation in which certain extents of political transformation and innovation take place, but these are disjointed from changes in civil society that are occurring at an even higher speed" (Cho, H., 2000). While Cho's argument is quite suggestive to the subject of this chapter, namely, the historically triggered structural dislocation among the different domains of societal transformation (i.e., civil society, industrial class structure, and democratic politics), his allusion to "lag" is not acceptable due to its inherent supposition of linear modernization.

9. There is a critical argument that the regionalist degeneration of South Korean politics resulted from the dismantling of the political competition landscape and its ultimate split into pro- and anti-democracy forces (Lee, K., 1998; Cho, K., 2000). The question is why and how such dismantling was tied to regionalism.

10. See "DJ's Rule for Three Years Has Aggravated the Regionalist Bigotory" (*Sisa Journal*, 25 January 2001; http://www.sisajournal.com/news/articleView.html?idxno=78924).

11. Most key leaders of the Grassroots Party—Lee Jae-Oh, Jang Gi-Pyo, and Kim Mun-Su—ultimately turned to rightwing positions as they got alienated from both organized labor and the ruling political factions under Kim Dae-Jung and Roh Moo-Hyun. In South Korean politics, it is a highly intriguing question why and how many progressive nationalist politicians have converted into rightwing populism and allied with the military-succeeding political faction.

12. A significant example in this respect was the National Poor Alliance (Jeongukbinminyeonhap), which was widely influential and effectively active. However, many other organizations and movements refused to join the DLP because of its allegedly conservative nature.
13. This perception was detected in the words of an executive of the DLP as follows, "People from student movement circles, or those who personally support the progressive parties, have often joined the party through brief personal connections.... In the future, to further broaden our support base, it is most expedient to carry out activities appealing to KCTU union members" (Chang and Chang, 2002).
14. There was a political opportunity to change the single member electorate system (*soseongeoguje*) during the political reform in 1987, but at the shortsighted urgings of the Peace and Democracy Party (Pyeonghwaminjudang), the ruling Democratic Justice Party (Minjujeonguidang) chose to retain it. This was a practical compromise between Minjujeonguidang, seeking to profit from the split of votes for the opposition parties, and Pyeonghwaminjudang, with a high concentration of support in its regional base (Yoon, S., 1997: 203).
15. In Ulsan and Changwon, the nation's two largest heavy industrial cities, organized labor have been able to translate their socioeconomic influence into the successful election of progressive candidates representing the working class formally or informally in various local and national parliamentary elections.
16. In exchange for its cooperative voting in major reform bills, Justice Party (Jeonguidang), which broadly succeeds the DLP, hard pressed the ruling Democratic Party (Deobuleominjudang) to agree in 2019 to revising the proportional representation system in the national parliamentary election for the sake of minority parties' enlarged shares. Even this agreement ended up being practically nullified by the two competing dominant parties because they set up a sort of affiliate minority parties for garnering most of proportional representation votes under the pretext of preventing their respectively dangerous enemy party from dominating the parliament (*The Briefing*, 18 March 2010; http://www.thebriefing.co.kr/news/articleView.html?idxno=630).

17. Albert Hirschman (1970) presents two lines of reaction to organizational crisis, namely, "voice" and "exit". Both voice (criticism or resistance concerning the current organizational practices) and exit (from the troubled organization) of certain members can stimulate the concerned organization to recover its normal processes and functions. If exit occurs to an excessive extent, however, the concerned organization will ultimately perish. If voice accumulates seriously, the organization can avoid its collapse only by implementing a fundamental reform which incorporates the demands of concerned members. It is members' "loyalty" (to the concerned organization) that critically divides the two possibilities of reaction to the organizational crisis. If members normally maintain strong moral attachment to the organization, they are more likely to voice than exit at a time of organizational crisis. It is apparent that a great majority of South Korean ruralites—youth in particular—have opted to exit, rather than to voice, in response to the rural socioeconomic depression. But many parents have remained in villages permanently to grow old and die therein. Perhaps those elderly who have stayed in their home villages have done so out of some loyalty. But even their loyalty is at best a sharply divided one. They have remained in their villages and cultivated farmland not so much as because they have believed in a possibility of renewed rural development as because their children have left for the cities to exploit urban economic and social opportunities on their behalf. Rural parents have rarely hoped their children to succeed their agricultural enterprise (see Chapter 8). In this sense, the rural elderly have taken an option of *indirect exit* through their urban-migrating family members. Their physical bodies have remained in villages but they have felt more gratification from their urban-based children's success than from their own immediate livelihood.

CHAPTER 4

1. Bryan S. Turner's (1990) discussion on the "passive" or "active" nature of citizenship is another complementary critique of T. H. Marshall from a comparative historical perspective.
2. The rule by semi-feudal oligarchies, often with strong landed interests, is not likely to promote social democratic policies, in which

they may have to give up many of their entrenched material interests. See Cho, et al. (2008).
3. For a latest account of developmental politics, see Chang, Fine, and Weiss, eds. (2012), *Developmental Politics in Transition: The Neoliberal Era and Beyond*. Also see Desai (2008) and Hein (2008) on "developmental nationalism".
4. Bryan S. Turner (2016) indicated the increasing prevalence of denizenship as a result of the neoliberally caused erosion of social citizenship, particularly in the UK and the USA. A corresponding neoliberal erosion of developmental citizenship and its pervasive degeneration into denizenship seem to haunt many societies in East Asia that used to boast rapid yet socially inclusionary economic development (see Chang, K., 2019, Ch. 4).
5. On Americans' Tocquevillian animosity to social rights, see Isin and Turner (2007).
6. However, the United States supported the (illiberal) developmental promotion policy of the South Korean government in consideration of the Cold War. This helps to explain why the United States turned rather predatory to South Korea in the post-Cold War era (Cumings, 1998).
7. The United States used to be the only one among all advanced industrial societies, lacking the compulsory public health insurance until the Obama administration's decisive yet half-way action on the issue. This American situation is sometimes taken in South Korea as a rationale for proposing an autonomous right of medical institutions to choose among different (public and private) insurance schemes for patients with private insurance coverage. Such right may fundamentally demolish the universality principle of the South Korean public health insurance because the profit motive of medical institutions is certain to induce their attention focused on those (rich) patients with expensive private insurances.
8. As of the mid 2000s, South Korea's social wage remained at the lowest level among the OECD member countries (*Kukminilbo*, 16 April 2009).
9. This included the archaically termed "one hundred day plan of the New Economy", a tragically failed policy that ultimately led to the national financial collapse in 1997.

10. The land reform recommended by the United States and then reluctantly implemented by the Rhee government was by nature a citizenship establishment project.
11. This differs from the European instance of inter-class social solidarity as the basis of the welfare state (see Baldwin, 1990).
12. See Chang, K. (2010a), and Kang, M. (1996) for the sociopolitical status and functions of *chaebol*.
13. The sincerity of such ruling cannot but be suspected because actual corporate managers are treated much less favorably than members of *chaebol*'s ruling families.
14. The Lee Myung-Bak government proudly announced its policy of allowing businessmen to use the VIP room of major airports in South Korea (*Korea Policy Portal*, 31 March 2008), but many businessmen felt burdensome about the political connotation attached to such favoritism.
15. Moon, W. (2020) applies this concept to analyze the mutual differences between local Chinese and transnational enterprises in their respective relationship with the Communist party-state.
16. See Chang, K. (2018) on implications of this situation for women (of poor families) in terms of *dual feudalism*.
17. For details on South Korea's jobless economic recovery, see Chang, K. (2019, Ch. 4).
18. See OECD (2007). South Korean singer Jang Ki Ha's extreme popularity can be explained in this regard. In particular, see the lyric of his "Living without Any Problem" which calls for such lifestyle and personal attitude as implicitly ignore social and political realities.
19. See Stephens (1979) on the sociopolitical efficacy of organized labor in heavy industries, but this very success, in the South Korean context, has caused a historical segmentation of heavy industrial labor from underclass people in other sectors.
20. Some *chaebol* have tried to become not only the financial and but also the political center of this new ruling coalition. See Chang, K. (2010a).
21. See *Newsweek* (7 April 2008) on "the politics of practical nostalgia" across Asia.
22. See the special issue of *Citizenship Studies*, volume 24, number 7 (October 2020), on "Developmental Citizenship in China:

Economic Reform, Social Governance, and Chinese Post-Socialism", edited by Chang Kyung-Sup.

23. Some rudimentary social security programs were adopted during the military-controlled developmental era in order to contain impoverished and handicapped population with "liberal" measures of minimum relief and to developmentally mobilize certain strategic groups of civil service and labor with "conservative-corporatist" measures of social insurance (cf. Esping-Andersen, 1990). Noting the strategic developmental intent behind the general passivity and pragmatic syncretism in these programs, I earlier classify the social policy regime of the South Korean developmental state as *developmental liberalism* (Chang, K., 2019).

CHAPTER 5

1. When I served as a member of the Social Welfare Policy Appraisal Committee of the South Korean government in 1994–1995, the Ministry of Health and Welfare prepared a preliminary draft of the general welfare policy reform, beginning with an apparently neoliberal statement on the potential inhibitive effects of social welfare on economic growth. As my only meaningful contribution in that capacity, I successfully discouraged the Ministry to delete such self-betraying statement from the reform draft.
2. Kim Dae-Jung thereby ended up being called "the IMF's man in Seoul" by Bruce Cumings (1998: 60).
3. The confirmed history of public welfare in the Korean peninsula dates back to almost three millennia ago (Nam and Cho, 1995: 84–85). In 843 BC, a poverty relief law called *yunhwanbeop* was established in Gijajoseon. In 675 BC, a public institution called *jeyangwon* was established to support "the four deprived" (i.e., widowers, widows, orphans, and childless elderly).
4. Despite continual changes in its name, the land system of *gyunjeon* (equal field) has been upheld over two millennia, including the contemporary farmland law.
5. The total amount of the American foreign aid to South Korea surpassed the combined amount of the American foreign aid to all Latin American countries (Lee, H., 2009).

6. The distribution of Japan's "enemy-left assets" in the 1950s to those select figures connected with state elites served a historical precursor to the later developmental creation and transformation of many strategic industries and firms. See Kang, M. (1996).
7. Police often worked together with privately organized or purchased force of *gusadae* (company-saving corps) in cracking down on workers. See Koo, H. (2001).
8. An interesting type of labor resistance is "law-abiding struggle" (*junbeoptujaeng*) by which workers challenge the labor-abusive industrial system by abiding by regulations and/or laws strictly. See Chang, K. (1998) and, also, Chapter 9 in this book.
9. See Laslett and Brenner (1989) on a general sociological introduction to social reproduction.
10. Among these non-state welfare providers, the role of Protestant churches has been particularly significant. As many of the most sizable and influential Protestant churches in South Korea were founded and have been dominated by extremely conservative ministers who had fled North Korea during the communist takeover or the Korean War, their welfare (and education) functions have often been politically contaminated as an ideological tool against North Korean communism and progressive causes in South Korea. See Chang, K. (2019) on conservative sectarian welfare pluralism in South Korea as a component of developmental liberalism in social policy.
11. For the European experiences of such social solidarity, see Baldwin (1990), *The Politics of Social Solidarity: Class Bases of the European Welfare State, 1875–1975*.
12. See a series of lucid collective work by Lee, S. on the specific nature of various types of non-regular employment (Lee, S., et al., 2017; Kim, Y., et al., 2018; Baek, S., et al., 2017; Lee, B., and Lee, S., 2017), the concerned workers' disadvantages in the public social security programs (Lee, S., et al., 2019), and the situational structural necessity of "the basic income" in the post-crisis neoliberal conditions of South Korea (Lee, S., et al., 2016).
13. See Esping-Andersen (1990) for an authoritative classification of different welfare state regimes. While Esping-Andersen did not include South Korea in his early classification, local South Korean scholars have applied his categories in order to classify South Korea.

14. This study flew in the face of the Kim Dae-Jung administration which was in a self-congratulatory mood amid rapid economic recovery. Officials expressed doubt about the validity of the study on the ground that its reliance on consumption data could be misleading because of people's tendency to reduce consumption under economic difficulty (*Hankyoreh*, 19 November 1999). However, since consumption can be considered as a measurement of the actually realized quality of life, the conclusion of the study does not appear seriously mistaken. On the other hand, officials tried to pressure a para-governmental research institute to lower the official level of the minimum living expenses below which households would be classified as absolutely poor (*Hankyoreh*, 23 November 1999).
15. This remark was by Roh, on 16 May 2005, at "the win–win cooperation measure meeting" with business leaders including major heads of *chaebol*. At this meeting, he was practically begging *chaebol* to be lenient and generous to *jungsogieop* (SMEs; small and medium-sized enterprises) and thereby enhance their social legitimacy and reputation.
16. For instance, *Kyunghyang Daily*, a center-left newspaper, ran a special series on "Saying the Welfare State" for nearly two months, between May 8 and July 6, 2011 (http://welfarekorea.khan.kr/). *The Hankyoreh*, another progressive newspaper, also covered welfare state issues through extensive special reports, conferences, interviews, and so forth. Such media coverage functioned as public venues for the civic debates on the welfare state as South Korea's future among prominent academics, experts, activists, and ordinary citizens.
17. For a useful critical account of the welfare state's limit in South Korea's post-crisis transition, see Kuk, M. (2012), *Developmental State, Welfare State, and Neoliberalism*.
18. During her presidential election campaign in 2012, under the urge of expert advisors, she pledged to construct a significant welfare state supposedly as her father's unfulfilled dream. Even in 2009, at the 30th commemoration of Park Chung-Hee's death, she dubbed in her eulogy, "Father's ultimate dream was the construction of the welfare state. Although he made such [hard] effort for economic growth, economic growth itself was not the goal" (*OhmynewsTV*, 11 October 2017; https://www.youtube.com/watch?v=4V9Yln b5ZWA).

19. It was during the Roh Tae-Woo administration (1987–1992) that social welfare was upheld as a core policy agenda, in order to materially fend off social challenges to the military's succession of state leadership even after democratization. The expansion of welfare expenditure during this period was greater than any previous government terms and even most of the subsequent government terms (Seo, B., 1997).
20. His ten major pledges included: "job creation, reform of political and institutional state powers, anti-corruption and *chaebol* reform, strengthening of the ROK-US alliance and securing of self-reliant national defense, youth-empowering nation, abolition of gender discrimination, nation of happy elderly, state responsibility for education and childrearing, rescuing of self-employed and small business people, and safe and healthy nation" (*The Hankyoreh*, 14 April 2017).
21. For instance, self-employed service traders whose number has increased explosively since the national financial crisis have been extremely unhappy about their business conditions being rather worsened under these labor market reforms, whereas yet-to-be-employed youth have been frustrated at the very sluggish pace of corporate job expansion (*Hankookilbo*, 21 December 2018).
22. In an interesting poll by *Realmeter*, President Moon's approval rate was the lowest (29.4%) among those men in their twenties, which was worse than the approval rate among those in their sixties and above. Thanks to a series of gender equity campaigns, those women in their twenties showed the highest approval rate of 63.5% (*Realmeter*, 17 December 2018; www.realmeter.net).
23. In the presidential election race in 2012, for instance, all major candidates pledged to transform South Korea into a welfare state. This included Park Geun-Hye, who in fact initiated the welfare state slogan ahead of even the progressive candidates in the race.
24. See Yang, J. (2017), *The Political Economy of the Small Welfare State in South Korea* for a succinct persuasive analysis of the inhibitive political economic and social institutional conditions to South Korea's advancement to a full-scale welfare state.
25. For instance, see Shin, K. (2015), *Swedish Social Democracy: Labor, Welfare, and Politics* (in Korean) and Song, H. (1997), *The Market and Welfare Politics: A Study of Sweden's Social Democracy* (in Korean).

Chapter 6

1. Amanda Ripley (2014), *The Smartest Kids in the World, and How They Got That Way*.
2. According to the ROK Statistics Research Institute (SRI), the average length of sleep in 2019 was 6.1 hours for high school students, 7.4 hours for middle school students, and 8.7 hours for 4–6 grade primary school students (*Yonhapnews*, 24 December 2019; https://www.yna.co.kr/view/AKR20191224069000002). Consequently, in a survey by the ROK Ministry of Health and Welfare, 49% of youth aged 12–17 years complained sleep shortage, all due to study burdens (*YTN*, 25 August 2019; https://www.ytn.co.kr/_ln/0103_201908252224242005).
3. Most of the private universities and colleges have depended on tuition revenue for more than 60% of their operational expenses (Korea Higher Education Research Institute (KHEI), 2017; https://khei-khei.tistory.com/2097).
4. "The lonely deaths of wild geese fathers" have frequently been sensationalized in media (e.g., *Kyunghyang Daily*, 26 March 2003; *Yeongnam Daily*, 5 July 2003; *Dong-A Ilbo*, 28 October 2003; *Maeil Economic Daily*, 19 October 2005).
5. *Education at a Glance: OECD Indicators*, since its inauguration in 2001, revealed that the private share of the public educational expenses in South Korea was consistently the highest in the 2000s among all member countries of the OECD, while the recent demographic shrinkage of its youth population has gradually but slightly lowered such ranking (OECD, 2001–2019). However, the key burden of South Korean families consists in their spending on children's private lessons (*sagyoyuk*) with individual tutors and/or special cram institutions.
6. See "Children's education prior to old-age preparation? Old-age measure vs. children's education expenses" (Kim, C., 2017; https://www.lifentalk.com/1635).
7. See Kariya's work on Japan in a similar perspective on the critical significance of education in condensed modernization and development (Kariya, 2013; Kariya and Rappleye, 2010).
8. The legal platform for free middle school education was prepared in 1985, but it took 17 years before the South Korean government

actually implemented it in 2002. As to free high school education, South Korea remains the only country without it among all OECD countries (*JoongAng Daily*, 25 September 2018; https://news.joins.com/article/22997524). The currently incumbent Moon Jae-In government has expressed a strong willingness to implement free high school education.
9. Annually, variable supplies of youth for military conscription determine the educational criteria for exemption of the national military service. Those without a high school diploma are often subject to such exemption.
10. There is controversy over who, among conservative politicians, should claim the copyright to the policy idea of halving the tuitions (*bangapdeungrokgeum*). See "The birth secret of the halved tuition policy from Hannara Party" (*Monthly Chosun*, 10 July 2011; http://monthly.chosun.com/client/news/viw.asp?ctcd=C&nNewsNumb=201107100009&page=23). In the subsequent presidential elections, even most of the progressive and less conservative candidates—including the current president, Moon Jae-In—also upheld the same policy.
11. On 29 August 2011, about seven hundred organizations and individuals officially formed "The National Headquarter for Realizing the Halved Tuitions" and declared to stage a strong struggle ahead (PSPD, 29 August 2011; http://www.peoplepower21.org/index.php?mid=StableLife&search_target=tag&search_keyword=%EB%B0%98%EA%B0%92%EB%93%B1%EB%A1%9D%EA%B8%88%EA%B5%AD%EB%AF%BC%EB%B3%B8%EB%B6%80&document_srl=818404&listStyle=list).
12. On the latest presidential election in 2017, see "Education pledges that should be presented by the presidential candidates" (*DTNews 24*, 18 April 2017; http://www.dtnews24.com/news/articleView.html?idxno=420238).
13. This is explained as "complex culturalism" in my separate book, *The Logic of Compressed Modernity* (2022). Also see Kim, M. (2010) on the political economic context of cultural complexity in South Korea.
14. See Chang, K. (2022), *The Logic of Compressed Modernity*, Chapter 4. On the conceptual differentiation between "reflexive" and "reflective" in modernity, see Chang, K. (2017b), "Reflexive

modernization" in *The Wiley Blackwell Encyclopedia of Social Theory*.

15. I conceptualize this as dialectical modernity as one of the (internal) multiple modernities in modern South Korea. See Chang, K. (2022), *The Logic of Compressed Modernity*," Chapter 4. Internal Multiple Modernities".

16. In "A Study on the Measures for Reducing the Required Subjects at High Schools" by Korea Institute for Curriculum and Evaluation (KICE, 2002), Taiwan and South Korea showed striking similarities in the excessive diversities and pluralities in the school subjects of secondary public education. This is largely due to the two countries' similar international and civilizational positions as the key condition of their respective liberal institutional(ist) modernization.

17. As such, school entrance exams and civil service recruitment exams have tested examinees' remembrance and understanding of West-derived textbook knowledge. For both exams, private cram institutions, respectively called *ipsihagwon* and *gongsihagwon*, have been heavily popularized across the nation. In an interesting recent trend, the abrupt demographic shrinkage of college/university applicants and the rapidly increasing seekers of *cheolbaptong* (iron rice bowl, meaning life-time employment in civil service) under the neoliberal employment crisis have made "star instructors" transfer from *ipsihagwon* to *gongsihagwon*. Such transfers are feasible particularly due to the similar natures of the two exams. See "Number-one-star instructors in *suneung* transferring to '*gongsi*'" (*DongA Ilbo*, 16 October 2019; http://www.donga.com/news/article/all/20191016/97895401/1). *Suneung* is the South Korean SAT. In recent years, these two groups of examinees are largely similar in number.

18. Davies and Mehta (2013) defines educationalization as "the way in which practices, processes, and forms associated with schooling increasingly penetrate other social spheres, as well as the ways in which formal schooling is assigned more responsibility for social problems that originate in those spheres". Also see Depaepe (2008) and Depaepe and Smeyers (2008).

19. For instance, the nation's leading comprehensive university, Seoul National University has, as of 2020, 15 undergraduate colleges which in turn have 82 academic disciplinary departments (http://

www.snu.ac.kr/organization). Its general graduate school has 5 areas, 70 departments, and 28 cooperative programs at the Masters level, and 5 areas, 72 departments, and 29 cooperative programs at the Ph.D. level. It also has 12 specialized graduate schools. Each department or graduate program operates basically as an independent institution with mutually segmented educational and research functions, with a faculty-hiring practice of strong inbreeding in terms of undergraduate departmental affiliation. It can hardly be a universal university.
20. This phenomenon is often called *hagyeon* (school connection), but *gwayeon* (department connection) may be more precise. On the concerned situation in the area of law, for instance, see Choi, J. (2013), *The Era of the Seoul National University College of Law: The Half Century of Seoul National University in My Observation*. According to the screening by *Beopryulsinmun* (*Law Times*, 7 November 2019; https://m.lawtimes.co.kr/Content/Article?serial=157021) of the five hundred career judges newly appointed between 2015 and 2019, the graduates of Seoul National University accounted for 49.2% (246 judges), followed by those of Korea University (15.6%; 78 judges) and Yonsei University (10.2%; 51 judges). These so-called SKY universities produced three fourths of the newly appointed career judges in this period.
21. A survey of corporate personnel managers revealed that the intra-firm cliques of employees are formed, in the order of significance, by employees' alma mater university/college, home region, major (academic department), and high school (KRIVET, 2008).
22. In my earlier work (Chang, K., 2010a, Ch. 6), such familial investment is explained as *social transition costs of industrialization*.
23. The Moon government set up the Presidential Committee on the Fourth Industrial Revolution in October 2017 (https://www.4th-ir.go.kr/). As an official state organ, this is the very first of its kind in the entire world. Accordingly, the Ministry of Education announced, "The Supporting Measures for University Innovation to Cope with Demographic Restructuring and the Fourth Industrial Revolution" (6 August 2019).
24. An interesting aspect of such pluralist cultural consumption is that cultural forms are enjoyed, appropriated, and/or reprocessed by flexibly neglecting their philosophical or ideational basis (e.g., Kang, M., 1999).

25. The role of media in sustaining and intensifying such practices in South Koreans' adulthood should also be recognized. The culture sections of major newspapers cover virtually unconstrained ranges and types of cultural production and experience as embodied in South Korean life (Park, S., 2018).
26. For instance, Seoul National University, the domestically dominant university in virtually every subject, has nationally separate departments of languages and literature as to Chinese, English, French, German, Russian, Spanish, as well as Korean (https://www.snu.ac.kr/about/overview/organization/sub_organ). Its education in history, philosophy, music, and fine arts is also finely divided according to world regional origins.
27. For instance, 168 South Korean students applied for the school of music at Berlin Arts University in spring 2003, outnumbering 107 German applicants. A local newspaper could not help making a cynical comment, "When will Koreans take over this school?", and sarcastically added "German degrees offer good marriage opportunities for female students, not to mention admission to Korean orchestras" (reported in *Digital Chosun*, 8 October 2003).
28. Religious institutions—Catholic churches in particular—were also understood similarly, making some religious leaders heavily influential in the democratization process (e.g., Chang, Y., 2014).
29. For a closely related argument, see the theory of *jungmin* (middling grassroots) by Han, S. (1991).
30. The British proposal of "the social investment state", despite its similar emphasis on human capital, should be carefully differentiated from "social investment" in the reform of Continental Europe's welfare states and economic systems. The latter is succinctly explained by Leoin (2016: 194) as follows,

> Policies that support human capital formation and labour market activation can prevent negative outcomes such as educational dropout, (long-term) unemployment and early labour market exit. These policies can represent investments, which in the medium and long run generate returns by enhancing welfare and avoiding benefit dependency.

"Social investment" here is to strengthen, not replace, social welfare with a systematic focus on the enhancement and activation

of human capacity, thereby strengthening the earlier active labor market policy.
31. See Colin Crouch (2003), *Commercialization or Citizenship: Education Policy and the Future of Public Services*, for an influential critical account in the neoliberalized European context.
32. According to "The Report of the Retirement Market in 2018" by Korea Insurance Development Institute (KIDI, 2019), those metropolitan urbanites in their 40s and 50s expected to spend, after retirement, an average amount of 72.6 million won for a child's remaining education, and another average amount of 139.5 million won for a child's marriage. These burdens would be multiplied by the number of their children. Consequently, 56.6% of them were worried about the burden of supporting children after retirement.
33. Domestically, the television drama in 2018–2019, *Sky Castle* (*JTBC*; http://tv.jtbc.joins.com/skycastle) enjoyed a record viewer rate by vividly showing upper class housewives' strategic and often desperate efforts to help promote their children's educational success.
34. These districts have led *budongsan geopum* (real estate bubble), thereby harming poor families and individuals in their housing situation as well. For instance, Gangnamgu in Seoul, Haeundaegu in Busan, and Suseonggu in Daegu are where upper class desires and privileges are consolidated into a tangible class culture, closely approximating Bourdieu's (1979) "distinction".
35. The ministry's organizational and personalized collusion with *sahak* (private schools; more precisely, owners/operators of private schools) and concomitant corruption have led media describe its former and current members as *Gyopia* (educational mafia). *Maekyung*, a key business newspaper, even ran a special series of featured reports, "*Gyopia* blocks education reform" in April–May 2019 (https://www.mk.co.kr/news/economy/view/2019/04/247524/).
36. "Dissolving the Ministry of Education" has recently become popularized both as a main pledge in the political elections and as a political demand of civil activists. Particularly in the 2017 presidential election race, for instance, a few major candidates emphatically declared their willingness to dissolve the Ministry of Education and

substitute a more socially acceptable organization (*Eduinnews*, 23 January 2017).
37. In a sense, the state's role in housing is similar in that it has mostly regulated the supply and allocation of chronically insufficient urban housing by various complicated requirements and preconditions for purchase application while its direct provision of housing units and allowance for the needy has been negligible. In this context, the notion of *jugeobingon* (housing poverty) has been popularized among critical researchers on housing and welfare. See Park, S. (2012) for a succinct account of this problem. The basic policy parameters in both education and housing, reflecting the state's *developmental liberalism* in social policy (Chang, K., 2019), have been set apart from genuine social citizenship.
38. On a latest related incident, see "No one taking responsibility for 'mistaken questions in *suneung*'" (*Moneytoday*, 3 December 2016; https://m.blog.naver.com/PostView.nhn?blogId=onetop1605&logNo=220541575665&proxyReferer=https:%2F%2Fwww.google.co.kr%2F). *Suneung* is South Korea's college scholastic ability test (SAT).
39. Without doubt, their common use of English is also a very significant attraction.
40. See the above-introduced speech in January 2014 by Arne Duncan, the education secretary of the Obama government, in which the earlier held but recently lost leader status of the United States in tertiary education was lamented (*Washington Post*, 14 January 2014; https://www.washingtonpost.com/news/answer-sheet/wp/2014/01/18/arne-duncan-why-cant-we-be-more-like-south-korea/?utm_term=.810a73d7643f).

CHAPTER 7

1. This precipitous fertility transition even dwarfed the Chinese achievement with its most coercive and stringent birth control campaigns in human history. China's total fertility rate declined from the record-high 7.5 in 1963 to 2.2 in 1980, accounting for a 71% decline. But, in the 1980s, fertility increased for a few years and began to fluctuate (CFEPH, 1988).

2. During the first demographic transition accompanying rapid industrialization and urbanization, the proportion of the elderly aged 65 year or higher in the total population was only 2.9% in 1960 but rose to 5.0% in 1990. In contrast, the proportion of the youth population, aged less than 15 years, declined from 42.3% in 1960 to 25.8% in 1990 (Kim, et al., 1993).
3. Both releasing the result of ultrasonic detection and performing an abortion operation without special reasons were illegal. In April 2019, the Constitutional Court of South Korea ruled the anti-abortion law (enacted in 1953) as unconstitutional due to its infringement on the pregnant woman's basic right to self-determination in her own life, and ordered the state to make necessary legal changes by the end of 2020 (http://www.law.go.kr/LSW/detcInfoP.do?mode=1&detcSeq=150780). This decision reversed its earlier opposite ruling in August 2012.
4. South Koreans' generalized familial Confucianism is *neotraditional* in that it was a culturally and, more critically, materially aristocratic attribute during the precolonial dynastic era of Chosun, but became culturally universalized in the postcolonial democratic reorganization of South Korean society, along with farmland redistribution and general public education (see Chapter 8 in this book). These three elements practically constituted the initial setup of (politico-ideologically undeclared) social citizenship for the nation's predominantly agrarian population (more than 80% on the eve of the Korean War).
5. See Han, H. (1994) for a vivid description of this social dilemma from a journalist's viewpoint.
6. Male workers' mishaps frequently had a chain effect on female workers, who were asked to sacrifice first in labor reshuffling (Chang, K., 2019). However, the proportion of female workers at each workplace was generally low, so such gendered buffering was in no sense significant.
7. Kim, D. (2005) argues that the second fertility transition in South Korea began from 1985. While I do not fully disagree, it is important to acknowledge the particular velocity of fertility decline since the "IMF economic crisis".
8. I addressed this dilemma of South Korean families in terms of "risk family" (Chang, K., 2011b), as compared to Ulrich Beck's (1992) "risk society". Relatedly, perhaps a new theory of intergenerational

and inter-gender risk flows could be developed systematically. See Ochiai (2011) who extends this perspective to comparatively address the broader Asian situations in terms of "unsustainability" of familialist social practices and state policies.

9. This social intransigence is clearly evidenced by the still widespread social hostility and governmental indifference to *mihonmo* (unmarried mothers) (Kim et al., 2012). South Korean demographers occasionally underline the importance of out-of-wedlock births in sustaining European fertility and hint at the necessity for a similar sociodemographic change in South Korea. However, the fundamental sociocultural and legal-political nature of such non-marital or, more properly, *post-marital* fertility has not yet been carefully analyzed or discussed.

10. As this trend constitutes a key demographic dimension of South Korea's compressed modernity, such warnings have often been issued, quite ironically, by those same population experts who used to diagnose demographic issues in the service of anti-natal population control.

11. At a special forum, "youth talk", organized by the Presidential Committee on Ageing Society and Population Policy (PCASPP; https://www.betterfuture.go.kr/mainPage.do) on 30 August 2018, a participant uttered, "The more low fertility is highlighted as a crisis, the more reluctant we become about procreation because we are made to think that it is a really difficult world for childbirth" (*Newsis*, 2 September 2018).

12. According to OECD and South Korean data, South Korea's TFR has remained under 1.3 for a longer period (since 2001) than any other country (Lee and Choi, 2013). Other notable countries include Italy (1993–2003), Slovenia (1995–2005), Spain (1993–2002), and so forth.

13. In human history, voluntarily patriotic demographic behavior has been limited to migration, whereas national family planning has been carried out mostly as a coercive political project (e.g., in China, etc.) or a top-down technocratic program (e.g., in South Korea, etc.).

14. See Richardson and Turner (2001) and Turner (2008) on reproductive citizenship.

15. Apart from various local-level allowances for multi-children families, every family with children aged 0–5 can receive redemption

of childcare facility fees from the national government (http://onl ine.bokjiro.go.kr/apl/info/aplInfoNurView.do). As of April 2020, the monthly redemption allowance ranges between 240,000 and 470,000 Korean won, depending on age of children and (institutional or familial) childcare arrangement. Alternatively, if children aged less than 86 months remain home, direct child-care assistance between 100,000 and 200,000 Korean won, depending on age of children, is provided. From September 2019, the general child allowance in the amount of 100,000 Korean won is provided for children aged up to 83 months.
16. As a rich minority's accumulation of extreme wealth would not lead to any correspondingly high fertility by them, the fertility effect of economic bipolarization should be studied in full scale. Conversely, the sudden population growth of some former socialist countries (in particular, China) after socioeconomic collectivization and nationalization, despite their worsening economic stagnation, seems to have been facilitated by universalized (egalitarian) marriage and access to the basic means of social reproduction. The socialist institutions of work, however, had a quasi-proletarianization (negative) effect on fertility in both rural and urban areas by abolishing family-based production activities and thereby altering intergenerational wealth flows downward (Chang, K., 1990).

CHAPTER 8

1. This differs from West Europe (e.g., Germany, etc.) and North America (e.g., Canada, etc.) where multiculturalism as the government policy and/or civil society cause has been necessitated and promoted in respect to the long-term presence of foreign guest workers and their family members. See Triadafilos Triadafilopoulos (2012), *Becoming Multicultural: Immigrants and the Politics of Membership in Canada and Germany*.
2. Japan's colonial rule in Korea, embodying its capitalist imperialism, was based upon a sort of *fish farm modernity* in that institutional-legal, ideational, and technological modernizations were supported or implemented in such directions as to facilitate the maximum mobilization and exploitation of Korean resources. As to *yangban*'s

entrenched material and sociocultural status, the Land Survey Project (*Tojijosasaeop*) and the Standard Rules of Rituals (*Uiryejunchik*) were particularly significant (Lee, H., 2000, 2011). By the former project, Japan illicitly appropriated a great part of Koreans' communally owned (and thus formally unspecified in ownership) land, whereas *yangban*, as feudal landlords, were enabled to firmly reestablish their land ownership in national legal terms. By the latter decree, Japan attempted to establish formal authority (and legitimacy) in its practically oriented sociocultural governance (or Foucauldian governmentality) over civilian life, whereas *yangban*, whether by ancestral lineage or status aspiration, were formally ascertained about the universal social significance of Confucian familial rituals, albeit, in arbitrarily reduced or deformed contents.

3. On eldest sons' unpopularity in the marriage market, see Kim and Yoon (2013).
4. See Jeong, J. (1995) for a lively account of two villages in south-central South Korea in this regard.
5. There was an earlier trend of *yangbanization* in late Chosun (Kim, S., 2003), however, with a more materially driven purpose of evading state exploitation by various illicitly acquired statuses of *yangban*.
6. In rural marriages, in this regard, aristocratic ancestral lineages were still showed off in many conservative regions (Kim, J., 1994).
7. The implication of familial neotraditionalization for women has been diametrically different between these two cases (Chang, K., 2018)—namely, the overexploitation of South Korean women under extended family relations and rituals in addition to farm labor, in striking contrast to the affective romanticization of Western women as the cultural pillar of the modern nuclear family. It should be indicated that Korean women's status norms had also been influenced by the Japanese ideology of *ryosai kenbo* (wise mother, good wife; *hyeonmoyangcheo*) during the colonial period (Ahn, T., 2003). This influence was not incompatible with Confucian family norms but would intricately reinforce them, with a complex impact of nurturing a womanly status betrayed by their everyday realties of farm labor (or urban employment) besides home management.
8. For comprehensive collective accounts of the long-term socioeconomic and cultural changes in rural society, see KREI (2003),

The Change and Development of Rural Society in South Korea (in Korean); Yi, et al. (2014), *Compressed Modernity and Rural Society: Life, Community, and the State in Changpyeong Diary* (in Korean); and Kim, et al. (1998), *The Tradition and Change in Lineage Village* (in Korean).

9. I analyze the governmental, communal, and corporate dependence on ordinary people's familial norms, relations, and resources in economic development and social governance as *infrastructural familialism*(Chang, K., 2022, Ch. 7).
10. While, even after migrating to urban areas, women's such status did not fundamentally change, their recent (re)integration with natal family has been much stronger in urban areas, in part reflecting the new old-age culture (or dilemma) of increasing affectionate and instrumental dependence on (pious) adult daughters (Chang, K., 2022, Ch. 8).
11. This practical necessity did not differ between rural and urban areas, so the resultant sex ratio distortion was prevalent in both areas (Chang, K., 2018).
12. Sorensen (1988) observed that most rural families managed to maintain their (neo)traditional organizational structure and culture even after rapid industrialization and urbanization began. In fact, their strategic support of urban-headed/based children as a new basis of economic progress and status advancement enabled themselves to feel relaxed about not changing their comfortably accustomed way of livelihood.
13. The latest revision of this rule (presidential decree) was carried out on 30 December 2015 during the presidency of Park Geun-Hye (i.e., Park Chung-Hee's daughter)—namely, The Standard Rules on Healthy Family Rituals, presidential decree, no. 26774 (http://www.law.go.kr/lsEfInfoP.do?lsiSeq=177881#).
14. There are numerous anecdotal observations on young factory girls' devotion to rural families in the early industrialization period, for instance, by saving and sending their meager wages (e.g., Lim, B., 2013). Even this (urban-to-rural) sacrifice was frequently channeled back into the urban economy because their peasant parents would use the sent money to finance the urban schooling of sons.
15. A comprehensive survey in the early 1990s showed that no urban parents or children desired agriculture as the children's prospective occupation and that even most of rural parents and children

excluded it in the same respect (The Center for Rural Studies, Ewha Womans University, 1994).
16. South Korean media have consistently dealt with this issue mainly in terms of moralistic self-sacrifice on the part of village-remaining parents. Currently, as many villages are inhabited by elderly persons only (aged women in particular), television channels frequently romanticize such social setting as an angelic community to be revered (and culturally consumed) by the whole society. Highly popular programs in this regard include, among others, *Hangukgihaeng* (*Korea Travel Note*) by *EBS* (2020b; https://home.ebs.co.kr/ktravel/main), *Yeoseotsi Naegohyang* (*Six O'Clock My Home Village*) by *KBS* (http://program.kbs.co.kr/1tv/culture/sixhour/pc/index.html).
17. As part of South Korea's desperate efforts at overcoming "the IMF economic crisis", it reached out for known and potential resources of overseas Koreans across the world, including financial, social, and human capital. This set off a course of *compatriotic globalization* both outward and inward (Chang, K., 2014a). Its neoliberal nature, however, has frequently frustrated and angered those overseas Koreans economically less attractive to the domestic economy and society (Park, W., 2020).
18. Taiwan preceded South Korea in rural marriage transnationalization by several years (Lee, H., 2016; Jones and Shen, 2008; Jones, 2012). Given Taiwan's multicultural ethnic composition and historico-cultural environment, the expansion of rural international marriages has been perceived and accommodated more practically than ideologically (Jeong, J., 2015).
19. See Chang, K. (2014b), "Asianization of Asia" for a discussion of this trend in a broad political economic context of Asia's intraregional integration.
20. In fact, the aggressive governmental and social drive for ad hoc multiculturalization has increasingly estranged many native South Koreans themselves, whose initial curious paternalism is being gradually mixed with indifference and refusal (Yoon, I., 2016).
21. So many South Korean scholars and students from across nearly all social sciences have studied this issue, that a foreign scholar visitor in this area told me a joke, "There seem to be more researchers on this issue than foreign brides investigated".

22. There is even a long-running weekly television show since October 2013 on this subject, *Damunhwa Gobuyeoljeon* (*Multicultural Mother-in-Law and Daughter-in-Law Biographic Notes*) (*EBS*, 2020a; https://home.ebs.co.kr/gobu/main). See Jung and Choi (2015) for a content analysis of how this subject is represented in public media.
23. In particular, many students from multiethnic families have complained about being called "Hey, multicultural(s)!" by their friends and, sometimes, teachers. See "'Hey, multicultural'… the homeroom teacher calls my friend like this" (*Seoul Times*, 30 July 2018); "'Hey, multicultural'" the scarlet letter inscribed in second generations…caused the tragedy of the Incheon student's death by 'fall'" (*AsiaToday*, 29 November 2018); "Multiculturals, raise your hands" (*OhmyNews*, 11 August 2016).
24. In his influential work, *Liquid Modernity* (2000), Zigmund Bauman characterizes late modern society as "cloakroom community" as follows:

> The name 'cloakroom community' grasps well some of their characteristic traits..... It is the evening performance which brought them all here – different as their interests and pastimes during the day could have been. Before entering the auditorium they all leave the coats or anoraks they wore in the streets in the playhouse cloakroom..... During the performance all eyes are on the stage; so is everybody's attention. Mirth and sadness, laughter and silence, rounds of applause, shouts of approval and gasps of surprise are synchronized – as if carefully scripted and directed. After the last fall of the curtain, however, the spectators collect their belongings from the cloakroom and when putting their street clothes on once more return to their ordinary mundane and different roles, a few moments later again dissolving in the variegated crowd filling the city streets from which they emerged a few hours earlier. (Bauman, 2000: 200)

In my other work (Chang, K., 2022, Ch. 5), I described the sociocultural nature of South Korea's multiculturalism drive as *cloakroom cosmopolitanism*.

Chapter 9

1. I also analyzed China as a post-socialist instance of complex risk society (Chang, K., 2017c).
2. It was as lately as 22 June 2021 that South Korean president, Moon Jae-In, deplored the latest gigantic disasters of a backward risk society—i.e., the sudden collapse of a high-rise building in Gwangju during demolition, killing many pedestrians and bus passengers, and the fire of a mega-size warehouse in Icheon, damaging the health of thousands of neighbors—by remarking before his cabinet, "We are an advanced nation at certain times, but have not outgrown a backward nation" (*Republic of Korea Policy Brief*, 22 June 2021; https://www.korea.kr/news/stateCouncilList.do).
3. This political trend has continued into the twenty-first century. For instance, as noted in Chapter 4 in this book, Lee Myung-Bak won the presidential election in 2007 with the so-called 747 pledge—namely, average annual economic growth of 7 percent, per capita income of 40,000 US dollars, and the world's seventh largest economy, to be achieved within his possible presidency. Unfortunately, none of his economic pledges were fulfilled, whereas his presidency would later be criticized as the worst political instance of ecological destruction, due to his nationwide river development project.
4. In one of the most infamous scandals in this regard, Hwang Woo-Suk, a professor at Seoul National University, was once upheld as a foremost national hero in science by his supposedly world-leading research in stem cell (as published in *Science*, *Nature*, etc.). However, he was soon revealed by investigative media and peer scientists to have fabricated key experimentations and committed serious ethical violations. This incident came to shock the entire nation and solemnly induced its critical self-reflection about the widespread fetishism in national technoscientific leap. The pros and cons about this national ambition continue even now, particularly in terms of fervently awaiting the very first South Korean Nobel Prize winners in sciences.
5. Such discourses are often blended with militaristic vocabulary and ethos, due to both the military's long held dictatorship and all men's obligatory military service experience (see Moon, S., 2005).

6. In particular, South Koreans' overwhelming preference for high-rise apartments has been discussed from various interesting angles (Gelézeau, 2013; Jun, S., 2009).
7. As the post-IMF crisis era has forced a majority of youth to helplessly become the so-called precariat amid the chronic employment crisis, they have been disproportionately subjected to particularly risky categories of work (Lee, S., et al., 2017). Also, see Seol, D. (2002, 2014) on foreign guest-workers' subjection to discriminatory and exploitative conditions of work.
8. The Samsung *chaebol* (conglomerate) has been particularly criticized in this respect by industrial labor, progressive media, critical intellectuals, and activist NGOs, who agree to see their nation as "the Samsung Republic," pointing to various state organs' habitual collusion with the conglomerate in labor relations and many other social affairs (*Hankyoreh*, 22 January 2020; https://www.hani.co.kr/arti/opinion/column/925402.html). As a crucial example, the leukemia incident in the semiconductor production lines of Samsung Electronics has drawn a particularly intense criticism from the affected workers and their advocates in civil society, leading to the company's ultimate acceptance of most responsibilities.
9. The most crucial part of this de facto industrial policy was financial subsidies and bail-outs for so many *chaebol* firms through government-controlled/manipulated banks. This bank-ruining practice reached its worst point in the latter part of Kim Young-Sam's presidency, ultimately causing the unprecedented national financial crisis. Many major South Korean banks ended up getting bankrupt and, under the coercive urge of the IMF, taken over by global financial capital.
10. Park Geun-Hye's political fall from presidency practically began with the sinking of Sewol Ferry, in which hundreds of teenage students got killed without any sensible rescue efforts by the state leadership or responsible government organs (Suh and Kim, eds., 2017).
11. For instance, such celebrated national landmarks as Burj Khalifa in Dubai, Petronas Twin Towers in Malaysia, and Marina Bay Sands Hotel in Singapore were built by South Korean construction companies.

12. This type of labor protest has been particularly popular and effective among public transportation workers such as subway workers and bus drivers (Chang, K., 1998).
13. Such political economic knack, coupled with leadership careers in the expert associations, would also serve as a very useful platform for political opportunities and appointments.
14. The collapse of Sampoong Department Store in June 1995, then the nation's biggest department store, sacrificed more than five hundred lives instantly. It would be comparable only to the sinking of Sewol Ferry in April 2014, claiming more than three hundred lives (mostly of teenage students), in terms of the intensity of public trauma and anger.
15. There were some interesting analogies developed to call for deregulations. Conservative media collaborated by loudly demanding the government to "remove *daemot* (big nails)," whereas the neo-developmentalist president, Lee Myung-Bak, pledged to "remove *jeonbotdae* (power poles)."
16. Vilifying economic and other regulations has been the most favored topic for expert columns in the biggest conservative newspapers for so many years.
17. When this trend disturbs the general public and/or burdens the government, media frequently step in by deploring the supposed loss or missing of *siminjeongsin* (civic virtue or citizen spirit). Interestingly, it has also been during the grave social, economic, environmental, or other disasters that astonishing numbers of ordinary citizens have suddenly devoted themselves to voluntarily helping overcome them. As one of the most notable instances, when the collision of a super oil tanker led to oil spill in 12,547 kls in one of South Korea's most cherished seashores in December 2007, as many as 1.23 million citizens from across the nation volunteered to help clean up the spill and recover the area's ecological conditions. By 2004, it was officially assessed that the concerned seawater had been completely cleaned, whereas in 2016, the area was environmentally evaluated, in an apparent miracle, as Category II (national park-level nature) by the International Union of Conservation for Nature (IUCN).
18. Reflexivity has a double meaning or usage for Ulrich Beck, Anthony Giddens, and many other intellectual-scholars—namely,

referential appraisal and self-conscious judgment. Perhaps, reflexivity had better be replaced by reflectivity if it is to exclusively signify self-conscious intellectual and/or scientific judgments (see Chang, K., 2017b). Reflexivity in this section implies both reflexive and reflective dimensions.
19. Anjeonsahoesiminyeondae (Citizens' Alliance for Safe Society) is a most exemplary organization in this respect.
20. See Kim and Kim (2020) for a lucid account of the South Korean situation under Covid 19.
21. Besides, in April 2021, the ruling party of Moon was badly defeated in the make-up elections for mayorship in Seoul and Busan, the nation's two largest cities.

CHAPTER 10

1. See Kang, S. (2020), *The Risen State and Deserted Citizens: Japan Since Meiji* for a revealing analysis of the Japanese situation in an interestingly related perspective.
2. Such common bewilderment led Ulrich Beck (2016) to argue about the "metamorphosis" of the world through the fundamentally unexpected emancipatory effect of all kinds of modern catastrophes—for instance, an associative awakening of the world as a risk community under the wholesale interconnected climate crisis in all parts of the world.

REFERENCES

Abrahamson, Peter. 2012. "European Welfare States: Neoliberal Retrenchment, Developmental Reinforcement, or Plural Evolutions." Chang Kyung-Sup, Ben Fine, and Linda Weiss, eds., *Developmental Politics in Transition: The Neoliberal Era and Beyond*, pp. 92–115. Basingstoke/New York: Palgrave Macmillan.

Ahn, Taeyoon. 2003. "Wartime Politics and the Colonization of Motherhood in Late Colonial Korea (1937–1945)" (in Korean). *Journal of Korean Women's Studies* 19(3): 75–116.

Amsden, Alice. 1989. *Asia's Next Giant: South Korea and Late Industrialization*. New York: Oxford University Press.

Amsden, Alice. 1994. "Why Isn't the Whole World Experimenting with the East Asian Model to Develop? Review of the East Asian Miracle." *World Development* 22(4): 627–633.

AsiaToday. 2018. "'Hey, Multicultural' the Scarlet Letter Inscribed in Second Generations ...Caused the Tragedy of the Incheon Student's Death by 'Fall'" (in Korean). 29 November 2018.

Badie, Bertrand. [1992] 2000. *The Imported State: The Westernization of the Political Order*. Stanford: Stanford University Press.

Baek, Seung-Ho, An Juyoung, and Lee Sophia Seung-Yoon. 2017. "A Comparative Study on Precarious Labor Market in Korea and Japan: Gender and Occupational Division of Precarious Work" (in Korean). *Korean Social Policy Review* 24(2): 1–29.

Bauman, Zigmund. 2000. *Liquid Modernity*. London: Polity.

Beck, Ulrich. [1984] 1992. *Risk Society: Towards a New Modernity*. London: Sage.
Beck, Ulrich. 1999. *World Risk Society*. Cambridge: Polity.
Beck, Ulrich. 2009. *World at Risk*. Cambridge: Polity.
Beck, Ulrich. 2016. *The Metamorphosis of the World: How Climate Change Is Transforming Our Concept of the World*. Cambridge: Polity.
Beck, Ulrich, Anthony Giddens, and Scott Lash. 1994. *Reflexive Modernization: Politics, Tradition and Aesthetics in the Modern Social Order*. Stanford: Stanford University Press.
Beopryulsinmun (*Law Times*). 2019. "Career Judges in the Recent Five Years, Abundant among Those from Kim & Chang and Seoul National University" (in Korean). 7 November 2019.
Bloch, Ernst. [1935] 1991. *Heritage of Our Times*. Berkeley: University of California Press.
Blue House. 2021. *Republic of Korea Policy Brief*, 22 June 2021 (https://www.korea.kr/news/stateCouncilList.do).
Bokjiro. 2020. "Multicultural Family Support Programs" (http://www.bokjiro.go.kr/welInfo/retrieveGvmtWelInfo.do?searchIntClId=01&welInfSno=169).
Bourdieu, Pierre. 1979. *Distinction: A Social Critique of the Judgment of Taste*. Cambridge: Polity.
Brun, Ellen, and Jacques Hersh. 1976. *Socialist Korea: A Case Study in the Strategy of Economic Development*. New York: Monthly Review Press.
Byun, Yong-Chan, Dong Hoe Kim, and Song Hee Lee Lee. 2010. *A Study of the Relationship between Marriage Behavior Changes and Fertility* (in Korean). Seoul: Korea Institute for Health and Social Affairs.
Cai, Yongshun. 2002. "The Resistance of Chinese Laid-off Workers in the Reform Period." *China Quarterly* 170: 327–344
Caldwell, John C. 1982. *Theory of Fertility Decline*. London: Academic Press.
Carney, Michael, and Eric Gadajlovic. 2003. "Strategic Innovation and the Administrative Heritage of East Asian Family Business Groups." *Asia Pacific Journal of Management* 20(1): 5–26.
Center for Rural Studies, Ewha Womans University. 1994. *The Current Situation and Measures Concerning the Rural Youth Problem in South Korea* (in Korean). Research report.
Chang, Dae-oup. 2009.*Capitalist Development in Korea: Labour, Capital and the Myth of the Developmental State*. London: Routledge.
Chang, Ha-Joon. 1994. *The Political Economy of Industrial Policy*. London: Palgrave Macmillan.
Chang, Kyung-Sup. 1990. "Socialist Institutions and Family Wealth Flows Reversal: An Assessment of Post-Revolutionary Chinese Rural Fertility." *Journal of Family History* 15(2): 179–200.

Chang, Kyung-Sup. 1992. "China's Rural Reform: The State and Peasantry in Constructing a Macro-Rationality." *Economy and Society* 21(4): 430–452.
Chang, Kyung-Sup. 1993. "The Peasant Family in Transition from Maoist to Lewisian Rural Industrialisation." *Journal of Development Studies* 29(2): 220–244.
Chang, Kyung-Sup. 1994. "Latent Civil Society in North Korea: The Second Consciousness, the Second Economy, and the Second Society" (in Korean). *Phenomenon and Cognition* 18(4): 133–156.
Chang, Kyung-Sup. 1997. "The Neo-Confucian Right and Family Politics in South Korea: The Nuclear Family as an Ideological Construct." *Economy and Society* 26(1): 22–42.
Chang, Kyung-Sup. 1998. "Risk Components of Compressed Modernity: South Korea as Complex Risk Society." *Korea Journal* 38(4): 207–228.
Chang, Kyung-Sup. 1999. "Compressed Modernity and Its Discontents: South Korean Society in Transition." *Economy and Society* 28(1): 30–55.
Chang, Kyung-Sup. 2001. "Accidental Pluralism in Family Ideology: Compressed Modernity and Korean Families" (in Korean). *Korean Studies Quarterly* 24(2): 161–202.
Chang, Kyung-Sup. 2003. "Politics of Partial Marketization: State and Class Relations in Post-Mao China." Alvin So, ed., *China's Developmental Miracle: Origins, Transformations, and Challenges*, pp. 265–288. Armonk: M. E. Sharpe.
Chang, Kyung-Sup. 2006. "From Developmental Liberalism to Neo-Liberalism: Globalization, Dependent Reflexivity and Social Policy in South Korea." Goran Therborn, and Habibul Haque Khondker, eds., *Asia and Europe in Globalization: Continents, Regions and Nations*, pp. 183–206. Leiden: Brill.
Chang, Kyung-Sup. 2007. "The End of Developmental Citizenship? Restructuring and Social Displacement in Post-Crisis South Korea." *Economic and Political Weekly* 42(50): 67–72.
Chang, Kyung-Sup. 2010a. *South Korea Under Compressed Modernity: Familial Political Economy in Transition*. London: Routledge.
Chang, Kyung-Sup. 2010b. "The Second Modern Condition? Compressed Modernity as Internalized Reflexive Cosmopolitisation." *British Journal of Sociology* 61(3): 444–464.
Chang, Kyung-Sup. 2011a. "Social Reproduction in an Era of 'Risk Aversion': From Familial Fertility to Women's Fertility?" (in Korean). *Journal of the Korean Family Studies Association* 23(3): 1–24.
Chang, Kyung-Sup. 2011b. "Developmental State, Welfare State, Risk Family: Developmental Liberalism and Social Reproduction Crisis in South Korea" (in Korean). *Korea Social Policy Review* 18(3): 63–90.

Chang, Kyung-Sup. 2012a. "Economic Development, Democracy, and Citizenship Politics in South Korea: The Predicament of Developmental Citizenship." *Citizenship Studies* 16(1): 29–47.
Chang, Kyung-Sup. 2012b. "Predicaments of Neoliberalism in the Post-Developmental Liberal Context." Chang Kyung-Sup, Ben Fine, and Linda Weiss, eds., *Developmental Politics in Transition: The Neoliberal Era and Beyond*, pp. 71–90. Basingstoke: Palgrave Macmillan.
Chang, Kyung-Sup. 2014a. "Transformative Modernity and Citizenship Politics: The South Korean Aperture." Chang Kyung-Sup, ed., *South Korea in Transition: Politics and Culture of Citizenship*, pp. 163–180. London: Routledge.
Chang, Kyung-Sup. 2014b. "Asianization of Asia: Asia's Integrative Ascendance Through a European Aperture." *European Societies* 16(3): 1–6.
Chang, Kyung-Sup. 2017a. "Compressed Modernity." Bryan S. Turner, Chang Kyung-Sup, Cynthia F. Epstein, Peter Kivisto, J. Michael Ryan, and William Outhwaite, eds., *The Wiley Blackwell Encyclopedia of Social Theory, Volume I*. Hoboken: Wiley Blackwell.
Chang, Kyung-Sup. 2017b. "Reflexive Modernization." Bryan S. Turner, Chang Kyung-Sup, Cynthia F. Epstein, Peter Kivisto, J. Michael Ryan, and William Outhwaite, eds., *The Wiley Blackwell Encyclopedia of Social Theory, Volumes IV*. Hoboken: Wiley Blackwell.
Chang, Kyung-Sup. 2017c. "China as Complex Risk Society: Risk Components of Post-Socialist Compressed Modernity." *Temporalités*, number 26 (2017/2), A special issue on "'Compressed Modernity' and Chinese Temporalities" (https://journals.openedition.org/temporalites/3810).
Chang, Kyung-Sup. 2018. *The End of Tomorrow? Familial Liberalism and Social Reproduction Crisis* (in Korean), Seoul: Jipmundang.
Chang, Kyung-Sup. 2019. *Developmental Liberalism in South Korea: Formation, Degeneration, and Transnationalization*. Basingstoke: Palgrave Macmillan.
Chang, Kyung-Sup. 2020a. "Why Developmental Citizenship, Why China? An Analytic Introduction." *Citizenship Studies* 24(7): 847–855.
Chang, Kyung-Sup. 2020b. "Developmental Pluralism and Stratified Developmental Citizenship: An Alternative Perspective on Chinese Post-Socialism." *Citizenship Studies* 24(7): 856–870.
Chang, Kyung-Sup. 2022. *The Logic of Compressed Modernity*. Cambridge: Polity.
Chang, Kyung-Sup, and Chang Gwi-Yon. 2002. "Cold War, Compressed Modernity, and Labor Politics: Dislocated Political Society and Democratic Labor Party in South Korea" (in Korean). *Studies in International Affairs* 24:151–191.
Chang, Kyung-Sup, Ben Fine, and Linda Weiss, eds. 2012. *Developmental Politics in Transition: The Neoliberal Era and Beyond*. Basingstoke: Palgrave Macmillan.

Chang, Kyung-Sup, and Song Min-Young. 2010. "The Stranded Individualizer Under Compressed Modernity: South Korean Women in Individualization without Individualism." *British Journal of Sociology* 61(3): 540–565.

Chang, Sang Hwan. 1999. "Political Empowerment of the Laborers and the Necessity and Realities of Progressive Parties" (in Korean). *Trends and Outlooks* 42: 21–49.

Chang, Young Min. 2014. "A Study on the Bishop Chi Hak Son's Fight for Democracy Based on the ROK-US Diplomatic Documents Centered on the Perception and Response of the Actors" (in Korean). *Memory and Vision* 31: 40–85.

Chin, Meejung. 2013. "Portrait of Unmarried One-Person Households in Early Adulthood: Delayed Transition or Achieved Individualization." Proceedings of the International Conference on "Life and Humanity in Late Modern Transformation: Beyond East and West", organized by SNU Center for Social Sciences, Korea Institute for Health and Social Affairs, and Korean Sociological Association, 30–31 May 2013, Seoul National University.

China Financial and Economic Publishing House (CFEPH). 1988. *New China's Population*. New York, Macmillan.

Cho, Hiyeon. 2000. "The Transfer of Democracy and Institutional Politics, Mass (*Minjung*) Politics, Civil Politics" (in Korean). *Economy and Society* 46: 170–198.

Cho, Hiyeon, Lawrence Surendra, and Eunhong Park, eds. 2008. *States of Democracy: Oligarchic Democracies and Asian Democratization*. Mumbai: Earthworm Books.

Cho, Hyo-Rae. 1995. "Democratization and Labor Politics: A Comparative Study of Korea, Brazil, Spain" (in Korean). Ph.D. dissertation, Department of Sociology, Seoul National University.

Cho, Kisuk. 2000. *Regionalistic Elections and the Rational Voter* (in Korean). Seoul: Nanam Publishers.

Cho, Moon-Young. 2020. "The Hierarchy of Corona Inequalities in South Korean Society" (in Korean). *Hwanghaemunhwa* 108(2020/09): 16–34.

Cho, Myung-Rae. 2007. "Developmentalism and Democracy" (in Korean). *Bipyeong* (Critique), Winter 2007.

Choi, Hyaeweol. 1991. "The Societal Impact of Student Politics in Contemporary South Korea." *Higher Education* 22(2): 175–188.

Choi, Jang Jip. 1992. "Why Is the Korean Labor Movement Failing to Become Politically Organized?" (in Korean). Korean Political Science Association, ed., *The State and Civil Society in Korea*, pp. 230–254. Seoul: Hanul Publishers.

Choi, Jang Jip. 1994. "The Transition to Democracy and the Labor Movements" (in Korean). Jang Eulbyeong, et al., eds., *Structure and Outlook of South and North Korean Politics*, pp. 135–170. Seoul: Hanul Publishers.

Choi, Jang Jip. 2002. *Democracy after Democratization: The Conservative Origins and Risks of Korean Democracy* (in Korean). Seoul: Humanitas Publishers.
Choi, Jang Jip. 2006. "Transformation Toward Democracy Without Labor: Analyzing the Failure of Japan Socialist Party" (in Korean). *Journal of Asiatic Studies* 124: 112–146.
Choi, Jong-Go. 2013. *The Era of the Seoul National University College of Law: The Half Century of Seoul National University in My Observation* (in Korean). Seoul: Seoul National University Press.
Chu, Byeong-Wan. 2011. *Multicultural Society and Global Leader* (in Korean). Seoul: Daegyo.
Chua, Beng Huat, and Koichi Iwabuchi, eds. 2008. *East Asian Pop Culture: Analyzing the Korean Wave*. Hong Kong: Hong Kong University Press.
Crouch, Colin. 2003. *Commercialization or Citizenship: Education Policy and the Future of Public Services*. London: Fabian Society.
Cumings, Bruce. 1981. *The Origins of the Korean War: Liberation and Emergence of Separate Regimes, 1945–1947*. Princeton: Princeton University Press.
Cumings, Bruce. 1997. *Korea's Place in the Sun*. New York: W.W. Norton & Company.
Cumings, Bruce. 1998. "The Korean Crisis and the End of 'Late' Development." *New Left Review* 231: 43–72.
Danuri. 20 April 2020 (https://www.liveinkorea.kr/portal/main/intro.do).
Davies, Scott, and Jal Mehta. 2013. "Educationalization." James Ainsworth, ed., *Sociology of Education: An A-to-Z Guide*. London: Sage (https://sk.sagepub.com/reference/sociology-of-education/n127.xml).
Depaepe, Marc, ed. 2008. *Educational Research: The Educationalization of Social Problems*. Berlin: Springer.
Depaepe, Marc, and Paul Smeyers. 2008. "Educationalization as an Ongoing Modernization Process." *Education Theory* 58(4): 379–389.
Desai, Radhika. 2008. "Developmental and Cultural Nationalisms in Historical Perspective." *Japan Focus* (on line), 26 June 2008.
Dickson, Bruce J. 2003. *Red Capitalists in China: The Party, Private Entrepreneurs, and Prospects for Political Change*. Cambridge: Cambridge University Press.
Digital Chosun (www.chosun.com).
Dong-A Ilbo (www.donga.com).
Dore, Ronald. 1973. *British Factory-Japanese Factory: The Origins of National Diversity in Industrial Relations*. Berkeley: University of California Press.
DTNews 24. 2017. "Education Pledges That Should Be Presented by the Presidential Candidates" (in Korean), 18 April 2017.
e-Narajipyo. 2020. "The Current Situation of Population in Urban Areas" (http://www.index.go.kr/potal/main/EachDtlPageDetail.do?idx_cd=1200).

Eastman, Lloyd E. 1972. "Fascism in Kuomintang China: The Blue Shirts." *China Quarterly* 49: 1–31.
EBS. 2020a. "Multicultural Mother-in-Law and Daughter-in-Law Biographic Notes" (*Damunhwa Gobuyeoljeon*; https://home.ebs.co.kr/gobu/main).
EBS. 2020b. "Korea Travel Note" (*Hangukgihaeng*; https://home.ebs.co.kr/ktravel/main).
Economic Planning Board (EPB) and National Statistical Office (NSO), Republic of Korea. 1990. *The Population and Housing Census Report* (in Korean).
Economic Planning Board (EPB) and National Statistical Office (NSO), Republic of Korea. Every five years. *The Population and Housing Census Report* (in Korean).
Eduinnews. 2017. "Dissolving the Ministry of Education, Abolishing Seoul National University... The Education Policies of Presidential Candidates." 23 January 2017.
Esping-Andersen, Gøsta. 1990. *The Three Worlds of Welfare Capitalism*. Princeton: Princeton University Press.
Estevez-Abe, Margarita. 2003. "State-Society Partnerships in the Japanese Welfare State." Frank J. Schwartz, and Susan J. Pharr, eds., *The State of Civil Society in Japan*, pp. 154–173. Cambridge: Cambridge University Press.
Eun, Ki-Soo. 2013. "Pathways to Post-Patriarchal Society: Global Convergence of Gender (Non-)Preference and East Asian Particularities." Proceedings of the International Conference on "Life and Humanity in Late Modern Transformation: Beyond East and West", organized by SNU Center for Social Sciences, Korea Institute for Health and Social Affairs, and Korean Sociological Association, 30–31 May 2013, Seoul National University.
Eun, Soo Mi. 2006. "The Relationship Between the Student Movement and the Labour Movement of Korea in 1980s" (in Korean). *Memory and Vision* 15: 199–238.
Evans, Peter. 1995. *Embedded Autonomy: States and Industrial Transformation*. Princeton: Princeton University Press.
Forbes (https://www.forbes.com/?sh=7496b1b02254).
Gallagher, Mary E. 2004. "China: The Limits of Civil Society in a Late Leninist State." Muthiah Alagappa, ed., *Civil Society and Political Change in Asia: Expanding and Contracting Democratic Space*, pp. 419–453. Stanford: Stanford University Press.
Garon, Sheldon. 1997. *Molding Japanese Minds: The State in Everyday Life*. Princeton: Princeton University Press.
Garon, Sheldon. 2003. "From Meiji to Heisei: The State and Civil Society in Japan." Frank J. Schwartz, and Susan J. Pharr, eds., *The State of Civil Society in Japan*, pp. 42–62. Cambridge: Cambridge University Press.
Geertz, Clifford. 1973. *The Interpretation of Cultures*. New York: Basic Books.

Gelézeau, Valérie. 2013. *Séoul, Ville Géante, Cités Radieuses*. Paris: CNRS Éditions.
Georgescu-Roegen, Nicholas. 1960. "Economic Theory and Agrarian Economics." *Oxford Economic Papers* 12(1): 1–40.
Georgescu-Roegen, Nicholas. 1970. "The Economics of Production." *American Economic Review* 60(2): 1–9.
Giddens, Anthony. 1990. *The Consequences of Modernity*. Stanford: Stanford University Press.
Giddens, Anthony. 1998. *The Third Way: The Renewal of Social Democracy*. Cambridge: Policy Press.
Goodman, Roger, Gordon White, and Huck-ju Kwon, eds.1998. *The East Asian Welfare Model: Welfare Orientalism and the State*. London: Routledge.
Grieder, Jerome B. 1983. *Intellectuals and the State in Modern China: A Narrative History*. New York: Free Press.
Gu, Shengzu, Yang Wei, and Hong Qunlian. 2012. "Corporate Citizenship in Contemporary China: Social Responsibility for Saving Jobs." Chang Kyung-Sup and Bryan S. Turner, eds., *Contested Citizenship in East Asia: Developmental Politics, National Unity, and Globalization*, pp. 105–114. London: Routledge.
Han, Hye-Jin. 1994. "Unwelcome Daughters: Son Preference and Abortion in South Korea." Judith Mirsky and Marty Radlett, eds., *Private Decisions, Public Debate: Women, Reproduction and Population*, pp. 33–42. London: Panos.
Han, Sang-Jin. 1991. *An Investigation into Middle Class (Jungmin) Theory* (in Korean). Seoul: Munhakgwajiseongsa.
Hankookilbo (www.hankookilbo.com).
Hankyoreh (www.hani.co.kr).
Hareven, Tamara. 1982. *Family Time and Industrial Time: The Relationship Between the Family and Work in a New England Industrial Community*. New York: Cambridge University Press.
Hirschman, Albert O. 1958.*The Strategy of Economic Development*. New Haven: Yale University Press.
Hirschman, Albert O. 1970. *Exit, Voice, and Loyalty*. Cambridge: Harvard University Press.
Hochschild, Arlie. 1990 *The Second Shift: Working Parents and the Revolution at Home*. New York: Avon Books.
Hwang, Yeojung. 2013. "The Stress of Students" (in Korean). ROK National Statistical Office, ed., *Korean Social Trends 2013*, pp. 119–126.
Hyman, R. 1998. "An Emerging Agenda for Trade Unions?" ILO Discussion Paper Series No. 98. Geneva: International Institute for Labour Studies.
Isin, Engin F., and Bryan S. Turner. 2007. "Investigating Citizenship: An Agenda for Citizenship Studies." *Citizenship Studies* 11(1): 5–17.

Jacoby, Sanford M. 2004. *The Embedded Corporation: Corporate Governance and Employment Relations in Japan and the United States.* Princeton: Princeton University Press.

Jeon, Jonghan. 2015. "A Study on the Landscape Elements and Construction of Eupseong (County Seat) in the Late Chosun Dynasty" (in Korean). *Journal of the Korean Association of Regional Geographers* 21(2): 319–341.

Jeong, Jin-sang. 1995. "The Dismantlement of the Social Estates During the Liberation Periods: A Case Study of Two Villages in Jinyang-gun" (in Korean). *Social Science Research* 13(1): 331–351.

Jeong, Jong-Ho. 2011. "From Illegal Migrant Settlements to Central Business and Residential Districts: Restructuring of Urban Space in Beijing's Migrant Enclaves." *Habitat International* 35(3): 508–513.

Jin, Hong-Goo. 2015. "A Study on the Conclusion Strategy and Agricultural and Fishery Sector Plans under Korea's FTA" (in Korean). *Journal of Korea Trade* 40(2): 161–189.

Johnson, Chalmers. 1982. *MITI and the Japanese Miracle: The Growth of Industrial Policy, 1925–1975.* Stanford: Stanford University Press.

Jones, Gavin W. 2012. "International Marriage in Asia: What Do We Know, and What Do We Need to Know?" Asia Research Institute Working Paper Series, No. 174.

Jones, Gavin, and Hsiu-hua Shen. 2008. "International Marriage in East and Southeast Asia: Trends and Research Emphases." *Citizenship Studies* 12(1): 9–25.

Jun, Sang-In. 2009. *Crazy about Apartments: Sociology of Residence in Contemporary South Korea* (in Korean). Seoul: Esoope.

Jung, Sun Joo, and Choi Sung Bo. 2015. "The Content Analysis on the Media Representation of Korean Multiculturalism: Focusing on EBS 'Multicultural Mother-in-Law and Daughter-in-Law Biographic Notes'" (in Korean). *Multicultural Education Studies* 8(2): 97–122.

Jung, Young-Tae. 1995. *A History of Social Democratic Parties in Korea* (in Korean). Seoul: Semyeongseogwan.

JungAng Daily (www.joins.com).

Justice Policy Institute, Justice Party. 2015. "National Citizens, Has Your Livelihood Somehow Improved?" (in Korean), 24 June 2015 (https://future-view.tistory.com/375).

Kang, Bogjeong. 2012. "The Status of Multicultural Family Policies and Services in Korea: Centering Around Multicultural Family Support Centers" (in Korean). *Journal of Multicultural Society* 5(1): 143–184.

Kang, Byung Ik. 2016. "The Conservative Parties' Reform of Welfare State: The Case of South Korea and UK" (in Korean). *Korean Politics Studies* 25(2): 145–174

Kang, Myung Hun. 1996. *The Korean Business Conglomerate: Chaebol Then and Now*. Berkeley: Institute of Asian Studies, University of California.
Kang, Myung Koo. 1999. "Postmodern Consumer Culture without Postmodernity: Copying the Crisis of Signification." *Cultural Studies* 13(1): 18–33.
Kang, Sang Jung. 2020. *The Risen State and Deserted Citizens: Japan Since Meiji* (translated in Korean from Japanese). Seoul: Sagyejeol.
Kariya, Takehiko. 2013. *Education Reform and Social Class in Japan: The Emerging Incentive Divide*. London: Routledge.
Kariya, Takehiko, and Jeremy Rappleye. 2010. "The Twisted, Unintended Impacts of Globalization on Japanese Education." *Research in the Sociology of Education* 17: 17–63.
KBS. 2020. "Six O'Clock My Home Village" (in Korean; http://program.kbs.co.kr/1tv/culture/sixhour/pc/index.html).
KBS News. 1996. "The Severity of Sex Ratio Imbalance among Primary School Children" (in Korean). (http://mn.kbs.co.kr/news/view.do?ncd=3762490)
Kim, Bo-Young. 2011. "Excess, or Absence of Welfare Politics" (in Korean). *Monthly Welfare Trend* 151: 66–68.
Kim, Chi-Wan. 2017. "Chilren's Education Prior to Old-Age Preparation? Old-Age Measure vs. Children's Education Expenses" (in Korean). *Life and Talk*, 4 December 2017 (https://www.lifentalk.com/1635).
Kim, Chul. [1966] 2000. "Is a Revolutionary Political Party Possible?" (in Korean). Kim Chul, ed., *The Reality of the People and Social Democracy: Complete Works of Kim Chul 1*. Seoul: Haenaem Publishers.
Kim, Dae-hwan. 1991. "Social Roles and Political Activities of the Korean Labor Parties" (in Korean). Labor Issues Research Institute, ed., *Korean Labor Issues*, pp. 197–219. Seoul: Bibong Publishers.
Kim, Dae Jung. 1994. "Is Culture Destiny? The Myth of Asia's Anti-Democratic Values." *Foreign Affairs* 73(6): 189–194.
Kim, Dong-Choon. 1993 "The Korean Labor Movement's Failure to Organize Politically" (in Korean). *Economy and Society* 20: 316–345.
Kim, Dong-Choon. 1995. *Research on Laborers in Korean Society* (in Korean). Seoul: Yeoksabipyongsa.
Kim, Dong-Choon. 1997. *National Division and Korean Society* (in Korean). Seoul: Yeoksabipyongsa.
Kim, Dong-Choon. 2000. *War and Society: What Was the Korean War to Us* (in Korean). Seoul: Dolbegae.
Kim, Dong-Choon. 2006. "How Did the Formation of Divided State Create the Character of Citizenship in Korea: 'Nationhood' and Citizenship Under the Korean War and the Early National Security State" (in Korean). *Economy and Society* 70: 168–189.

Kim, Doo-Sub. 2005. "Theoretical Explanations of Rapid Fertility Decline in Korea." *Japanese Journal of Population* 3(1): 1–25.
Kim, Eun-Jae, and Choi Hyunmi. 2016. "Experiences of Cultural Acceptance and Perception of Former Inhabitants Which the Immigrant Parties Perceived" (in Korean). *Journal of Korean Social Welfare Administration* 18(4): 143–167.
Kim, Eung-Seok, et al. 1993. *Structural Characteristics of Rural Households and Family Support System* (in Korean). Seoul: Korea Institute for Health and Social Affairs.
Kim, Gyoung Rae. 2011. "The Philosophy and Value of Work-Life Balance: Toward Paradigm Change" (in Korean). *Contemporary Social Science Research* 15: 1–18.
Kim, HeeJoo, Jong Hee Kwon, and Hyeong Suk Choi. 2012. "A Case Study on Discrimination Experienced by Unmarried Mother" (in Korean). *Korean Journal of Family Welfare* 36: 121–155.
Kim, Hung-Ju. 2002 "Modernization Project of Korean Society and Family Politics: On the Basis of Family Planning Programs" (in Korean). *Korea Journal of Population Studies* 25(1): 51–82.
Kim, Hyun Mee. 2012. "The Emergence of the 'Multicultural Family' and Genderized Citizenship in South Korea." Chang Kyung-Sup and Bryan S. Turner, eds., *Contested Citizenship in East Asia: Developmental Politics, National Unity, and Globalization*, pp. 203–217. London: Routledge.
Kim, Hyun Mee. 2014. "The State and Migrant Women: Diverging Hopes in the Making of 'Multicultural Families'." Chang Kyung-Sup, ed., *South Korea in Transition: Politics and Culture of Citizenship*, pp. 147–160. London: Routledge.
Kim, Il-Chul, et al. 1998. *The Tradition and Change in Lineage Village* (in Korean). Seoul: Baeksanseodang.
Kim, Jongyoung. 2015. *The Ruled Ruler: Studying in the US and the Birth of South Korean Elites* (in Korean). Seoul: Dolbegae.
Kim, Ju-Suk. 1994. *Woman and Family in the South Korean Countryside* (in Korean). Seoul: Hanul Academy.
Kim, Kyung Keun. 2019. "Major Trends in the Education Area" (in Korean). *Korean Social Trends 2019*, pp. 121–133. Sejong: National Statistical Office (NSO), Republic of Korea.
Kim, Myoung Soo. 2010. "Catch-up Economic Growth and Cultural Complexity in Korea" (in Korean). *Review of Culture and Economy* 13(2): 307–341.
Kim, Sang-Jun. 2003. "Yangbanization of the Entire Country: The Confucian Equalization Mechanism in Late Chosun" (in Korean). *Society and History* 63: 5–29.

Kim, Se-Kyun. 2013. "The Launching of the Park Geun-Hye Regime and the Development Prospect for South Korean Society" (in Korean). *Tomorrow-Opening History* 50: 79–86.
Kim, Seung-Kwon, et al. 2010. *The 2009 National Survey Study of Real Conditions of Multicultural Families* (in Korean). Ministry of Health, Welfare, and Family, Ministry of Justice, Ministry of Gender Equality, and Korea Institute for Health and Social Affairs.
Kim, Sunhyuk. 2000. *The Politics of Democratization in Korea: The Role of Civil Society*. Pittsburgh: University of Pittsburgh Press.
Kim, Sunhyuk. 2004. "South Korea: Confrontational Legacy and Democratic Contributions." Muthiah Alagappa, ed., *Civil Society and Political Change in Asia: Expanding and Contracting Democratic Space*, pp. 138–163. Stanford: Stanford University Press.
Kim, Tae-Heon. 1996. "The Characteristics of Rural Population, Korea, 1960–1995: Population Composition and Internal Migration" (in Korean). *Korean Journal of Population* 19(2): 77–105.
Kim, Tae-Heon. 2001. "Transition of the Korean Rural Society: On the Basis of Population and Family Changes" (in Korean). *Korean Journal of Population* 24(1): 5–40.
Kim, Tae-Heon, Hong Moon-Sik, and Chang Young-Sik. 1993. *The Size and Structure of the Korean Population* (in Korean). Seoul: National Statistical Office.
Kim, Tae-Hoon. 2012. "The 2012 Presidential Election, Analysis of Welfare Policy" (in Korean). *Social Movement* 109: 71–86.
Kim, Tae-Sung, and SeongKyoung-Ryung. 1993. *Social Welfare Policy* (in Korean). Seoul: Nanam.
Kim, Taekyoon, and Bo Kyung Kim. 2020. "Enhancing Mixed Accountability for State-Society Synergy: South Korea's Responses to COVID-19 with Ambidexterity Governance." *Inter-Asia Cultural Studies* 21(4): 533–541.
Kim, Yong-Hak, and Yoon Ho Young. 2013. "Value Exchange in Marriage Market" (in Korean). *Korea Journal of Population Studies* 36(3): 69–95.
Kim, Youna, ed. 2013. *The Korean Wave: Korean Media Go Global*. London: Routledge.
Kim, Youngsu. 1999. *The Political Movement of the Korean Laborer Class* (in Korean). Seoul: Hyeonjangeseomiraereul.
Kim, Yu-Seon. 2003. "The Direction of Reform in Labor Relations in South Korea" (in Korean). Presented at the Symposium on "The New Search for South Korean Labor Relations and the Implication of European Models," 5 September 2003.
Kim, Yun-Young, Seung-Ho Baek, and Sophia Seung-Yoon Lee. 2018. "Precarious Elderly Workers in Post-Industrial South Korea." *Journal of Contemporary Asia* 48(3): 465–484.

Ko, Se-Hoon. 1999. *History of the British Labor Movement* (in Korean). Seoul: Nanam Publishers.

Koh, Won. 2006. "Development, Acculturation and Modernization in South Korea during the Park Chung-Hee Regime with Focus on Simplified Family Ritual Standards" (in Korean). *Discourse 201* 9(3): 191–223.

Kong, Eun-Suk. 2009. "A Case Study on the Conflict Between a Korean Mother-in-Low and a Vietnamese Daughter-in-Low" (in Korean). *Korean Journal of Research in Gerontology* 18(1): 123–134.

Koo, Hagen. 1993a. "Strong State and Contentious Society." Hagen Koo, ed., *State and Society in Contemporary Korea*, pp. 231–249. Ithaca: Cornell University Press.

Koo, Hagen. 1993b. "The State, Minjung, and the Working Class in South Korea." Hagen Koo, ed., *State and Society in Contemporary Korea*, pp. 131–162. Ithaca: Cornell University Press.

Koo, Hagen. 2001. *Korean Workers: The Culture and Politics of Class Formation.* Ithaca: Cornell University Press.

Korea Confederation of Trade Unions (KCTU). 1999, 2001. *Report on Surveys about the Living Circumstances and Awareness of Union Members.* Internal survey reports.

Korea Higher Education Research Institute (KHEI). 2017. Unpublished Report (https://khei-khei.tistory.com/2097).

Korea Institute for Curriculum and Evaluation (KICE). 2002. "A Study on the Measures for Reducing the Required Subjects at High Schools" (in Korean). Research report submitted to the Ministry of Education and Human Resources Development.

Korea Insurance Development Institute (KIDI). 2019. "The Report on the Retirement Market in 2018" (in Korean). Research report.

Korea Policy Portal (www.korea.kr).

Korea Research Institute for Vocational Education and Training (KRIVET). 2008. *The Perception Trends of Ordinary Citizens and Corporate Personnel Managers on Capability and Educational Background* (in Korean). Research Report 2008-2. Seoul: KRIVET.

Korea Rural Economic Institute (KREI). 2003. "The Change and Development of Rural Society in South Korea" (in Korean). *The Papers on the Century History of Agriculture and Rural Community in South Korea*, volume 2. Seoul: KREI.

Korea Rural Economic Institute (KREI). 2004. "The Medium and Long-Term Prospect for the Rural and Farm Household Population and the Agricultural Labor Force and the Policy Tasks" (in Korean). Research Report R491. 2004.12.

Korea Statistical Office (KSO). 2021. "The Tentative Result of Birth and Death Statistics in the Survey of Population Changes in 2020." Media brief.

Korea Women's Development Institute (KWDI). 2016. "The Analysis of the National Survey of the Realities of Multicultural Families in 2015" (in Korean). Research Report 2016–03, submitted to The Ministry of Gender Equality and Family.
Korean Statistical Information Service (KOSIS). Each year. "Urban Household Income by Deciles Distribution Ratio" (http://kosis.kr/statHtml/statHtml.do?orgId=101&tblId=DT_1L9I008).
Krugman, Paul. 1994. "The Myth of Asia's Miracle." *Foreign Affairs* 73(6): 62–78.
Kuk, Min Ho. 2012. *Developmental State, Welfare State, and Neoliberalism* (in Korean). Gwangju: Chonnam National University Press.
Kukminilbo (www.kukinews.com).
Kyeonggilbo (https://www.kyeonggi.com).
Kyunghyang Daily (www.khan.co.kr).
Laslett, Barbara, and Johanna Brenner. 1989. "Gender and Social Reproduction: Historical Perspectives." *Annual Review of Sociology* 15: 381–404.
Lee, Byoung-Hoon, and Sophia Seung-Yoon Lee. 2017. "Winning Conditions of Precarious Workers' Struggles: A Reflection Based on Case Studies from South Korea." *Relations Industrielles-Industrial Relations* 72(3): 524–550.
Lee, Chang Eon. 2012. "A Study on the Relation Between the Collective Identity and Resistance of Student Movement Under the Yushin System: Focusing on the Role of the Intramural Network in the Universities" (in Korean). *Historical Studies* 23: 7–42.
Lee, Cheol-Sung. 2016. *When Solidarity Works: Labor-Civic Networks and Welfare States in the Market Reform Era*. Cambridge: Cambridge University Press.
Lee, Ching Kwan. 1999. "From Organized Dependence to Disorganized Despotism: Changing Labour Regimes in Chinese Factories." *China Quarterly* 157: 44–71.
Lee, Hee Jae. 2011. "The Nature of the Change in the Confucian Rituals During the Japanese Colonial Occupation Period: Focusing on Family Rituals in 'The Standard Rules of Rituals' in the 1930s" (in Korean). *Japan Studies* 15: 565–584.
Lee, Hong Yung. 1991. *From Revolutionary Cadres to Party Technocrats in Socialist China*. Berkeley: University of California Press.
Lee, Hui-Jei. 2000. "Capital Accumulation of Korean Landlord in Colonial Period" (in Korean). MA thesis in Sociology Department, Yonsei University.
Lee, Hyun-jin. 2009. *The American Economic Aid Policy to the Republic of Korea, 1948–1960* (in Korean). Seoul: Hyean.
Lee, Hyunok. 2016. "Changing Care Regime and Feminization of Migration: A Comparison of Taiwan and South Korea" (in Korean). *Economy and Society* 110: 239–269.

Lee, Kap-Yun. 1998. *Elections and Regionalism in Korea* (in Korean). Seoul: Oreum Publishers.
Lee, Keun. 2016. *Economic Catch-up and Technological Leapfrogging: The Path to Development and Macroeconomic Stability in Korea*. Cheltenam: Edward Elgar.
Lee, Myung-Bak. 2007. "Korea 747" (http://english.mbplaza.net/default/korea/?type=html/747_01&wgrp=42&m=2).
Lee, Sam-Sik, and Hyo-Jin Choi. 2013. "The National Reproductive Crisis: South Korea's Fertility Shock." Proceedings of the International Conference on 'Life and Humanity in Late Modern Transformation: Beyond East and West', organized by SNU Center for Social Sciences, Korea Institute for Health and Social Affairs, and Korean Sociological Association, 30–31 May 2013, Seoul National University.
Lee, Sophia Seung-Yoon, Baek Seung Ho, Kim Migyoung, and Kim Yoon Young. 2017. "Analysis of Precariousness in Korean Youth Labour Market" (in Korean). *Journal of Critical Social Policy* 54: 487–521.
Lee, Sophia Seung-Yoon, Lee Jung-Ah, and Baek Seung-Ho. 2016. "Korean Precarious Youth Labour Market and Policy Ideas for Youth Basic Income" (in Korean). *Journal of Critical Social Policy* 52: 365–405.
Lee, Sophia Seung-Yoon, Park Kyoung-jin, and Kim Gyu-hye. 2019. "A Qualitative Study of Young Freelancers' Experience of Work and Social Protection System in South Korea" (in Korean). *Journal of Critical Social Welfare* 64: 181–239.
Leoin, Thomas. 2016. "Social Investment as a Perspective on Welfare State Transformation in Europe." *Intereconomics* 51(4): 194–200.
Lewis, W. Arthur. 1954. "Economic Development with Unlimited Supplies of Labour." *Manchester School of Economics and Social Studies* 22(1): 139–191.
Lie, John. 1998. *Han Unbound: The Political Economy of South Korea*. Stanford: Stanford University Press.
Lim, Byung-Do. 2013. "'Female Workers' in Guro Industrial Area Who Lived with 'Queen Bee' in Honeycomb" (in Korean). *Power of Truth*, 1 May 2013.
Lim, Hyun-Chin. 1986. *Dependent Development in Korea, 1963–1979*. Seoul: Seoul National University Press.
Lim, Hyun-Chin, and Jin-Ho Jang. 2006. "Between Neoliberalism and Democracy: The Transformation of the Developmental State in South Korea." *Development and Society* 35(1): 1–28.
Lim, Hyun-Chin, Lee Se-Yong, and Chang Kyung-Sup, eds. 1998. *Koreans' Quality of Life: Physical and Psychological Safety* (in Korean). Seoul: Seoul National University Press.
Lim, Sungyun. 2019. *Rules of the House: Family Law and Domestic Disputes in Colonial Korea*. Berkeley: University of California Press.

Lim, Young-Il. 1997a. *South Korea's Labor Movement and Class Politics in South Korea, 1987–1995* (in Korean). Masan: Kyungnam University Press.
Lim, Young-Il. 1997b. "Institutionalization of the Labor Movement and Citizenship" (in Korean). *Economy and Society* 34: 51–66.
Lim, Young-Il. 2014. "KLDP and Labor Politics in Korea" (in Korean). *Economy and Society* 64: 65–85.
Lipton, Michael. 1977. *Why Poor People Stay Poor: Urban Bias in World Development*. Cambridge: Harvard University Press.
Löw, Martina, and Hubert Knoblauch. 2020. "Dancing in Quarantine: The Spatial Refiguration of Society and the Interaction Orders." *Space and Culture* 23(3): 221–225.
Maeil Economic Daily (www.mk.co.kr).
Maeil Labor News (http://www.labortoday.co.kr).
Mann, Michael. 1987. "Ruling Class Strategies and Citizenship." *Sociology* 21(3): 339–354.
Marshall, T. H. 1964. *Class, Citizenship, and Social Development*. Garden City: Doubleday.
Marx, Karl. [1852] 1951. *The Eighteenth Brumaire of Louis Bonaparte*. New York: International Publishers.
McGinn, Noel F., Donald R. Snodgrass, Shin-Bok Kim, Quee-Young Kim, and Yung Bong Kim. 1979. *Education and Development in Korea*. Cambridge: Harvard University Press.
McQuarrie, Michael. 2017. "The Revolt of the Rust Belt: Place and Politics in the Age of Anger." *British Journal of Sociology* 68(S1): S120–S152.
Ministry of Education (MOE), Republic of Korea. 2019. "The Supporting Measures for University Innovation to Cope with Demographic Restructuring and the Fourth Industrial Revolution" (in Korean). Policy announcement, 6 August 2019.
Ministry of Gender Equality and Family (MOGEF), Republic of Korea. 2019. *The National Survey Study of the Actual Conditions of Multicultural Families* (in Korean).
Mobrand, Erik. 2019. *Top-Down Democracy in South Korea*. Seattle: University of Washington Press.
Money Today (www.moneytoday.co.kr).
Monthly Chosun (http://monthly.chosun.com/).
Monthly Report on Legislation (National Congress of the Republic of Korea).
Moody, Kim. 1997. *Workers in a Lean World: Unions in the International Economy*. London: Verso.
Moon, Seungsook. 2005. *Militarized Modernity and Gendered Citizenship in South Korea*. Durham: Duke University Press.

Moon, Woojong. 2020. "Corporate Social vs. Developmental Responsibility: Corporate Citizenship in the Restructuring of China's Pharmaceutical Industry." *Citizenship Studies* 24(7): 887–903.

Nam, Se-Jin, and Cho Heung-Sik. 1995. *Social Welfare in Korea* (in Korean). Seoul: Nanam.

National Election Commission (NEC), Republic of Korea. 2020. "The Election History of the Republic of Korea" (in Korean) (http://museum.nec.go.kr/museum2018/bbs/2/1/1/20170912155756377100_list.do?article_category=1#year2000).

National Statistical Office (NSO). Republic of Korea. 1998. *Fifty Years' Economic and Social Change Seen Through Statistics* (in Korean).

National Statistical Office (NSO), Republic of Korea. 2000. *The Appearance of the Republic of Korea Seen through Statistics* (in Korean).

National Statistical Office (NSO), Republic of Korea. 2019. *Korean Social Trend 2019* (in Korean).

National Welfare Planning Commission, Republic of Korea. 1995. "The Basic Plan of National Welfare for the Globalization of 'the Quality of Life'" (in Korean).

Newsis (www.newsis.com).

Newsweek (www.newsweek.com).

Nosajeongwiwonhoe (Labor-Business-Government Committee). 1998. "Nosajeong Co-declaration" (in Korean), 20 January 1998.

Ochiai, Emiko. 2011. "Unsustainable Societies: The Failure of Familialism in East Asia's Compressed Modernity." *Historical Social Research* 36(2): 219–245.

Oh, Young Ran. 2019. "Analysis on the Formation of the Family Planning Policy in Korea: Focused on the Perspective of Policy Diffusion" (in Korean). *Korea Social Policy Review* 26(3): 195–223.

Ohmynews. 2016. " Multiculturals, Raise Your Hands" (in Korean). 11 August 2016.

Ohmynews. 2019. "Seoul National University with Only Those Haves... Devils Love 'South Korean Elites'" (in Korean). 19 June 2019.

OhmynewsTV. 11 October 2017 (https://www.youtube.com/watch?v=4V9Yln b5ZWA).

Ohno, Taiichi. [1978] 1988. *Toyota Production System: Beyond Large-Scale Production*. New York: Productivity Press.

Oi, Jean C. 1989. *State and Peasant in Contemporary China*. Berkeley: University of California Press.

Organisation for Economic Cooperation and Development (OECD). 2007. *Jobs for Youth: Korea*. Paris: OECD.

Organisation for Economic Cooperation and Development (OECD). 2011, 2019. *Education at a Glance: OECD Indicators*. Paris: OECD (https://data.oecd.org/eduatt/population-with-tertiary-education.htm).

Park, Bo-Young. 2006. "Family Policy in an Ageing and Low Fertility Society: Work-Family Life Balance Policies" (in Korean). *Situation and Welfare* (22): 119–153.

Park, Chai Bin, and Nam-Hoon Cho. 1995. "Consequences of Son Preference in a Low-Fertility Society: Imbalance of the Sex Ratio at Birth in Korea." *Population and Development Review* 21(1): 59–84.

Park, Dong-jin. 1995. "Change in Political Relations Laws and Party Politics" (in Korean). An Heui-su, ed., *A Theory of Korean Party Politics*, pp. 349–394. Seoul: Nanam Publishers.

Park, Kangwoo. 2014. "The College Wage Premium in Korea (1974–2011): A Supply and Demand Factor Decomposition" (in Korean). *Journal of Industrial Economics and Business* 27(1): 477–505.

Park, Mee-Hae. 1991. "Patterns and Trends of Educational Mating in Korea." *Korea Journal of Population and Development* 20(2): 1–16.

Park, Myoung-Kyu. 2014. *National, People, Citizen* (in Korean). Seoul: Sohwa.

Park, Myung-Lim. 1996. *Outbreak and Origins of the Korean War* (in Korean). Seoul: Nanam Publishers.

Park, Myung-Lim. 1998. "Democracy and Authoritarianism in the 1950s' Korea" (in Korean). Historical Issues Research Institute, ed., *Choice and Refraction of the Two Koreas in the 1950s*, pp. 72–127. Seoul: Yeoksabipyeongsa.

Park, Song-Yong. 2019. "A Study of Place Names Representing Socio-Spatial Hierarchy and Distinction in a Village with Yangban Lineage: A Case of Sinchon in Cheongdo County" (in Korean). *Folk Studies* 45: 55–89.

Park, Sunny. 2018. "The Transformation of Korean Cultural Journalism: From 1960s to 2010s" (in Korean). *Media Economics and Culture* 16(1): 57–98.

Park, Tae Gyun. 2008. "The First Korean Government and the US in 1948" (in Korean). *Citizen and the World* 14: 95–109.

Park, Woo. 2020. *Chaoxianzu Entrepreneurs in Korea: Searching for Citizenship in the Ethnic Homeland*. London: Routledge.

Park, Young-Ho. 2000. "Why Did the Democratic Labor Party Lose?" (in Korean). *Trends and Outlooks* 45: 92–99.

Pekkanen, Robert. 2003. "Molding Japanese Civil Society: State-Structured Incentives and the Patterning of Civil Society." Frank J. Schwartz and Susan J. Pharr, eds., *The State of Civil Society in Japan*, pp. 116–134. Cambridge: Cambridge University Press.

Pekkanen, Robert. 2004. "Japan: Social Capital without Advocacy." Muthiah Alagappa, ed., *Civil Society and Political Change in Asia: Expanding and Contracting Democratic Space*, pp. 223–257. Stanford: Stanford University Press.

Peng, Ito, Joseph Wong, and Andrew DeWit. 2010. "East Asian Welfare Regimes." *The Asia-Pacific Journal* 48-4-10 (29 November 2010).

People's Solidarity for Participatory Democracy (PSPD). 1998. *White Book on Public Interest Foundations: Accusing Public Interest Foundations That Are Chaebol's Camouflaged Affiliate Firms* (in Korean). Seoul: Jijeong.
People's Solidarity for Participatory Democracy (PSPD). 2011. "The Launching of the National Headquarter for Realizing the Halved Tuitions and Strengthening the Public Nature of Education" (in Korean), 29 August 2011.
Perrow, Charles. 1984. *Normal Accidents: Living with High-Risk Technologies*. New York: Basic Books.
Peters, Michael A. 2018. "The End of Neoliberal Globalisation and the Rise of Authoritarian Populism." *Educational Philosophy and Theory* 50(4): 323–325.
President Parkchunghee Memorial Foundation. 2020. "The National Chart of Education, 5 December 1968" (https://www.youtube.com/watch?v=3Syifr u8BR8).
Presidential Committee on Ageing Society and Population Policy (PCASPP). 2018a. "The Roadmap of the Low Fertility-Ageing Society Policy for 'the Improvement of the Quality of Life for All Generations and the Realization of the Inclusionary State'" (in Korean). Report Agenda, 7 December 2018.
Presidential Committee on Ageing Society and Population Policy (PCASPP). 2018b. "Youth Talk". 16–30 August 2018 (https://www.yna.co.kr/view/AKR20180901018400017).
Presidential Committee on the Fourth Industrial Revolution. October 2017 (https://www.4th-ir.go.kr/).
Rawls, John. 2001. *The Law of Peoples*. Cambridge: Harvard University Press.
Realmeter (www.realmeter.net), 17 December 2018.
Rhyu, Mina. 2005. "'Collaboration and Frustration' to Japanese Colonial Government: Focusing on the Relationship of Kyonghagwon, Hyangyo and Munmyou" (in Korean). *Korean Culture* 36: 157–191.
Rhyu, Mina. 2007. "The Joseon Governor General Office's Policy Regarding the Yurim (Confucianists) Society During the Wartime Period" (in Korean). *History and Reality* 63: 309–341.
Richardson, Eileen H., and Bryan S. Turner. 2001. "Sexual, Intimate or Reproductive Citizenship?" *Citizenship Studies* 5(3): 329–338.
Ripley, Amanda. 2014. *The Smartest Kids in the World, and How They Got That Way*. New York: Simon & Schuster.
Riskin, Carl. 1987. *China's Political Economy: The Quest for Development Since 1949*. Oxford: Oxford University Press.
Roh, Joongkee. 1995. *Research on the State's Labor Control Policies: 1987–1992* (in Korean). Ph.D. dissertation, Department of Sociology, Seoul National University,
Roh, Joongkee. 2012. "A Study on the 1987 Great Labour Struggle" (in Korean). *Economy and Society* 96: 178–209.

Ryoo, Woongjae. 2008. "Globalization, or the Logic of Cultural Hybridization: The Case of the Korean Wave." *Asian Journal of Communication* 19(2): 137–151.
Sautman, Barry. 1992. "Sirens of the Strongman: Neo-Authoritarianism in Recent Chinese Political Theory." *China Quarterly* 129: 72–102.
Schurmann, Franz. 1966. *Ideology and Organization in Communist China*. Berkeley: University of California Press.
Selden, Mark. 1971. *The Yenan Way in Revolutionary China*. Cambridge: Harvard University Press.
Seo, Bong Seob. 1997. "Welfare Policies and Democratization in Korea" (in Korean). *Korean Public Administration Review* 31(1): 95–111.
Seo, Joong-Seok. 2000. *Cho Bong-am and the 1950s* (in Korean). Seoul: Yeoksabipyeongsa.
Seol, Dong-Hoon. 2002. "The Discrimination of Gastarbeiter and Their Civil Right" (in Korean). *Citizen and the World* 2: 345–356.
Seol, Dong-Hoon. 2014. "The Citizenship of Foreign Workers: Stratified Formation, Fragmented Evolution." Chang Kyung-Sup, ed., *South Korea in Transition: Politics and Culture of Citizenship*, pp. 131–146. London: Routledge.
Seong, Eun Young, Kwon Ji Eun, and Hwang Soon-Taeg. 2012. "A Qualitative Study on the Conflict of Mother-in-laws of Multicultural Families: Focusing on the Rural Areas" (in Korean). *Korean Journal of Woman Psychology* 17(3): 363–383.
Seoul Times. 2018. ""Hey, Multicultural" ... the Homeroom Teacher Calls My Friend like This" (in Korean). 30 July 2018.
Seth, Michael. 2002. *Education Fever: Society, Politics, and the Pursuit of Schooling in South Korea*. Honolulu: University of Hawaii Press.
Shin, Gi-Wook. 2006. *Ethnic Nationalism in Korea: Genealogy, Politics, and Legacy*. Stanford: Stanford University Press.
Shin, Kwang-Yeong. 2013. "Economic Crisis, Neoliberal Reforms, and the Rise of Precarious Work in South Korea." *American Behavioral Scientist* 57(3): 335–353.
Shin, Woo Cheol. 2008. "The Origins of the Korean Constitutional Drafts (1945~1948): Influences of the Constitutional Documents during the Provisional Government" (in Korean). *The Journal of the Korean Public Law Association* 36(4): 389–434.
Shin, Yong-Ha. 2001. *Ethnonational Movement and Social Movement in Early Modern Korea* (in Korean). Seoul: Munhakgwajiseongsa.
Shue, Vivienne. 1988. *The Reach of the State: Sketches of the Chinese Body Politic*. Stanford: Stanford University Press.

Sisa Journal. 2001. "DJ's Rule for Three Years Has Aggravated the Regionalist Bigotory", 25 January 2010 (http://www.sisajournal.com/news/articleView.html?idxno=78924).

Social Welfare Policy Appraisal Committee, Republic of Korea. 1994. *The Development Direction for Social Welfare Policy* (in Korean).

Solidarity for Economic Reform. 2007. "Analysis of the Factors for Offense Assessment Concerning White Collar Crimes in the Courts of Our Country: Under What Reasons Convicted White Collar Criminals Are Released." *Economic Reform Report* 2007(9).

Solinger, Dorothy J. 1992. "Urban Entrepreneurs and the State: The Merger of State and Society." Arthur Lewis Rosenbaum, ed., *State and Society in China: The Consequences of Reform*, pp. 121–142. Boulder: Westview.

Solinger, Dorothy J. 1999. *Contesting Citizenship in Urban China: Peasant Migrants, the State, and the Logic of the Market.* Berkeley: University of California Press.

Son, In-Su. 1992. *The American Military Rule and Educational Policy* (in Korean). Seoul: Minyoungsa.

Song, Ho-Keun. 1995. *Korea's Company Welfare: An Empirical Research* (in Korean). Seoul: Korea Labor Institute.

Song, Ho-Keun. 1997. *The Market and Welfare Politics: A Study of Sweden's Social Democracy* (in Korean). Seoul: Nanam.

Song, Won Keun, Shin Hak-Rim, Lee Won-Jae, and Lee Il-Young. 2016. "*Chaebol* (Conglomerates) in Korea, *Chaebol*'s Korea?" (in Korean). *Quarterly Changbi* 44(4): 449–476.

Sorensen, Clark K. 1988. *Over the Mountains Are Mountains: Korean Peasant Households and Their Adaptation to Rapid Industrialization.* Seattle: University of Washington Press.

Soresen, Clark K. 1994. "Success and Education in South Korea." *Comparative Education Review* 38(1): 10–35.

Stephens, John D. 1979. *The Transition from Capitalism to Socialism.* London: Macmillan.

Suh, Hee Kyung. 2006. "The Historical Origins of the 1948 Founding Constitutional Law in the Modern Korea, 1898–1919: Focusing on the Understanding of Democratic Republic in the General People's Assembly, March 1 Independence Movement, and the Korean Provision Government" (in Korean). *Korean Political Science Review* 40(5): 139–163.

Suh, Jae-Jung, and Mikyoung Kim, eds. 2017. *Challenges of Modernization and Governance in South Korea: The Sinking of the Sewol and Its Causes.* London/New York: Palgrave Macmillan.

Sung, Nak Il, Lee Hye Kyeong, and Cho Dong Hyuk. 2012. "Regional Imbalance in Sex Ratio and Marriage Rate: Empirical Analysis" (in Korean). *Applied Economics* 14(1): 187–220.

Suzuki, Akira. 2003. "The Death of Unions' Associational Life? Political and Cultural Aspects of Enterprise Unions." Frank J. Schwartz and Susan J. Pharr, eds., *The State of Civil Society in Japan*, pp. 195–213. Cambridge: Cambridge University Press.

Thaxton, Ralph A. 1983. *China Turned Rightside Up: Revolutionary Legitimacy in the Peasant World*. New Haven: Yale University Press.

Thompson, E. P. 1963. *The Making of the English Working Class*. New York: Vintage Books.

Tocqueville, Alexis de. [1835–1839] 1988. *Democracy in America*. New York: Harper and Row.

Triadafilopoulos, Triadafilos. 2012. *Becoming Multicultural: Immigrants and the Politics of Membership in Canada and Germany*. Vancouver: University of British Columbia Press.

Tsujinaka, Yutaka. 2003. "From Developmentalism to Maturity: Japan's Civil Society Organizations in Comparative Perspective." Frank J. Schwartz and Susan J. Pharr, eds., *The State of Civil Society in Japan*, pp. 83–115. Cambridge: Cambridge University Press.

Turner, Bryan S. 1990. "Outline of a Theory of Citizenship." *Sociology* 24(2): 189–217.

Turner, Bryan S. 1993. "Contemporary Problems in the Theory of Citizenship." Bryan S. Turner, ed., *Citizenship and Social Theory*, pp. 1–18. London: Sage.

Turner, Bryan S. 2001. "The Erosion of Citizenship." *British Journal of Sociology* 52(2): 189–209.

Turner, Bryan S. 2008. "Citizenship, Reproduction and the State: International Marriage and Human Rights." *Citizenship Studies* 12(1): 45–54.

Turner, Bryan S. 2016. "We Are All Denizens Now: On the Erosion of Citizenship." *Citizenship Studies* 20(6/7): 679–692.

Turner, Bryan S., and Chang Kyung-Sup. 2012. "Whither East Asian Citizenship?" Chang Kyung-Sup and Bryan S. Turner, eds., *Contested Citizenship in East Asia: Developmental Politics, National Unity, and Globalization*, pp. 243–255. London/New York: Routledge.

United Nations Economic and Social Council, the Committee on Economic, Social and Cultural Rights. 2001. "Concluding Observations of the Committee on Economic, Social and Cultural Rights on Non-Compliance with Reporting Obligations by States Parties: Republic of Korea", 9 May 2001.

Wade, Robert. 1990. *Governing the Market: Economic Theory and the Role of Government in East Asian Industrialization*. Princeton: Princeton University Press.

Wade, Robert. 1998. "The Asian Debt-and-Development Crisis of 1997–?: Causes and Consequences." *World Development* 26(8): 1535–1553.

Walder, Andrew. 1986. *Communist Neo-Traditionalism: Work and Authority in Chinese Industry*. Berkeley: University of California Press.
Wando Times. 2013. "'Uncomfortable' Because of Being Mobilized for Various Multicultural Family Events" (in Korean). 9 January 2013 (http://wandonews.com/news/articleView.html?idxno=192595).
Washington Post. 14 Jan 2014.
Watson, Iain. 2010. "Multiculturalism in South Korea: A Critical Assessment." *Journal of Contemporary Asia* 40(2): 337–346.
Watson, Iain. 2011. "Global Korea: Foreign Aid and National Interests in an Age of Globalization." *Contemporary Politics* 17(1): 53–69.
Weber, Max. 1946. *From Max Weber: Essays in Sociology*, edited by H. H. Gerth, and C. Wright Mills. New York: Oxford University Press.
Whittaker, D. Hugh. 1990. "The End of Japanese-Style Employment?" *Work, Employment & Society* 4(3): 321–347.
Whittaker, D. Hugh, Timothy Sturgeon, Toshie Okita, and Tianbiao Zhu. 2020. *Compressed Development: Time and Timing in Economic and Social Development*. Oxford: Oxford University Press.
Wiarda, Howard J. 2003. *Civil Society: The American Model and Third World Development*. Boulder: Westview.
Windolf, Paul. 1998. "Privatization and Elite Reproduction in Eastern Europe." *European Journal of Sociology* 39(2): 335–376.
World Bank. 2020 "Fertility Rate, Total (Births per Woman): All Countries and Economies" (https://data.worldbank.org/indicator/SP.DYN.TFRT.IN).
Yan, Yunxiang. 2010. "The Chinese Path to Individualization." *British Journal of Sociology* 61(3): 489–512.
Yang, Heung-Sook, and Kong Yoon-Kyung. 2016. "Rural Women's Everyday Life and Roles Described in the Diary" (in Korean). *Korean National Culture* 61: 41–79.
Yang, Hyunah. 2006. "Vision of Postcolonial Feminist Jurisprudence in Korea: Seen from the 'Family-Head System' in Family Law." *Journal of Korean Law* 5(2): 12–28.
Yang, Hyunah. 2011. *Reading the Korean Family Law: At the Intersection of Tradition, Coloniality and Gender* (in Korean). Seoul: Changbi.
Yang, Jae-Jin. 2017. *The Political Economy of the Small Welfare State in South Korea*. Cambridge: Cambridge University Press.
Yeongnam Daily. 2003. (https://www.yeongnam.com/web/).
Yi, Hwang Jik. 2014. "A Study on Confucian Organizations in Post-Liberation Period" (in Korean). *Phenomenon and Cognition* 122: 115–149.
Yi, JeongDuk, et al. 2014. *Compressed Modernity and Rural Society: Life, Community, and the State in Changpyeong Diary* (in Korean). Jeonju: Jeonbuk National University Press.
Yonhapnews (http://www.yonhapnews.co.kr).

Yoon, In-Jin. 2008. "The Development and Characteristics of Multiculturalism in South Korea: With a Focus on the Relationship of the State and Civil Society" (in Korean). *Korean Journal of Sociology* 42(2): 72–103.

Yoon, In-Jin. 2016. "Characteristics and Changes of Koreans' Perceptions of Multicultural Minorities" (in Korean). *Journal of Diaspora Studies* 10(1): 125–154.

Yoon, Jin-Ho, Yu-Sun Kim, Jang-Ho Kim, Dae-Myung Roh, and Jae-Eun Seok. 2005. "The Direction of Labor and Welfare Policies for Allied Growth and Bipolarization Annulment" (in Korean). Report submitted to the Presidential Commission on Policy and Planning, November 2005.

Yoon, Jong-Seok. 2020. "The Local State and *Nongmingong* Citizenship: Local Welfare as Developmental Contributory Rights in Guangdong Province." *Citizenship Studies* 24(7): 871–886.

Yoon, Sang-Chul. 1997. *Political Change of the Authoritarian Regime in Korea, 1983–1990* (in Korean). Seoul: Seoul National University Press.

Yun, Yeong-Ho. 1998. "Tardy and Dull, the Structural Adjustment of Five Largest *Chaebol*: 'Mighty *Chaebol*' Head-On Contest Against D.J. Reform" (in Korean). *Shin Dong-A* 41(11): 160–171.

Zakaria, Fareed, and Lee Kuan Yew. 1994. "Culture Is Destiny: A Conversation with Lee Kuan Yew." *Foreign Affairs* 73(2): 109–126.

Zaretsky, Eli. 1973. *Capitalism, the Family, and Personal Life*. New York: Harper & Colophon Books.

Zhou, Kate Xiao. 1996. *How the Farmers Changed China: Power of the People*. Boulder: Westview.

INDEX

A
Absolute poverty, 130
Activist students, 154, 155
Advanced risk society, 196
Anti-communism, 34, 81
Antinatal policy, 170
Aristocratization, 179
Aristocratization of democracy, 45
"Aristocratization" of politics, 33

B
Backward risk society, 197, 252
Bauman, Zigmunt, 251
Beck, Ulrich, 196, 197, 204, 207, 208, 224, 245, 254, 255
Birth control, 170, 244
Bismarck, 20, 74, 112
Bismarckian social insurances, 135
Bismarckian social security system, 103, 215
Blair, Tony, 135, 156, 157
Bourgeoisie, 47, 61, 84, 89, 94, 101, 103, 117, 179

British labour party, 74

C
Capitalism, 9, 26, 39, 95, 115, 119, 120, 132, 147, 150, 153, 167, 176, 179, 196, 214, 216, 217
Chaebol, 36, 84, 100, 101, 105, 112, 113, 119, 124, 125, 169, 209, 233, 236, 237, 253
Children, 14, 21, 23, 43, 84, 103, 122, 139, 140, 142, 143, 150, 156–158, 163–167, 169, 170, 172–174, 183, 185, 188, 189, 215, 216
China, 6, 17, 27–30, 37–41, 43–48, 50–52, 103, 107, 108, 110, 146, 185, 193, 194, 207, 221, 226, 227, 244, 247, 252
Choi, Jang Jip, 9, 57, 67, 68, 76
Chosun, 32, 177, 179
Citizenship, 85
Citizenship politics, 17, 29, 41, 45, 47, 53, 109

Citizenship rights, 3
Civil rights, 20, 34, 43–47, 49, 51, 58, 65, 85, 90, 97, 100, 107, 109, 110, 116, 122, 133, 224, 227
Civil society, 7–10, 14, 17, 18, 27–38, 40–47, 50–52, 57–62, 64–68, 70–72, 74, 77, 79, 81–83, 94, 120, 121, 123, 132, 135, 136, 143, 146, 147, 154, 225, 226, 229, 247, 253
Civil war, 34, 60, 81, 180
Cold War, the, 59–61, 81, 83, 95, 103
College/university education, 22
College/university entrance examination, 22, 144, 158
Colonialism, 7
Complex risk society, 24, 25, 193, 195, 196, 199, 201, 205, 206, 208, 218, 219, 252
Compressed modernity, 10, 12, 22, 25, 81, 82, 173, 246
Compressive risk society, 196, 198
Confucian, 23, 24
Confucian familialism, 120
Confucian norms, 24, 180, 181, 191
Confucianism, 49, 177–179, 227, 245
Continental Europe, 95, 242
Continental European, 20, 112
Continental European-style social security system, 128
Continental European welfare state, 103
Contributory rights, 11
Coronavirus, 3–6, 207, 208, 218
Cosmopolitan citizenship, 176
Cosmopolitanization, 186
Crisis politics, 122
Critical academics, 154
Critical intellectual, 40, 253
Cultural aristocratization, 180

Cultural citizenship, 21, 23, 24, 143, 145, 153, 177, 179, 181, 186, 192, 217
Cultural rights, 92
Cumings, Bruce, 8, 33, 51, 59, 60, 66, 113, 125, 146, 154, 208, 232, 234

D
Democracy, 5, 6, 8, 18, 34, 35, 37, 42, 43, 45–47, 52, 61, 67, 78, 82, 83, 85, 90, 92, 94, 97, 100, 108, 110, 122, 123, 132, 145, 147, 154, 160, 205, 227–229
Democratic Labor Party (DLP), 56, 57, 72–75, 77, 79–81, 83
Democratic representation, 19, 85
Democratic social representation, 18, 81, 82
Democratic succession of developmental politics, 104
Democratization, 11, 20, 21, 30, 36, 45, 56, 62, 64, 66, 68, 76, 78, 82, 83, 91, 94, 97, 100, 104, 110, 122, 142, 145, 154, 155, 157, 170, 195, 204, 206, 214, 237, 242
Demographic behavior, 22, 23, 174
Demographic meltdown, 23, 165, 172, 174
Demographic patriotism, 171
Demographic restructuring, 22, 165, 173
Demographic transition, 245
Developmental citizenship, 91, 97, 99–101, 103–110, 113, 118, 121, 128, 131, 136, 215, 232
Developmental liberalism, 20, 111, 112, 114, 115, 117, 121, 122, 124, 125, 128, 133, 136, 215, 234, 235, 244

Developmental politics, 19, 90–92, 94, 96–98, 104–106, 109, 110, 232
Developmental risk society, 204
Developmental state, 8, 12, 13, 36, 41, 46, 101, 103, 106, 110, 114, 117, 119–121, 124, 131, 150, 151, 183, 185, 192, 199, 201, 214, 217, 234
Developmental workfare, 149, 151
Dictatorship, 45, 46, 58, 65, 85, 97, 108, 116, 145, 207, 252
Divorce, 22, 23, 164, 169, 174

E
East Asia, 12–14, 16–18, 27–29, 47, 49, 50, 52, 106, 117, 161, 202, 220, 221, 224–227, 232
East Asian, 7, 12–18, 28, 29, 45–53, 161, 227
East Asian capitalism, 49
Eastern Europe, 220
Education, 8
Education as citizenship, 155
Education as social citizenship, 155
Education zeal, 12, 14, 144, 145, 155, 159–161
Educationalization, 146, 147, 149, 153, 155, 158, 240
Educationalized citizenship, 216
Erosion of citizenship, 134, 135
Esping-Andersen, 94, 112, 115
Ethno nationalism, 8, 171
Europe, 7, 114, 135

F
Familialism, 169, 170
Familialization, 24, 122, 191
Family planning, 23, 163, 166, 174
Fertility, 4, 17, 22, 23, 164–167, 169–174, 180, 217, 244–247

Fertility transition, 164, 165, 244, 245
Financial crisis, 129
Financialization, 135
Foreign brides, 24, 175–178, 182, 186–188, 190, 192, 193, 218
Foreign guest worker, 176, 190

G
Gender bias, 167
Gender discrimination, 168
Germany, 20, 74, 112, 135, 247
Giddens, Anthony, 156, 227, 254
Globalization, 11, 20, 113, 124, 131, 164, 172, 177, 185, 186, 191, 214, 221
Growth first, distribution later, 20, 43, 109, 111, 121, 133, 136, 199, 200, 202, 216, 219
Growth first, safety later, 202

H
Hakchul, 71
Higher education, 22, 144
Hospice migration, 193
Household indebtedness, 4
Housing poverty, 244
Human rights, 11, 43, 52, 119

I
IMF economic crisis, 62, 97, 153, 202, 206, 245
Immigration, 191
Individualization without individualism, 170
Industrial policy, 5, 34, 119, 122, 201, 253
Industrialization, 166, 174, 175, 180–183, 185, 196, 214, 221, 245, 249

Inequalities, 91, 92, 103, 127, 130, 158, 194, 199, 201, 208, 215, 216, 218, 219
Inequality in risk citizenship, 201
Infrastructural familialism, 249
Institutional modernization, 21, 112, 133, 142, 147, 149, 156, 161
Intergenerational interactions, 23
Intergenerational relations, 50, 173
Intergenerational wealth flows theory, 166
International marriage, 185, 218, 250
International Monetary Fund (IMF), 56, 105, 113, 125, 127, 130, 208, 209, 234, 250, 253

J
Japan, 7, 17, 27–33, 40–42, 44–46, 48, 50–52, 59, 101, 111, 146, 177, 178, 180, 213, 225, 227, 228, 235, 247, 248
Japanese colonialism, 6, 180

K
Kariya, Takehiko, 12, 238
Kim Chul, 71, 83
Kim Dae-Jung, 9, 66, 67, 69, 97, 105, 106, 113, 125, 126, 208
Kim Young-Sam, 9, 56, 57, 66, 67, 70, 97, 123, 124
Koo, Hagen, 27, 32, 35, 57, 63–65, 71, 182
Korean bourgeoisie, 47
Korean Cold War, 34
Korean Confederation of Trade Unions (KCTU), 57, 72, 73, 75, 77
Korean War, the, 6, 34, 60, 71, 99, 147, 235, 245
Kwon Young-Gil, 72, 75, 79

L
Labor politics, 119, 228
Labor relations, 13, 14, 33, 35, 36, 103, 119
Labor unionism, 47
Labor unions, 39, 59, 76, 77, 123, 124
Lee Myung-Bak, 9, 98, 106, 114, 131, 132, 143, 233, 252, 254
Lewisian industrialization, 149
Lewis, W. Arthur, 63, 149, 163, 182
Liberal bourgeoisie, 40, 47
Liberal democracy, 8, 30, 33, 41, 154
Liberal modernization, 146, 147, 149, 154, 155, 159
Liberalism, 50, 135
Liberation, 10, 59–61, 154, 180
Liberation from Japan, 21, 59, 142, 178
Lim, Hyun-Chin, 35
Lowest-low fertility, 165

M
Marriage, 22, 152, 153, 164, 165, 168–171, 173, 174, 176, 178, 180, 181, 183, 185, 188, 189, 192, 217, 218, 242, 243, 247, 248
Marshall, T.H., 12, 90, 91, 108, 231
Marshallian evolution in citizenship politics, 19, 85
Marshallian theory, 12
Migration, 22, 23, 63, 150, 166, 173, 174, 183, 217, 246
Military, 8, 9
Military dictatorship, 8, 19
Military state, 9
Mobrand, Erik, 8, 56, 62, 65, 68, 74, 228
Modernity, 6
Moon Jae-In, 5, 43, 132, 133, 207–209, 224, 239, 252

Mortality, 165
Multicultural bride, 189
Multicultural child and youth, 189
Multicultural citizenship, 24, 177
Multicultural family, 189
Multicultural family support policy, 185, 190
Multiculturalism, 24, 152, 175, 176, 185, 187, 189, 192, 218, 247, 251
Multiculturals, 189

N
National Chart of Education, 160
National citizenship, 3
National financial crisis, 164, 168, 208, 209
Nationalism, 32, 33, 50, 51
Nationalist, 9
Nation-states, 3
Neoliberal globalization, 26, 135, 176, 185, 214
Neoliberal hospice state, 191
Neoliberalism, 20, 32, 36, 95, 105, 110, 112, 113, 122, 123, 125, 127, 128, 135, 191, 205
Neoliberalization, 21, 113, 114, 125, 134, 135
Neotraditional familialism, 24
Neotraditionalism, 191
North Korea, 6, 27, 30, 51, 60, 61, 81, 99, 103, 147, 171, 172

O
Obama, Barack, 139, 140, 157
Old age, 217
Old-age poverty, 4, 157, 216
Omni-pandemic era, 208, 218
Organized proletariat, 47

P
Pandemic, 207, 208
Pandemic risk, 208
Parenthood, 23, 164, 165, 174
Parents, 14, 24, 43, 84, 139, 141–143, 149, 150, 155–158, 163, 166, 167, 172, 173, 183, 185, 186, 188, 191, 192, 217, 218, 231, 249, 250
Park Chung-Hee, 9, 24, 34, 42, 56, 60, 61, 65, 68, 78, 97, 99, 104, 108, 109, 111, 112, 116, 119, 121, 122, 132, 133, 149, 159, 179, 181, 191, 200, 216
Park Chung-Hee marketers, 9
Paternalism, 121, 250
Patriotic fertility, 22
People's Solidarity for Participatory Democracy (PSPD), 130, 239
Pluralist cultural citizenship, 152, 153
Political citizenship, 18, 19, 40, 46, 50, 58, 81–83, 85, 91, 97, 108, 121, 123, 155, 204
Political economic citizenship, 91
Political modernity, 13, 18, 28
Political party, 6, 19, 56, 58, 68, 71, 72, 74, 78, 83, 85
Political rights, 14, 20, 34, 43, 44, 46, 47, 49, 51, 65, 67, 78, 90, 100, 107, 109, 110, 116, 133, 227
Post-familialist fertility, 171
Post-socialist transition, 106, 107, 221
Poverty, 103, 113, 116, 127, 135, 180, 202, 206, 215, 216
Poverty line, 129
Poverty relief law, 234
Private lessons (*sagyoyuk*), 238
Procreation, 163, 164, 168, 170–172, 217, 219
Proletariat, 47, 58, 63, 64, 89, 101, 128, 146, 179

Pronatal policy, 170, 173
Public education, 21, 116, 135, 142–147, 150–153, 155–161, 179, 216, 238, 240, 245

R
Referential communities, 48–50
Reflexive modernization, 152, 155, 159, 196, 224
Reflexivity, 152, 206, 207, 254, 255
Relative poverty, 142
Representative politics, 19, 85
Reproductive citizenship, 171–173, 217
Reproductive contributory rights, 176
Risk-based inequalities, 201, 204
Risk citizenship, 194, 201, 202, 206, 209, 218
Risk democracy, 202, 205
Risk society, 196, 204, 218
Rural marriage, 176, 184, 248, 250
Rural youth, 183
Russia, 220

S
Scandinavia, 135
Second fertility transition, 169
Seoul National University, 240–242, 252
Sex ratio, 167–169, 217
SKY universities, 241
Slapdash risk society, 198, 199
Social citizenship, 14, 15, 19, 20, 22–24, 43, 47, 49, 50, 52, 58, 85, 91, 92, 94, 95, 97, 98, 100, 103–105, 108–116, 118–123, 127, 131, 134–136, 144, 151, 153, 156, 165, 172, 174, 191, 194, 215, 232, 244, 245
Social citizenship politics, 119
Social democracy, 71, 132

Social investment family, 156
Social investment state, 135, 156, 242
Social policy, 13, 20, 45, 48, 94, 110, 112, 114, 115, 117–120, 123, 124, 133, 134, 136, 151, 225, 234, 235, 244
Social policy liberalism, 111
Social policy regime, 94, 95, 112, 118, 125, 220
Social policy state, 92, 116, 122
Social reproduction, 24, 120, 164, 169, 170, 173, 176, 177, 184, 186, 188, 191, 192, 218, 235, 247
Social rights, 11, 14, 42, 47–49, 90, 92, 94, 99, 100, 104, 105, 108, 117, 121, 168
Social safety net, 47, 124, 127, 202
Social security, 14, 21, 47, 103, 113, 114, 116, 127, 128, 135, 201, 202, 215
Social security system, 4, 23, 126, 127, 174
Social transition costs of industrialization, 241
Social welfare, 17, 20, 52, 92, 100, 112, 113, 116, 122–124, 132, 133, 151
Socioeconomic rights, 9, 205
Southeast Asia, 208
Soviet Union, 6, 30, 103
State-business entrepreneurial merge, 119
State-civil society relations, 29, 30, 41
State-society relations, 13, 16, 17, 29, 37, 38, 41, 43, 49, 50, 52
Suicide, 4, 23, 141, 164, 174, 219
Sweden, 136

T
Taiwan, 27, 169, 240, 250

Tertiary education, 22, 140, 143, 145, 147, 151–153, 157, 160, 161, 216
The Korean wave (*Hallyu*), 151
Third Way, 132, 156
T. H. Marshall's theory of citizenship, 89
Tocqueville, Alexis de, 48, 225
Total fertility rate (TFR), 165, 169, 244, 246
Transformative citizenship, 12, 17, 23, 26, 144, 164, 174, 214, 219–221
Transformative collectivism, 7, 10
Transformative contributory rights, 6, 11, 12, 17, 25, 26, 176, 214
Transformative contributory risk, 25, 194, 199, 201
Transformative victim, 26, 214–217, 219, 220
Transformative victimhood, 25, 26, 213, 214, 219–221
Turner, Bryan S., 7, 11, 29, 91, 231, 232

U
UK, 5, 23, 135, 143, 174, 208, 232
Unbalanced growth, 182, 200
Unemployment, 103, 113, 125–129, 202, 206
United States, 8, 23, 59, 94, 105, 115, 117, 128, 142, 146, 148, 160, 174, 185, 223, 225, 232

Urbanization, 48, 63, 165, 166, 182, 183, 185, 245, 249
Urban youth, 39

V
Vietnam, 27, 107, 108, 110, 218, 221
Vietnamese women, 185

W
Welfare pluralism, 120, 123, 235
Welfare state, 20, 31, 48, 94, 97, 112, 114, 115, 120, 123, 131–133, 135–137, 156, 173, 201
Western Europe, 47, 135, 136, 170
Women's citizenship, 168
Women's right, 168
Working class, 20, 27, 55–57, 62–65, 70, 71, 74, 75, 82, 83, 85, 95, 96, 110, 112
Working class party, 72, 76
Working class politics, 72

Y
Youth, 5, 50, 84, 103, 129, 136, 143, 157, 171, 209, 215–217

Z
Zaretsky, Eli, 179